Randy D.

LINCOLN'S SONS

LINCOLN'S SONS

by
RUTH PAINTER RANDALL

With Illustrations

Little, Brown and Company

Boston　　　　　　　　Toronto

*Published simultaneously in Canada
by Little, Brown & Company (Canada) Limited*

PRINTED IN THE UNITED STATES OF AMERICA

To these two:

F. V. N. PAINTER

who was my father

and

J. G. RANDALL

who was my husband

Foreword

AFTER I had completed *Mary Lincoln: Biography of a Marriage*, it seemed logical to continue the narrative of the Lincoln family with a special study of the second generation. This book attempts to recover, strictly from historical evidence, the personalities and lives of the sons of Abraham and Mary Lincoln. It is the story of four boys born into a typical American family in the eighteen forties and fifties and their growing up, first in a primitive little town in Illinois and then in the White House, the storm center of the nation engaged in a great civil war. It was against the backdrop of one of the most colorful and dramatic periods of our history that these young personalities developed and family relationships were maintained.

After the assassination of Lincoln the strangely tangled lives of the eldest and youngest sons are followed to the end. The last three chapters are devoted to the later life of the enigmatic Robert Lincoln. It is not within the scope of this book to deal in detail with his public and business career. The main events are given and I have tried to answer the questions people usually ask about him. The primary purpose here is to present Robert Lincoln's personality through its varying phases to its ripe maturity and to deal with that personality in relation to his father and mother. The fact that he was his father's son conditioned his whole life. The question could be raised as to whether Abraham Lincoln did not have more effect upon Robert after his death than he did while living.

One of the leading topics of this book is Lincoln as a father. When I adjusted the focus of my study on the Lincoln sons and attempted to relegate the father and mother to a minor role as mere parents, I found that Mr. Lincoln firmly refused to take a back seat. His fatherhood was so basic a part of his life that he remained prominently in the picture.

I have tried at all times to walk the tightrope of historical research. While it has been decided to publish the book without footnotes, the original manuscript in my possession is fully documented, and these references to the sources have been used to make up the bibliography.

R. P. R.

Urbana, Illinois
February 1955

Acknowledgments

FRIENDS have given me such generous assistance in this work that I am reminded of Lincoln's own words: "The better part of one's life consists of his friendships." As always in a years-long association, those scrupulous Lincoln scholars, Harry E. Pratt, State Historian of Illinois, and his wife Marion Dolores Pratt, assistant editor of *The Collected Works of Abraham Lincoln*, have stood by to help in every possible way. They have constantly furnished research clues and items and have carefully read the entire manuscript, making many safeguarding suggestions. I owe them more than I can well express.

I am deeply grateful to David C. Mearns, Chief of the Manuscripts Division, Library of Congress, who generously gave me the use of his extensive material on Robert Todd Lincoln which he had collected for the writing of the notable introduction to his two-volume work *The Lincoln Papers*. In addition to this invaluable aid, Mr. Mearns has constantly sent me further research suggestions and I have turned to him for guidance in certain special problems.

Through the courtesy of Willard L. King, who is writing the biography of David Davis, I had access to some unusual documents. Mr. King has in the David Davis papers a wealth of personal material such as most biographers can only dream of, and he has generously given me the use of letters from Mrs. Lincoln, Robert Lincoln, and the Davises which have added unique details to this story.

William H. Townsend has courteously permitted me to use more than fifty rare family letters from Robert Lincoln to his aunt, Emilie Todd Helm, and her son and daughter, Ben and Katherine Helm; new and revealing letters. Commander Philip R. Baker, great-grand-nephew of Mrs. Abraham Lincoln, in addition to giving me the use of special letters from Mrs. Lincoln and from his great-grandmother, Mrs. Ninian W. Edwards, has furnished the lovely photograph of Robert Lincoln's bride, Mary Harlan Lincoln. Mrs. Roy F. Donaldson, granddaughter of Elizabeth Todd Grimsley, has permitted me to quote from her delightful letter about Robert Lincoln. Frank H. West has given me permission to use three pictures from Julia Taft Bayne's *Tad Lincoln's Father*.

Alfred Whital Stern, from his great collection of Lincolniana, has sent me photostats of significant letters from Robert Lincoln. Frederick H. Meserve with his usual generosity has again let me use pictures from the Meserve Collection. Ralph Newman of the Abraham Lincoln Book Shop has contributed research clues and items.

Professor Richard N. Current, who has completed *Last Full Measure*, the fourth volume of J. G. Randall's *Lincoln the President*, which my husband left unfinished at the time of his death, has read the last three chapters of *Lincoln's Sons* in manuscript and made helpful comments. Wayne C. Temple, the authority on Noah Brooks, has called my attention to unusual writings by Brooks which relate to my subject and has found, out of his own thoughtfulness, many other ways in which to be helpful.

Librarians and guardians of historical records have been wonderfully altruistic, as usual. Paul M. Angle has helped me find the particular nuggets I needed from the treasures of the Chicago Historical Society. Dr. Louis A. Warren has rendered the same generous service for the historical material at the Lincoln National Life Foundation. Kimball C. Elkins of the Harvard Archives has answered each inquiry with the desired information or photostat. Director Robert B. Downs, Professor Leslie W. Dunlap, Nelle M. Signor, Dorothy M. Black, and Eleanor Blum of the University of Illinois Library have all aided in every pleasant and possible way. Norma Cuthbert has taken pains to see that I received what I needed from the Huntington Library. Margaret A. Flint, reference librarian at the Illinois State Historical Library, has welcomed each SOS for information and given it her expert attention. Elizabeth Baughman of the Chicago Historical Society has furnished careful reports on special problems.

It is not possible to name all who have assisted, but the following have found their own ways in which to be of service: David Rankin Barbee, Margaret Kahler Bearden, Professor Robert G. Bone, Mrs. W. A. Noyes, Dr. Charles W. Olsen, Mrs. Harrison Ruehe, and Martha Swain. Mrs. Verner Alexanderson especially has rendered thoughtful and deeply appreciated assistance.

Ned Bradford of Little, Brown and Company helped me plan this book, and throughout its writing I have been happy in having his guidance and skillful editing. To David Donald I owe the stimulation of delightful shop talks about this study and the privilege (which I have been using since his student days) of asking his advice.

Lida E. Voight not only has typed expertly the entire manuscript but has shown a delightful interest in the growing up of the Lincoln sons. Helen Hart Metz has again demonstrated her expert skill and cherished friendship by making the index of this book.

I feel also that I owe much to Caroline Woodruff, loved friend and helper for twenty-two years. She has freed me from household tasks so that I have had time for research and writing and has shown me at all times understanding sympathy and deep-rooted wisdom.

Such warmhearted generosity of friends truly belongs to "the better part of one's life." To all these benefactors I am profoundly grateful.

It was taking part in the Lincoln research of my husband, J. G. Randall, which led me into the study of the personal lives of the Lincolns. It was his generous backing that encouraged me to write my biography of Mrs. Lincoln. When I began the research for this book after his death, I found among his notes an indispensable file on Robert Lincoln. It seems symbolic of the way in which his scholarship and personality have guided and are still guiding me.

R. P. R.

Contents

List of Illustrations

LINCOLN'S SONS

CHAPTER 1

A Family on Eighth Street

MR. ABRAHAM LINCOLN used to walk home from his office. In the simple way of small towns he and other substantial citizens of Springfield, Illinois, when the day's work was ended, left their places of business around the public square and walked the few blocks to their homes, where each a little later was likely to be seen seated at his own dining table having supper with his wife and children. To have accompanied one of them would have been to get acquainted with his family.

In order then to meet the children of Mr. Lincoln one has only to follow him to his home on the corner of Eighth and Jackson Streets. A good time for this would be a summer evening in the year of our Lord 1857. That date is selected because the house had been enlarged and improved the year before and was looking its best and very much as one sees it today. Mrs. Lincoln would have preferred it to be viewed then, as she took pride in having a pretty and appropriate home.

Using only those details which are verified in the records, one can picture Mr. Lincoln putting on the tall hat which was the correct headgear for a gentleman in his position, leaving the dilapidated Lincoln and Herndon law office on the second floor, walking down the dusty stairs, and stepping out into the street on the west side of the public square. In the center of its green stood the sandstone State House which figured so largely in his life and in the life of the town which was the state capital. Turning to the right he would start with long loose strides toward home, a distance of nearly seven blocks, three of them east and the rest south.

The stores and offices of the business section would soon be left behind and he would be passing assorted small-town homes frequently set back of comfortable front yards, which might at this season of the year boast some flowers and a rosebush or two. He knew all the people who lived in these houses, knew them with the intimate knowledge of long-time neighborliness. He also knew and loved their children, who played with his own young sons.

This fact constituted a menace to his getting home on time. The neighborhood in which Mr. Lincoln lived was bountifully supplied with youngsters and he was very popular with them. As he walked along, probably with both hands clasped behind him and lost in deep thought, he was often awakened from his meditations by a boyish voice calling him and the sad, serious expression of his face would change as by magic into one of warm, sympathetic interest. It was as if a lantern had been lighted back of it. He would of course stop and exchange a few words of playful camaraderie with the child.

If he met a friend or neighbor, that was apt to prove even more delaying. They would have to stop and exchange small items of personal and public news, and then Mr. Lincoln was sure to be reminded of a story, and this meant that for Mrs. Lincoln and the children waiting at home supper was further postponed. The matter of being late at his meals never hurried or disturbed Mr. Lincoln; he could stroll in two hours after the appointed time completely unaware that he was late.

Getting "Father" home to meals was an undertaking that sometimes required the united efforts of the entire family. When the hour grew too late, "Mother" would send the three boys to fetch him.

Then might follow the comic scene described by one who had witnessed it more than once. Mr. Lincoln, his back turned toward the home where he was impatiently awaited, would be cordially shaking the hand of his friend while two little boys were swinging onto his coattails, pulling with all their might. The third son would co-operate by pushing in front. Mr. Lincoln would continue his conversation with complete imperturbability, but there probably was a twinkle deep in his eyes and one suspects he was getting his own enjoyment from the situation. He liked to romp and tussle with his little sons, to stiffen his powerful muscles against their fierce young tuggings; it was one of the ways they played together.

Whether it was by some such united effort or whether he got there on his own, Mr. Lincoln would ultimately reach the two-story frame dwelling at the corner of Eighth and Jackson. It was a house of simple and dignified lines that stood on a little elevation above the street and was painted a color variously described as "brown," "neutral," "a pale chocolate," and "a most beautiful dirty clay color." Its window blinds were a dark green. Mr. Lincoln would climb the few steps that came down to the sidewalk itself and open the little gate which was part of the paling fence that ran along the top of the brick retaining wall. Perhaps the fence had been put there to keep the children within bounds, and it is in the range of possibilities that the gate at times sagged a little because of the small boys' habit of swinging on it; at all events the home had an unmistakable air of domesticity. It is known that the Lincolns had a dog several years later and were devoted to pets, so it is quite possible the master of the house was greeted with a welcoming bark and wagging tail as he climbed the additional steps to the front door which bore a black name plate with "A. Lincoln" on it in silvered roman letters.

If they had not already sallied forth to bring him home, his two youngest sons might have been on the watch to give him a tumultuous greeting. A third possibility is that they were still playing at a neighbor's (since they were as irresponsible as their father about getting home on time) and that Mrs. Lincoln, busy with supper preparations, would send him to fetch them.

But assuming that the family were all at home, one can picture Mr. Lincoln turning to the right after entering the front door (probably taking off his coat as he did so, for he liked to go in shirt sleeves when at home) and going into the family sitting room. The formal parlor on the left was for special occasions only (the bric-a-brac on the whatnot would hardly have survived the activities of the lively boys), but one could relax and be comfortable in the sitting room. Back of it was the dining room; in a short time the family would assemble around the dining table. With father, mother, and three children seated there, this will be an excellent time to examine and describe them.

"Pa," as the boys called him, was probably still in shirt sleeves, though his wife frowned upon this if guests were present. It was a period of stiff conventionalities which she took much more seriously than he. He did not seem quite so tall when seated, though his long legs undoubtedly stretched far down the length of the table underneath. His black hair was probably tousled, as he had a habit of running his long fingers through it. His eyes were gray, but because they were deep-set in his swarthy face and shadowed by eyelids and brow, they gave at times the impression of being very dark. Most of the people in Springfield would have called the lean face ugly, but at the same time their eyes would be lingering on it, drawn by its kindliness and swift changes of expression and its power to be irresistibly droll.

The mother at the other end of the table was strikingly different from her husband; she was short and plump, so that when they stood side by side the contrast was a bit amusing. Her coloring was an attractive combination of rich light-chestnut hair, very fair skin, and blue eyes. When people began to write down their descriptions of her several years later, they often chose the words "amiable" and "motherly." Her motions and gestures were quick as opposed to her husband's deliberateness; she was an excitable and enthusiastic little woman. Color rose easily to her face and she was perhaps flushed now with the effort of getting her family and the supper assembled. The boys called her "Ma."

Where such contrast exists between father and mother, there is apt to be great variety in the offspring. This was true of the three sons who sat at the table. The youngest, called Tad or Taddie, was four years old in 1857, and as he was probably clamoring for attention (and getting it, too), one may as well begin with him.

His appealing little-boy face was sensitive and subject to quick changes of expression. It was probably evident even at that age that he was to have dark hair like his father's, and it would be revealed ultimately that he too was to have a tall, thin body. His mother in one of her letters referred to his eyes as "dark" and in one source they are even called "black," a rather unexpected product of gray- and blue-eyed parents. His maternal grandfather, Robert S. Todd, had brown eyes and it is possible Tad went back to him or some other ancestor for this dark eye coloring.

He was quick in his movements like his mother and like her too he talked rapidly, his baby words fairly tumbling over each other. As he had a pronounced impediment in his speech, only parental intuition was likely at this time to translate what he was trying to say. He was an imaginative, responsive, and happy little fellow, though it took little to upset him and plunge him into an explosion of anger or tears. Perhaps even this early his eyes turned constantly to his father's face, for the bond between them was strong and tender. One of his playmates later described Tad as a *"Mama* boy," explaining that this meant his personality was like hers; a spectator at that supper table might have been likely to agree. Yet deep within him, as time would show, lay the potentiality of several fundamental qualities of his father.

Somehow one pictures the two younger boys, Tad and Willie, on one side of the table together and the eldest son Robert, or Bob, on the other side alone. It is a grouping whose symbolism will become more apparent as the evidence about the three unfolds. Willie was going on seven in the summer of 1857, an attractive boy with light brown hair, fair skin, and blue eyes. His manner was more quiet than that of the unpredictable Tad; he was amiable, cheerful, mature for his age, and the one who was most popular with his playmates. According to his mother he "was a very beautiful boy, with a most *spiritual* expression of face," but one should not be misled by the word "spiritual" into thinking that Willie would not be ready, when Tad was a little older, to join that inventive sprite in any mischief he might think up. For that matter, Willie could think up some tricks of his own.

But his quiet thoughtfulness made him able, perhaps even at the age of seven, to understand and deal with his mother's excitability. There was a special bond between them; he called himself "mother's boy," and if her overflowing maternalness permitted a favorite, Willie was his mother's favorite. The reason is not hard to find: Willie was his father over again. As his development is traced it will be found that he had his father's qualities to an amazing extent; he even had Mr. Lincoln's mannerism of holding his head a little to one side. The mother called Taddie her "little troublesome *sunshine*" but Willie was her comfort. She said he scarcely seemed a child to her.

With Abraham and Mary Lincoln a trait in the one would fill a lack and need of that trait in the other. The two boys who resembled them were drawn together by the same attraction of complementary qualities. Willie and Tad were "so unlike," said their mother, "yet so devoted." "Their love for each other, was charming to behold." Both of the little boys were very affectionate (a quality possessed by each of the parents) and completely natural and spontaneous in the expression of this affection.

There had been another affectionate little boy; the family table should have been balanced with two sons on each side. Willie and Tad were not aware of this gap—it had all happened before they were born—but Robert had been old enough at the time to remember the dark days of his little brother's death. That loss had left a scar in the hearts of the parents which undoubtedly contributed toward their complete indulgence of the other children.

One can picture Mr. Lincoln after supper was over sitting down to read in the family living room, perhaps in the very same large rocker which is seen there today. Then was likely to follow a scene with Willie and Tad similar to the one described in detail by a somewhat disapproving journalist several years later. When Mr. Lincoln crossed his long legs, wrote this reporter, "the pendent foot swung almost to the floor. And all the while, two little boys, his sons, clambered over those legs. . . ." They "patted his cheeks" lovingly and then, with that quick transition from cherub to imp which parents just have to get used to, they would pull his nose. Any one of the long-suffering neighbors could have told this journalist, probably in a tone of indignation, that the Lincoln boys had no respect for the dignity of their elders. He himself was indignant that Mr. Lincoln let the children maul him around without "reprimand or even notice"; he was just finding out what the neighbors had known all along: that the Lincolns let their children do exactly as they pleased. The motto of the home was "Let the children have a good time," which frequently meant that the adults had a rather bad one.

But, as usual, the two lively younger boys have drawn attention away from Robert, the fifth member of the family supper group. He was fourteen on August 1 in that summer of 1857. A glance at him would reveal that he would never have the long-boned leanness of Mr. Lincoln; his build was on stockier and more compact lines. "Bob is 'short and low,'" his father had written when he was only three years old, "and, I expect, always will be." (But the boy was growing and it would one day be written on a passport that he was five feet nine and a half inches, which was six and a half inches shorter than his father.)

Bob's hair was brown and his eyes were gray. If one had looked closely it might have been noticed that one eye turned slightly inward. On that same passport of the future he would describe his nose as "ordinary" and acknowledge a dimple in his chin. Perhaps that dimple was inherited, as Mr. Lincoln, in his earliest picture, appears to have a deep one in his chin too. Bob's skin ultimately would be dark like his father's, but there the resemblance ended. His roundish face, as shown by his pictures taken several years later, was keen and determined but had none of the "spiritual" quality of Willie's or the appeal of the elfin Tad's. In the fragments of description which one collects to round out the portrait of a personality the various references to Robert in his growing-up years show a curious restraint; they lack the warmth and color found in the mention of his younger brothers. Mrs. Lincoln herself said he was entirely different from them.

He was a difficult boy passing through a difficult age. Good evidence can be given of the special bond between Tad and his father and of that between Willie and his mother, but evidence of responsiveness and affection on Robert's part at this time seems lacking. Some element in his nature (perhaps shyness was a part of it) apparently kept him from letting himself go in a wholehearted expression of such emotions. He lacked the quality of enthusiasm. The magnetism of his father, the vivacious friendliness of his mother had not been handed down to him. In the collected record he appears, as a boy, to have had an uncomfortable aloofness from the rest of the family, with perhaps a suggestion of antagonism.

The difference in their ages would explain a certain lack of common interests with the younger boys. It will be found that he disapproved of the way his parents indulged Willie and Tad, and, in this, Springfield solidly agreed with him. But, having been spoiled and indulged in exactly the same way when he was around their ages, it probably was difficult for him to adjust himself to giving in to them on all points. A fourteen-year-old ego likes to have its own way just as much as when it was seven or four.

At all events, a psychiatrist, viewing the family group and noting the happy spontaneousness of the younger boys and the lack of this quality in Robert, suspecting that he was the unadjusted child of the household, might have started to search back over his previous years to find the causes contributing to this maladjustment. The intricacies of psychiatry will be left to the psychiatrist, but going back to Robert's earlier life, with a view to fuller knowledge and understanding, seems a good plan.

CHAPTER 2

The First Two "Dear Codgers"

IF MR. LINCOLN, coming out of his office building on that summer evening in 1857, had turned right at the first crossing and walked about a block and a half west from the public square, he would have come to the place where Robert had been born fourteen years before, the Globe Tavern. The name is more impressive than the descriptions or later pictures of it. "It was a primitive sort of house—" said one who was living there at the time, "a big, ugly frame building." The Lincolns were living at this boardinghouse the first year of their marriage because it was inexpensive and Mr. Lincoln had little money and was in debt besides. They could get room and board at the Globe Tavern for four dollars a week.

It was in one of its plainly furnished rooms that Mary Lincoln had given birth to their first-born son on August 1, 1843, nine months less three days after she and Mr. Lincoln were married. She had no nurse to take care of her and a friend who happened to be staying at the tavern came in every day to wash and dress the baby, tidy up the room, and make the mother comfortable. The new arrival would find when he grew to knowledge of such things that he had a bountiful array of aunts, his mother's sisters and half sisters. Two sisters were living in well-to-do homes in Springfield at the time of his birth but the scanty records make no mention of their helping out on this occasion. Perhaps they did, but they had not wanted their gay and attractive sister Mary to marry Mr. Lincoln, who had grown up in a cabin in the backwoods, had had little schooling, and was not, according to their view, socially qualified to marry into the aristocratic and prosperous Todd family.

But sisters did not matter too much when the young wife could remember afterwards how ". . . my darling husband, was bending over me, with such love and tenderness" when this child was born.

Both Abraham and Mary Lincoln had a remarkable love for children. An instinctive understanding and fostering impulse flowed from each of them toward any child. It was a great fulfillment to these two to have a baby of their own. But there was one thing about this little son which must have troubled them: he had one crossed eye. At least it is known that he was a cross-eyed little boy and one presumes that he had the defect from birth. This must have troubled his mother greatly, for she was proud and sensitive to the point of touchiness and in her zest for living she glorified everything she loved and wanted it perfect. The subject of eye defects was probably painful to Mary Lincoln; Mr. Lincoln had an eye peculiarity too: in moments of excitement his left eye turned upward. That inward-turning eye was destined to cause the new arrival much trouble in the long run, both psychologically because of humiliation and physically because of the weakness of the eye itself.

He was named Robert Todd Lincoln for his mother's father, Robert S. Todd, who was one of the most prominent and influential citizens of Lexington, Kentucky. Mr. Todd came to Springfield that fall to see the numerous members of his family living there: the three daughters and various relatives, and now a little grandson named for him. Like Southerners in general he felt family ties strongly. "May God bless and protect my little namesake" was his benediction over the new baby. This would be the only one of the Lincoln children he would have the opportunity to know well and possibly influence.

By the time Mr. Todd arrived that autumn the Lincoln family may have moved to the three-room frame cottage at 214 South Fourth Street which they occupied during the winter of 1843–1844. It has been said that the baby cried so much at the Globe Tavern that other guests complained. But if he was noisy so was the tavern itself, with guests passing back and forth and stagecoaches lumbering up to the front door, their arrival heralded by the clanging of the big bell on the roof, a signal to the stablemen in the rear to come and take charge of the horses. The tavern was no more desirable for the baby than the baby was for the tavern.

When Robert, or Bobbie, as they called the baby, was about nine months old his parents bought a cottage on the corner of Eighth and Jackson Streets. It is hard to realize that this small story-and-a-half structure surrounded by mud or dust was the first version of the comfortable two-story house with neat fence and retaining wall to which Mr. Lincoln walked home in 1857. The house, the Lincoln family, and Springfield itself were destined to grow amazingly in the first thirteen years of Robert's life.

Housework was almost unbelievably laborious in the eighteen forties—there were no push-button conveniences—and the young mother, nervous, excitable, and unused to hard work, needed help. Not long after the family moved, Mr. Lincoln, who had been attending court in Charleston, Illinois, brought back with him in the wheeled vehicle, a buggy perhaps, by which he made the two-day trip a backwoods cousin of his, a girl named Harriet Hanks. She could attend school in Springfield and at the same time help Mary with household chores. Harriet's recollections give a close-up glimpse of Bobbie when he was the only child.

It appears that the Lincolns, later noted for not restraining their children in any way, at first made some faint attempts at discipline. Harriet told of an incident in which Mr. Lincoln tried to correct Robert and Mrs. Lincoln, who could not bear to see her baby made unhappy, interfered, becoming hysterical. Harriet reported that Mr. Lincoln continued the correction in spite of the mother's angry protests, a bit of firmness in regard to his offspring that was soon to become a rarity. Harriet also remembered that "one of his greatest pleasures when at home was that of nursing and playing with his little boy."

Harriet left the Lincoln home after about a year and a half, having learned to write a much better letter than the illiterate scrawls of her father, Dennis Hanks. Probably at the time she departed it was already evident that Mrs. Lincoln was going to have another baby and that the household, which was finding it hard enough to cope with the active and head-strong Robert, would have additional cares.

For posterity the birth announcement of the second child comes from the father himself. In the fall of 1846 Mr. Lincoln wrote his dear friend Joshua Speed in Kentucky: "We have another boy, born the 10th. of March last. He is very much such a child as Bob was at his age—rather of a longer order." He then referred to Bob as being short and low and continued with a telling description of his firstborn: "He talks very plainly—almost as plainly as any body. He is quite smart enough. I some times fear he is one of the little rare-ripe sort, that are smarter at about five than ever after."

The father's comments on Robert have a curious overtone that might imply disapproval. Here he is apparently taking no pride in his son's precocity; it seems rather as if he had already taken the measurements of the three-year-old, discovered the mold in which he was cast and was not quite satisfied with it.

Bob's personality at three was decidedly rambunctious. The father's description of him continued: "He has a great deal of that sort of mischief, that is the offspring of much animal spirits." Even as the father was writing he had a demonstration of this. "Since I began this letter a messenger came to tell me, Bob was lost; but by the time I reached the house, his mother had found him, and had him whiped —and, by now, very likely he is run away again."

There is a suggestion here that Robert might have been one of those first babies whose world gets out of adjustment when the second baby comes along. He had had nearly three years of being the central interest of two very indulgent parents, then he was suddenly dethroned from his absolute monarchy by a younger brother. As the old saying has it, "His nose was out of joint." The jealousy this situation may create very often takes the form of "acting up" to attract attention. Running away from home might also be a sort of rebellion against the changed order of things. That it proved an excellent method of attracting attention, lots of attention, is evident from the recollections of a neighbor. The young mother was apt to fly into a hysterical panic at any threat to her children, and this neighbor remembered how she would come to the front door of the cottage and scream in terror, "Bobbie's lost! Bobbie's lost!" Finding him became a neighborhood matter; even his father was sent for in such cases.

The same neighbor recalled another incident about Bobbie. The back yard of the cottage, like all the back yards in Springfield, had its privy, and frequently associated with privies was a "lime box." One day the little boy put some of the lime into his mouth. His mother, terrified by her child's distress, ran out screaming, "Bobbie will die! Bobbie will die!" Again neighbors came to the rescue, washing out the burned and painful mouth.

The whipping, or spanking, for running away seems to indicate that the Lincolns were still making some attempt at correcting their first-born, but not very successfully as the father surmised in his letter that it would just make Bob run away again. Perhaps spankings did not work well with him but only made him more antagonistic, as is sometimes the case with difficult children. But this punishment stands out in contrast to the complete indulgence which was soon the policy of the Lincolns. Eldest children are sometimes heard to complain that they got all the discipline for the whole family, ultimately wearing down any parental theories on the subject to the profit of the younger children; perhaps it was so in Robert's case.

The second baby was named Edward Baker Lincoln for Edward D. Baker, Mr. Lincoln's intimate friend and close associate in politics. Like all the Lincoln children he was promptly nicknamed. Little Eddie doubtless was put into the same long infants' dresses which Bobbie had worn and went through the usual developing stages so exciting to parents—that series of firsts: first smile, first tooth, first word, first step. The father delighted to lie down in the hall with his shoulders on a turned-down chair, his feet up on the newel post and dangle a baby over him. Now there were two little sons to romp with in the boyish way that Mr. Lincoln never outgrew.

When Bobbie was four his world suddenly widened into new dimensions. The family was going on a long journey. They would first visit grandfather Todd at Lexington, Kentucky, and then go on to a very desirable place called Washington. Mr. Lincoln had been elected to the United States House of Representatives. To the little boy's mind that fact probably appeared vaguely as something nice which had happened to his father. There was excitement and bustle of preparation; then a day came when he with his father, mother, and baby Eddie boarded a great stagecoach drawn by horses and rode right out of the familiar world of Springfield. This grand but jolting journey was adventure enough, but greater wonders were ahead; they came to a broad river on which there were big boats and they themselves got aboard one of these boats.

There followed for the little boy strange days and nights of riding along on the river. He could run around the deck (which fortunately for the parents' peace of mind had a good stout railing), a deck which constantly vibrated with the throb of a mighty engine below. He could watch the huge paddle wheel turning round and round with a tremendous splashing which scattered bright drops of water in all directions and left a wake of churned-up water and foam behind it. Black smoke came out of the tall smokestacks which seemed to reach right up into the sky, smoke that showered one with soot, and at intervals there was the whistle so loud and penetrating it could be heard for miles around. It sometimes hurt one's ears, that whistle, and one could hear it strangely at night when tucked into a peculiar little bed called a bunk. In Robert's future he would cross the ocean a number of times and travel in foreign countries, but probably never again would travel bring such wonder to him. There was enchantment in that journey too for the parents; they were at a happy stage of life with their two children and the high hopes of Mr. Lincoln's widening political success.

Judging by what followed, Bobbie was not popular with the other passengers on the boat. At least when the family disembarked to take a primitive little train to Lexington, one of the occupants of the coach made some observations and later gave an account of what it was like to travel with the Lincoln family. "I was never so glad to get off a train in my life," he said. "There were two lively youngsters on board who kept the whole train in a turmoil, and their long-legged father, instead of spanking the brats, looked pleased as Punch and aided and abetted the older one in mischief."

In Lexington the Todd carriage met the Lincolns at the station and took them to a stately brick house on Main Street. Perhaps Bobbie later remembered that homecoming: how his mother, holding baby Eddie in her arms, entered the front door first, her face glowing, and how his father followed carrying him into the wide hall where the whole family was assembled to welcome them. Mary Lincoln had returned to her father's house which she had left as an unmarried girl eight years before. Now at last she could show her stepmother and a whole stairsteps of young half brothers and sisters the husband and two children she had acquired in Illinois.

Among the children lined up in the hall were three little girls dressed in crimson merino dresses with little white ruffled aprons. They were, strangely enough, Robert's aunts, his mother's half sisters. For the first time he saw his Aunt Emilie Todd, then around eleven years of age. Down the long stretch of years which the future held for each of them, they would have many meetings under greatly varying circumstances and some of these meetings would be tied in with historic situations.

Emilie remembered well how Robert's father stooped to put the little boy down, and as he arose, unfolding his long legs until he reached his great height, he made her think of the hungry giant in "Jack and the Beanstalk." She was half frightened and shrank behind her mother's voluminous skirts, mothers' skirts at that time being very adequate hiding places. But her fears vanished when Mr. Lincoln stooped and lifted her in his arms saying, "So this is little sister." There was something about his smile and voice that made her feel very safe.

A whole new environment opened up for Robert in the three weeks of that visit in Lexington. For all his rambunctiousness he was probably shy of this aggregation of relatives at first; at least later evidence shows that he did not easily adjust to others. But the Todd children, the youngest being only a little older than Robert himself, doubtless helped him explore the rear lawn with its coachhouse, stable, and servants' quarters and the little stream that ran at the back where they could chase minnows. Perhaps Robert already knew how absorbing a small brook could be to a little boy—the Town Branch in Springfield ran close to the cottage on Eighth and Jackson.

At one side of the Todd home was a beautiful flower garden with a winding white-gravel walk and an enticing summerhouse. The grounds made the back yard and surroundings of the cottage in Illinois seem poor and drab by comparison. There were no servants' quarters in that back yard. Sometimes his mother had a girl or woman to help her and sometimes she did not. From later indications one suspects that Robert found things much to his taste at his grandfather Todd's. There was luxury, much to see and do, and these lively new relatives were interesting. One of the Todd sons came home from college while he was there and delighted to teach this four-year-old who talked so plainly to call him "Uncle Sam."

When the Lincoln family left Lexington, there was again the thrill and adventure of travel, but that travel was also rough and tedious, and when they arrived in Washington late at night a week later, on December 2, doubtless they all were frayed and weary. Shortly afterwards parents and children were settled at Mrs. Sprigg's boardinghouse on Capitol Hill, where they were to spend the winter months.

Very little is known of the family during those months. A doctor who also boarded at Mrs. Sprigg's remembered that Robert "was a bright boy" but "seemed to have his own way." Apparently the Lincolns had reached their characteristic attitude of letting their children do as they pleased.

Later, in the year when Robert graduated from college, he wrote a sketch of his life up to that time. Referring to the period when his father was in the House of Representatives he said, "Of my life at Washington my recollections are very faint—" but there did remain a memory of the time when his father took him to the Patent Office and they looked at the endless wonders of modern invention until it seemed as if there was nothing more that could be invented. Mr. Lincoln always had an absorbing interest in inventions and machinery. Anything mechanical fascinated him—he had a small boy's impulse to take it apart to see how it worked. It will be seen that even his children's toys were not safe from him. He and Robert were to have few tastes in common but perhaps this was one; at least Robert inherited his father's interest in mathematics.

It is pleasant to picture that tall father and the "short and low" four-year-old gazing at the curiosities in the cabinets, Lincoln's face alight with interest as he explained to his little boy as much as he could comprehend. It was his way to explain things to his children in simple terms. No one knew then that thirteen or fourteen years later, in 1861, this father and son would again journey to Washington, and in that year lines of triple-decked bunks would be placed between these exhibition cabinets when the Patent Office was used to quarter soldiers in a great civil war.

Living in a boardinghouse with two small and vocal children undoubtedly had its difficulties, and the spring of 1848 found Mary
Lincoln with the boys again visiting her father's home in Lexington,
Kentucky. Certain letters which the Lincolns wrote each other during
this separation have been preserved. Reading them, it is as if the
more than one hundred years between have vanished and one is
listening to this father and mother talking about their children.

A letter from Mr. Lincoln to his "Dear Mary" in April promptly discloses the fact that the members of the divided family were missing
each other. "I hate to stay in this old room by myself," wrote Congressman Lincoln to his wife. Apparently she had written him that the
youngest boy wondered where he was, as he continued: "Dear Eddy
thinks father is 'gone tapila.'" "Tapila" may have been the child's
attempt to say Capitol; it suggests a flashback scene at Mrs.
Sprigg's in Washington when the mother might have explained to
the little boys that their father had gone to his work at the Capitol.
She could have pointed out the flat-domed building which was
just across the way from Mrs. Sprigg's. The dining room of the boardinghouse had looked out on the trees in the Capitol Park, where the
Lincolns had sometimes gone on Saturday evenings to listen to the
public concerts.

"Mother" had commissioned "Father" to do some shopping in
Washington, giving him minute directions. This April letter reported
the result: "I went yesterday to hunt the little plaid stockings, as you
wished; but found that McKnight has quit business, and Allen had
not a single pair of the description you give, and only one plaid pair
of any sort that I thought would fit 'Eddy's dear little feet.'" But he
was not willing to accept defeat in the matter; he had "a notion to
make another trial to-morrow morning."

Mr. Lincoln worried about his family. He wondered whether his
wife had had any of the migraine headaches to which she was subject and he had had a distressing dream about one of the boys. "I
did not get rid of the impression of that foolish dream about dear
Bobby till I got your letter written the same day. What did he and
Eddy think of the little letters father sent them?" The unhappy
thought had crossed his mind that the children, not seeing him for
some months, might find him strange when they met again. "Don't
let the blessed fellows forget father," he wrote.

Of the letters Mary Lincoln wrote her husband at this time only
one is known to exist. It shows she too found the separation irksome:
"How much, I wish instead of writing, we were together this evening,
I feel very sad away from you." But she at least had the consolation

that the children were with her. She was writing on a Saturday night, she said, and "our *babies* are asleep." One of them had been ailing, but she had reassuring news: "Our little Eddy, has recovered from his little spell of sickness."

One can almost imagine the mother's warm voice talking about Eddie as her pen continued: "Dear boy, I must tell you a little story about him. Bobby in his wanderings to day, came across in a yard, a little kitten, *your hobby*, he says he asked a man for it, he brought it triumphantly to the house, so soon as Eddy, spied it his *tenderness*, broke forth, he made them bring it *water*, fed it with bread himself, with his *own dear hands*, he was a delighted little creature over it . . ."

Unfortunately Mrs. Lincoln's stepmother, the second Mrs. Robert Todd, keenly disliked "the whole cat race," and in what Mary Lincoln called "a very unfeeling manner, she ordered the servant near, to throw it out," the two-year-old Eddie "screaming & protesting loudly against the proceeding." His mother emphasized how "long & loud" those screams were; no Lincoln child was accustomed to having his wishes so disregarded. But there was more to it than this. Eddie was like his father in showing tenderness for a helpless kitten. When Mrs. Lincoln wrote "*your hobby*" she was referring to her husband's marked love for cats. It will be seen that this was a family devoted to pets.

The mother's letter ends with a reassurance to Lincoln's plea that she should not let the children forget father: "Do not fear the children, have forgotten you . . . Even E[ddie's] eyes brighten at the mention of your name."

Mr. Lincoln's letter to his wife in June is a short one, as he was writing in the House of Representatives. It is concerned with plans for her return to Washington and ends: "Come on just as soon as you can—I want to see you, and our dear—*dear* boys very much. Every body here wants to see our dear Bobby."

For a woman with two small children to take the rough week-long trip back to Washington required finding someone to go with her to help and protect her. Mrs. Lincoln was still in Lexington in July when her husband wrote with further mention of her trip, which seems to have been postponed. It is a sprightly letter full of bits of news about their friends. With her absorbing interest in babies, he knew she would be pleased with such an iten as this: "Mrs. Richardson is still here; and what is more, has a baby—so Richardson says, and he ought to know." But it ends on a note of concern about her overdoing and of affection for those all-important children. Lincoln had good reason to know that their offspring were very strenuous charges. "By the way, you do not intend to do without a girl, because the one you had has left you? Get another as soon as you can to take charge of the dear codgers. Father expected to see you all sooner; but let it pass; stay as long as you please, and come when you please. Kiss and love the dear rascals."

CHAPTER 3

Two More "Blessed Fellows"

MARY LINCOLN and her two boys remained in Lexington the summer of 1848. They undoubtedly spent some time at the Todd summer home "Buena Vista," a rambling frame dwelling some miles out on the Leestown Pike. It was a wonderful place for the children, especially Bobbie, who had lovely country acres to roam over and small Negro children from the stone slave cabins back of the house to do his bidding.

Scanty historical evidence makes it difficult to follow the movements of Mr. Lincoln's family in September. Certain things are known but details are hidden. He himself went to New England to make some political speeches. And on October 7 the *Daily Democrat* reported: "Hon. A. Lincoln and Family passed down to Springfield this morning on his way home from Congress." So it is evident that his family joined him somewhere before he got home.

Mrs. Lincoln wrote many years later that she and the two boys were with him in New England, where they were "detained by the illness of our youngest son [Eddie]." One also has the statement from Robert in his autobiographical sketch that during the winter of 1848–1849, "I lived with my Grandfather at Lexington Ky." It would seem that if he was going to stay in Lexington that winter, he would have been left there. On the other hand, plans are subject to change, and Eddie's illness might even have influenced the decision, though this is pure conjecture. Mr. Lincoln had to return to Washington late in November leaving his wife in Springfield. Eddie was not strong and if Mrs. Lincoln had an ailing child to take care of alone, it was undoubtedly a good plan to park the strenuous Bobbie elsewhere.

That winter with the Todds in Lexington undoubtedly had far-reaching effects on Robert and may explain many things in his personality. He was between the ages of five and six, an age in which a child is lastingly molded. He must have liked his Lexington relatives and have wanted to stay, or his indulgent parents would not have so arranged it. Ever after he would naturally have a deep sense of kinship with the Todds, both those in Lexington and those in Springfield.

Judging from evidence in his later life, Robert seems to have been born with the Todd tastes, abilities, and inclinations. The Todd relatives had so much to offer in contrast to the modest household of his odd lawyer father who had grown up in the backwoods. The Todd ancestors had a distinguished record, they had occupied positions of trust and honor, they were intelligent, gifted, determined people, excellent fighters as soldiers, and patriotic citizens. The Todd kin whom Robert knew had the things he liked, high standards of social correctness, prosperity and the comfortable type of living that goes with it. It is easy to see how he could have come under their influence and looked at matters through their eyes.

Perhaps even as young as he was that winter of 1848–1849 he absorbed some of their social attitudes and certainly he had opportunity to do so later from the powerful clique of his mother's relatives in Springfield. They were the socially prominent people of the town. There was his Aunt Elizabeth Todd Edwards, his mother's oldest sister, married to Ninian W. Edwards, son of a former governor of Illinois. The Edwardses lived in a mansion on "Aristocracy Hill," as it was called, and had lavish entertainments for the elite of Springfield. Robert's Aunt Frances was married to Dr. William Wallace, the Lincolns' family doctor, and was quite comfortably situated, as was his Aunt Ann, the wife of a Springfield merchant, Clark M. Smith. His mother's cousins the John Todd Stuarts were an outstanding family with a fine home. There they all were within easy walking distance with much family visiting back and forth and Robert, another child in the collection of small cousins, quick at picking up ideas.

Some of the Todd attitudes which would now seem snobbish were merely the views contemporary with their era, Southern origin, and upper-class position. But they were not the views of Robert's father. The point is that his ideals were not generally contemporary with the age in which he lived; they were ahead of it. His views in many things were completely opposed to the righteously held opinions of his in-laws.

Robert, as he grew up in Springfield, undoubtedly recognized in time the feeling of some of his Todd relatives, especially his Aunt Elizabeth Edwards, that his mother had married beneath her, had married a man "on a different social plane," one they considered "not capable," and a man with "radical" views. His mother, who had pas-

sionate faith in the greatness of the man she had married, constantly
had this attitude to contend with. It made things difficult for her,
and it is said she never quite forgave her sister Elizabeth for opposing
her marriage to Mr. Lincoln. If Robert, with the immature judgment
of a boy, absorbed any of this Todd feeling of superiority toward his
father, it might explain the curious restraint and suggestion of conflict that appear in Lincoln's comments on his first-born and the lack
of closeness between them. Perhaps it might also throw partial light
on Robert's strange reluctance later to tell about his father as he had
known him in his boyhood. This conjecture seems to fit in with known
facts. At all events, where Robert's personality seems off key in the
Lincoln family into which he was born, it harmonizes perfectly with
the Todds.

Following the winter spent in Kentucky, Robert presumably was
back in Springfield by the summer of 1849, fortunately so, as Lexington was panic-stricken and prostrate then with an epidemic of
the deadly plague cholera. In July Robert Todd, the grandfather for
whom he was named, died, apparently of this horrible disease. It
was probably the little boy's first real acquaintance with death. But
it was something that happened in Kentucky; death was on its way
to the cottage in Springfield.

When the New Year of 1850 came in, there was sickness and anxiety in the Lincoln home. Little Eddie had taken ill in December.
What the disease was it is now difficult to determine. Medical knowledge was rudimentary—and helpless—then and even if the contemporary diagnosis had come down, it would probably not have been
trustworthy. A doctor in this century has suggested diphtheria, but
this does not seem to harmonize with Mr. Lincoln's statement that
Eddie "was sick fiftytwo days." January dragged by with the father
and mother becoming more and more distressed and worn out with
their constant nursing. On the morning of February 1 the long vigil
ended; their little son lay dead.

Robert was old enough to remember the strangeness of that day.
Rain pattered on the roof of the cottage, inside the rooms were darkened, kind neighbors came to help make arrangements, speaking in
hushed voices, and he heard the sound of his mother's uncontrollable
weeping, a dreadful sound to a six-year-old child. His father's face
was haggard and filled with deep lines. People sat up all night beside the form of his little brother that was so strangely still. He doubtless heard strange new words like "grave," "cemetery," and "funeral."

Afterwards the house seemed lonely and quiet. His father had
none of his usual funmaking and playfulness; his mother's cheerful-

ness and gaiety were gone. It was a dark time for Bobbie, who had little buoyancy of spirit in his make-up but did have much vulnerability to hurts.

A few days after the funeral one of Springfield's newspapers, the *Illinois Journal,* printed "By Request" an unsigned poem called "Little Eddie." Its four stanzas seem stilted and Victorian now.

> The angel death was hovering nigh,
> And the lovely boy was called to die.

Yet there comes through these verses the picture of a little boy's soft hair lying still on his cold forehead and the sound of brokenhearted parents calling for the child who never again would answer. The poem ends:

> Bright is the home to him now given,
> For "of such is the kingdom of Heaven."

Perhaps Abraham or Mary Lincoln wrote the verses. The quotation in the last line seems to have been a comforting thought to them; at least they chose it for the inscription on the white marble tombstone that was placed on Eddie's grave:

> EDWARD B.
> *Son of*
> A. & M. LINCOLN.
> DIED
> Feb. 1. 1850.
> *Aged*
> 3 years 10 months
> 18 days.
> *Of such is the kingdom of Heaven.*

That marble slab would guard the little grave in Hutchinson's Cemetery for fifteen years; then it would be overturned and lie face down.

Little Eddie's portrait is drawn by a minimum of lines. Baby though he was, he noted the absence of the father who had "gone tapila" and his eyes brightened with love at the mention of that father's name. His tenderness broke forth at the sight of a forlorn kitten; he wanted to feed and comfort it with his *"own dear hands."* He was a "blessed fellow," a "dear codger." Only those few strokes of the pen are left but they are sufficient to sketch the picture of an affectionate and deeply loved little boy, whose loss left permanent scars in the hearts of his father and mother. She never afterwards could talk of him without tears, and when the day came for Mr. Lincoln to leave Illinois and he faced his neighbors to say good-by, remembering all that Springfield had held for him, his mind turned to that little grave.

It was desirable that the Lincolns get away from the lonely home, and a good reason for a trip had already presented itself. While Eddie was ill in January, Bobbie's maternal great-grandmother, Mrs. Robert Parker of Lexington, had died, and matters connected with the settlement of her estate called for a trip to that town. The Lincolns had made a similar journey the fall before because of a contest over the will of Mr. Todd. Lincoln represented the legal interests of the four heirs in Springfield.

Again there was the thrill and excitement of a journey under the slow, picturesque methods of the time. Bobbie was probably more of a nuisance to the other passengers than ever; after losing Eddie his parents could deny him nothing. He was quite a seasoned traveler by now and returning to Lexington after his winter there the year before must have seemed like a homecoming. Again he had the companionship of Emilie, now a beautiful girl in her teens, and the other Todd children. Mr. Lincoln had to return to Springfield (these trips were playing havoc with his law practice and income) but Mary Lincoln and her son remained with her stepmother and family at the country home, Buena Vista. Here Bobbie with his small uncles dashed about on ponies, slid down the icehouse roof, and frolicked with the dogs. Again there were colored people to wait on him. It is easy to understand why the Todd way of living had appeal for him. No other Lincoln son was to have such close association with the Todds or would be so influenced by them.

After Bobbie and his mother returned to Springfield, it was not long before people became aware that the Lincolns were going to have another baby. Springfield was full of helpful and sympathetic neighbors who shared each other's joys and sorrows. Doubtless many kind heads nodded approval, thinking that another baby would be the best possible thing for the Lincolns after the loss of their little boy.

The news spread when Mr. Lincoln went out on the judicial circuit that fall, traveling with other lawyers from town to town to hold court. It happened that his friend David Davis, one of those who made the rounds with him, had lost a baby daughter shortly before setting out. Being unwilling to leave his grieving wife alone, he took her and his eight-year-old son George with him on the circuit for a couple of months. Now Mr. Davis was so large and heavy he had to use two horses for the vehicle in which he and Mrs. Davis rode from town to town and there was no room for their boy at all. So the fatherly Mr. Lincoln took little George with him in his open one-horse buggy drawn by "old Buck."

Their common bereavement drew Lincoln and the Davises very close together, and he told them that he and Mary expected another child. So one can understand the interested feeling back of the words when Sarah Davis wrote her husband in January: "Has Mrs. Lincoln been confined yet & if so what has she? I am anxious to know." Everyone was anxious to know.

Mrs. Davis was behind the times; the baby had been born December 21, 1850, just in time for Christmas, a perfect boy. He was named William Wallace after the husband of Mrs. Lincoln's sister Frances, Dr. Wallace, who probably officiated at the birth as he was the Lincolns' family physician. The relation to a family doctor, especially when he functions as obstetrician, is very close. The child was promptly nicknamed Willie. Beautifully endowed, sweet-natured, bright and responsive, he brought a measure of healing to his parents, who soon gave him complete adoration.

Again those good friends, the David Davises, furnish a most intimate detail. Nearly a year and a half later Lincoln and Davis were out on the judicial circuit. Mr. Davis in a letter to his wife told her how much the arrival of the stagecoach with mail meant to these traveling husbands and fathers and added: "Lincoln got a letter from his wife. She says she has the nursing sore mouth—child 18 mos. old. I guess she ought to have quit nursing some time ago." (There seems to have been a belief that prolonged lactation led to this condition.) Mr. Davis also once wrote his wife a curious item about Robert. There had been much talk about a murder case in Boston for which the convicted murderer, Dr. Webster, had just been hanged. "Lincoln says that his little boy Robert has been counting the days that Dr. Webster had to live & Thursday he said that Thursday was the last night he had to live. Rather singular that the event should so mark itself . . . on a child of seven years."

With Willie's birth Robert's nose was once more out of joint, especially since he was in competition with such a lovable child. But he was older now and was going to school. He himself later gave the meager details of that early education: "I have a dim recollection of being under the slipper-guardianship of a Schoolmistress until 1850, when I became a pupil at the Academy of a Mr. Esterbrook, & under his instruction I remained for three years." The words "slipper-guardianship" create the picture of said slipper being forcibly applied to the seat of a small pair of pants. Bobbie apparently received some discipline at school even if he did not at home. From the standpoint of the schoolmistress he probably needed it. His father indicated later that Bob, the "little rascal," showed some resistance to learning his letters. Mr. Lincoln had not erred in saying he was "quite smart enough—" he was emphatically that under varying circumstances all his life; it was apparently a disinclination to be forced to apply himself to such "poky" matters when there were more active and interesting things for a very mischievous boy to do.

The seat of Bobbie's pants may well have been adorned with a patch. Being the first child of the Lincolns, his little boyhood came at a time when they were more limited financially than they were when the younger children came along. Mr. Lincoln's letters frequently complained of their being poor and Mrs. Lincoln earnestly practiced economy, including the patching of Bobbie's pants. It is possible this hurt that sensitive pride of his, especially as the Todds in Lexington could afford nice clothes. In contrast to his father, who had little awareness of what he wore, Robert in mature years was to dress with meticulous care. Perhaps such early humiliations contributed in some degree to that quality which shows in his letters as a young man—the determination to make money.

Much worse than the chagrin of wearing patches was the shame caused by that inward-turning eye. With the thoughtless and brutal cruelty of children his schoolmates called him "cockeye." Touchy to criticism of any kind, as was usual with the Todds, the little boy undoubtedly felt furious resentment and humiliation. What could be done to improve the eye condition was being done. An old document states that he cured it by peeping through the keyhole of a door, perhaps a case of strengthening the weak eye by using it. One notes that it was considered cured, which implies it became practically unnoticeable, but a photograph taken when he was approaching old age shows a slight inward turning of the left eye and in later life, by his own statement, he lost the sight of one eye, presumably that one. That eye defect may well have contributed to the shyness, and uncomfortable reserve, that became so marked a trait in his personality. Robert seems not to have been an adjusted child in his school days in Springfield.

He had, of course, the mishaps of boyhood. His Aunt Frances Wallace told later of his being bitten by a dog supposed to be mad. In the primitive medical development then, it was thought that danger of hydrophobia could be averted by what was called a "mad-stone."

The "stone" was applied for a time to the wound caused by the bite and was supposed to draw out the poison. Afterward it was soaked in milk or water and gave off a greenish-yellow scum which was considered convincing evidence that the poison had been drawn out. The stones were rare, and according to Mrs. Wallace's recollection, Mr. Lincoln took Bob to Terre Haute, Indiana, where one was available. People do not believe in mad-stones now, but the Lincolns provided for their children what they thought was the best medical treatment they could get. The feelings that revolved around that trip, the anxiety of the parents and the fright of the child, made it an ordeal for everybody concerned.

By the time Willie's second birthday came around, the Lincolns were looking forward to the birth of another child. They did so want this one to be a girl. Mr. Lincoln had talked with David Davis about it, as the Davises wanted a girl too. But the baby who was born in the Lincoln cottage on April 4, 1853, was destined to be an unpredictable little individual, and he started his career of doing the unexpected by turning out to be a boy.

It could not be denied that it was a disappointment. The following September Mrs. Davis wrote to her husband: "Is Mr. Lincoln with you on the circuit? And has he become reconciled to his little son?" She could write with a certain complacency as well as sympathy, for by that time the Davises had their wished-for daughter.

In a way the Lincolns were never quite reconciled; they continued to have an unfulfilled longing. Mr. Lincoln a few years later was to write to a little girl: "I regret the necessity of saying I have no daughters." And there is record that Mrs. Lincoln said repeatedly to an attractive sixteen-year-old miss: "I wish I had a little girl like you." But this in no way affected their adoration of the son who had arrived.

"Dear little Taddie was named, for my husband's father, Thomas Lincoln—no *T* for a middle name—was nicknamed Taddie by his loving Father," wrote Mrs. Lincoln a dozen years after his birth. That seemed fair enough—to name one son for the grandfather on the Todd side and one for the grandfather on the Lincoln side. The baby's head was larger than usual and Mr. Lincoln, viewing the contrast between head and tiny baby figure (perhaps looking on as his mother gave him a bath), called him a little Tadpole, and thus started a nickname that was ultimately to be known all over the nation.

With the coming of Willie and Tad, that incomparable pair, the Lincolns entered a new phase, one with more variety and sparkle.

The remaining years of the eighteen fifties formed the golden period of their family life. Springfield was expanding and so were Mr. Lincoln's fortunes. In and out of the home on Eighth Street first toddled, then raced two lovable, original little boys. Affectionate, mischievous, warmhearted, responsive, devoted to each other, and full of childhood's joy of living, they were indeed "blessed fellows."

CHAPTER 4

Growing Up in Springfield

SPRINGFIELD was not so sure as the parents about the blessedness of the Lincoln sons. By the time Willie and Tad came along the laissez-faire policy of the Lincolns toward their children was firmly established. Mrs. Lincoln later gave a good description of the situation and attitude: "Mr. Lincoln was the kindest man and most loving husband and father in the world. He gave us all unbounded liberty. . . . He was very—exceedingly indulgent to his children. Chided or praised them for what they did—their acts, etc. He always said: 'It is my pleasure that my children are free, happy and unrestrained by parental tyranny. Love is the chain whereby to bind a child to its parents.'"

In an age which was convinced that children should be seen and not heard, and that to spare the rod was to spoil the child, the Lincolns were anticipating an attitude of the present century that children's personalities should not be frustrated. Their use of praise as a method of encouragement to a youngster was not in favor then; sober, Bible-quoting citizens feared it might breed vanity. Mr. Lincoln was ahead of his time, as usual.

These advanced theories went rather hard with some of the inhabitants of Springfield. Mr. William H. Herndon, junior partner at the law office of Lincoln and Herndon on the west side of the public square, was often greatly frustrated in consequence, and left a flavorful and strongly emotional account of his sufferings. For Mr. Lincoln used to bring what Herndon called "*them* little devils" to the law office.

It usually happened on a Sunday morning when the father served as baby sitter so that Mrs. Lincoln could go to church. There again he violated the accepted idea of the day that baby tending was something strictly in woman's sphere. A dignified lawyer who wore a stovepipe hat had no business looking after the children. But Mr. Lincoln would put Willie and Tad into their little wagon and haul them through the streets on that familiar route to his office, help or carry them up the stairs, deposit them on the grimy floor, and then bury himself in legal papers. The children would proceed to tear up the office, scatter the books and papers, smash the pens, spill the ink, and sometimes as a grand climax heap up books, papers, inkstands, pens, and ashes from the stove in a pile on the floor and then dance on it. Herndon in his private correspondence even reveals in forthright terms that the children were brought to the office before they were housebroken. Mr. Lincoln, absorbed in his work, took no notice whatever of the wrecking that was in progress. Herndon said he "wanted to wring the necks of these brats and pitch them out of the windows." But he added: "Out of respect for Lincoln I kept my mouth shut."

Keeping his mouth shut under any circumstances must have been a terrific strain on the loquacious junior partner. Probably the real reason he kept quiet lies in his statement that Mr. Lincoln "worshipped his children and *what* they worshipped [;] he loved what they loved and hated what they hated. . . ." In other words, to incur the dislike of the children was to risk Mr. Lincoln's displeasure. Mr. Lincoln "was the great big man of our firm," once wrote Herndon, "and I was the little one. The little one looked *naturally* up to the big one. . . ." He did not care to offend the senior partner but he thought Lincoln was "a fool" in being so blind to his children's faults.

The benighted father actually seemed to admire the antics of the children as an indication of their brightness. To be sure, both he and their mother had liked to play pranks in their time; the boys came by their prankishness honestly. He expected others to be as tolerant in the matter as he was himself. It was the one thing on which the most reasonable Mr. Lincoln was not exactly reasonable. Mrs. Lincoln herself said that his one weakness was his indulgence to her and the children.

An incident which occurred after the family moved to Washington illustrates his attitude. Tad and his father had gone to the telegraph office and while Mr. Lincoln was looking over the latest dispatches, Tad strolled into the adjoining room where some very black ink and a very white marble table top gave him a bright idea. Dipping his fingers in the inkwell he began to draw designs on the marble, to the great indignation of the telegraph operator, one Madison Buell by name. Mr. Buell seized the boy by the collar (doubtless to his great amazement) and marched him into the cipher room, where Mr. Lincoln was reading. Tad with his usual honesty held up his inky fingers and the outraged Mr. Buell pointed through the open door at the ruined table tops. Lincoln lifted Tad in his arms, said briefly, "Come, Tad; Buell is abusing you," and left the office. Mr. Herndon was quite right—Mr. Lincoln would not have liked it if he had reproved that wrecking crew at the law office.

In one delightful reminiscence Mr. Lincoln was the one who played the prank and the joke was on Tad. The Lincolns were having an evening party and the youngest, much to his indignation, had been put to bed. He did not stay there but got up and, clad in a red flannel night gown, sat peeping through a door, complaining in loud whispers of the great injustice of his being shut out from the party. His father heard him, opened the door, picked Tad up, and carried him, squirming with embarrassment at being thus exhibited, the length of the room where the guests were assembled, introducing him right and left and laughing as he went.

The little wagon in which Mr. Lincoln hauled the children to his office apparently figured largely in his baby sitting. It was his custom to put the babies in it and pull them up and down the street in front of his house, usually holding a book with his free hand and reading as he walked. Once one of the children fell out and lay squalling on the ground while Mr. Lincoln went on completely unaware of anything wrong. Mrs. Lincoln, arriving on the scene, shrieked at the sight of the crying baby and gave Mr. Lincoln an unrestrained scolding. Afterwards the ridiculous baby spilling was a family joke whose very mention brought a laugh.

A friend of Mr. Lincoln's, Judge Samuel H. Treat, with whom he delighted to play chess, had an experience in which he undoubtedly shared the infanticidal impulses of Mr. Herndon. An absorbing game of chess between Mr. Lincoln and Judge Treat was in progress one morning at the Treat office when one of the Lincoln boys appeared to summon his father to dinner. It was the old hopeless problem of getting him home to meals. Lincoln promised to come, the boy left, and the game went on as before.

By and by the boy returned with an even more urgent announcement that dinner was ready. But the engrossed players did not even notice his presence. This is at least one case where a Lincoln child was completely frustrated. Exasperated at being so ignored, the boy moved nearer and deliberately kicked board and chessmen into the air. Judge Treat expected parental wrath to go into action, but Mr. Lincoln calmly arose, took the boy by the hand, and started to leave. At the door he turned with a good-natured smile and said to his friend, "Well, Judge, I reckon we'll have to finish this game some other time." After all, the boy had found a solution to what seemed an unsolvable problem; he had cut the Gordian knot. But Judge Treat remarked feelingly to Jesse Weik, to whom he told the story, ". . . I can assure you of one thing: if that little rascal had been a boy of mine he never would have applied his boots to another chessboard." (This incident has been told a number of times with variations, and sometimes the boy is identified as Bob and sometimes as Tad.)

All in all the Lincoln family furnished much food for conversation and considerable entertainment for the talkative town of Springfield. The recollections of friends and neighbors present a series of highly diverting street scenes. The tall, unique figure of Mr. Lincoln himself in the Sunday best of a Western lawyer—stovepipe hat, black cloth swallow-tailed coat, black satin vest open low down to display a broad expanse of shirt bosom, and collar turned down over a black silk neckerchief—was enough to enrich any picture. One reminiscence adds to this the wriggling form of little Tad, slung over his father's arm like a pair of saddlebags. Mr. Lincoln, having left church in the middle of the service one Sunday morning, was making long strides down the street toward home. Meeting a group of friends at one corner and anticipating the question which he saw in their faces, he said with twinkling eyes, "Gentlemen, I entered this colt, but he kicked around so I had to withdraw him."

If it were possible by some magic to witness one of these incidents that were free shows to the citizens of Springfield, a favorite choice, perhaps, would be one that occurred when Willie was three or four and Tad a baby. His mother had undressed Willie to bathe him and had left him by himself for a moment, possibly to give attention to Tad. Most mothers find out sooner or later that leaving an unclad child alone is a mistake. Willie saw his chance for a glorious freedom unhampered by clothes and buttons, and scampered out of the room and out of the house. He flew down the street, then ducked under a fence into a green field. His father, who happened to be on the front porch, stood laughing at the pleasing sight of the small cherub asserting his independence, but Mrs. Lincoln begged him to go after the boy. Mr. Lincoln gave chase across the field, finally captured the runaway and gathered him up in his arms to kiss the gleeful face and small white body in an outburst of father love. Then, both doubtless chuckling with the fun of the adventure, he mounted the boy on his shoulders, the little naked legs around his neck, and carried him back in triumph to his mother and the bath.

Sometimes the show was advertised by rounds of wailing. A neighbor, hearing children crying, hurried to his door to see Mr. Lincoln herding Willie and Tad along, both yelling at the top of their voices.

"Why, Mr. Lincoln, what's the matter with the boys?" he asked. "Just what's the matter with the whole world," was the salty answer; "I've got three walnuts and each wants two."

When Tad was very small and flew into one of his tempests of rage, it is said his father would hold him out at his long arm's length and laugh at the little fellow's attempts to kick him in the face. That might have amused the neighbors somewhat, but such disrespect to a parent shocked them. Mr. Herndon and Judge Treat were not the only citizens who had emotional opinions as to the manner in which the Lincolns were raising their children. It was probably a favorite grievance in conversations among the various relatives of Mary Lincoln, especially her three sisters, who were all rearing families of their own and could not have cared too much for the horrible example set by the Lincoln boys. Doubtless they offered unappreciated advice (the Todds were apt to be outspoken in giving advice but were not very good at receiving it), but only one mild incident of this seems to have come down in the records. Frances Wallace once saw her brother-in-law carrying Tad (who had probably outgrown the little wagon) to his office and said, "Why, Mr. Lincoln, put down that great big boy. He's big enough to walk." She might as well have saved her breath, for Mr. Lincoln answered amiably, "Oh, don't you think his little feet get too tired?"

He perhaps carried Tad slung over his shoulder, as that was not particularly tiring to one of Mr. Lincoln's great physical strength. But often he held Tad by the hand or the little fellow hung onto his long coattails. People in Springfield became quite accustomed to seeing Mr. Lincoln on the streets with his two younger boys, for he loved to take them with him. Mr. Herndon gave a delightful word picture of such a scene: "On a winters morning he might be seen stalking and stilting it toward the market house, basket on his arm, his old grey shawl wrapped around his neck, his little Willie or Tad running along at his heels, asking a thousand little quick questions which his father heard not. . . ."

One of the most engaging of these street scenes is pictured in a story told later by Mr. Lincoln's friend George T. M. Davis in his autobiography. Mr. Davis was visiting Springfield and happened to be standing on the shady side of his hotel when along came Mr. Lincoln with Tad holding onto the tail of his frock coat. Of course Lincoln stopped and the two men began to talk politics. Bob Lincoln came walking down the street, joined the group, and began to talk to Tad. The father's ear caught something in their conversation which made him pause and turn to the boys. "Tad," he said, "show Mr. Davis the knife I bought you yesterday." Then turning to the visitor, he added, "It's the first knife Tad ever had, and it's a big thing for him."

Tad hesitated and seemed embarrassed. "You haven't lost your knife, have you?" asked his father.

"No, but I ain't got any," the boy answered.

"What has become of it?" persisted Mr. Lincoln with a quizzical look. Tad again hesitated. He was a truthful child but apparently did not want to be a telltale about his brother. Lincoln waited and then Tad came out with it: "Bob told me if he was me, he'd swap my knife for candy."

Lincoln laughed and said to Bob, who in his turn was looking embarrassed, "Bob, how much did you pay for that candy?" Bob named the price and his father promptly said, "Why, Tad's knife cost three bits . . . ; do you think you made a fair trade with Tad?"

Robert was also truthful and evidently a bit ashamed. "No, sir," he replied, and taking the knife out of his pocket, he handed it to Tad.

The lawyer father conducting this adjustment continued, "I guess, Bob, that's about right on your part and now, Tad, as you've got your knife, you must give back to Bob the candy he gave you for the knife."

"I can't," exclaimed Tad, "'cause I ate up all the candy Bob give me, and I ain't got no money to buy it."

Mr. Lincoln insisted: "Bob must have his candy back to make things square between you."

All three were silent a moment over this quandary; then Lincoln without comment handed Tad one bit. Tad's face lighted up and he shrieked out joyfully, "Come on, Bob, I'll get your candy back for you." Mr. Lincoln had carried on the negotiation in a merry tone and the two men laughed heartily as the boys started off storeward.

Somehow Robert seems not to show up to advantage in the incidents which were preserved in the memories of the old-timers. One recollection tells of him and his friends giving shows in the Lincoln barn. Bob is the only Lincoln child mentioned; perhaps the other boys were too young to participate. Admission to these shows was paid in buttons and pins.

There were many dogs in the neighborhood and in this particular episode Bob and his friends were trying to train them for a show. For dramatic purposes the boys wanted the dogs to stand on their hind feet and growl, but the dogs did not co-operate very well. To make them stand up, someone suggested putting a rope around each dog's neck and over a rafter, which bade fair to turn the performance into a canine hanging. Hearing howls and screams coming from the

Lincoln barn, someone reported the matter to Mr. Lincoln, who speedily investigated. It is said that as he crossed the back yard he seized a stave from the ash barrel (Mrs. Lincoln had been making soap and had left the ash hopper standing) as a handy instrument for restoring order. The boys fled and Mr. Lincoln doubtless released the long-suffering animals. He hated cruelty and he had a great fondness for dogs and cats.

In fact, pets figured largely in the Lincoln household. The picture of three boys growing up in a small country town would not be complete without them. Mr. Herndon, still in disapproving vein, reported that if the Lincoln children "wanted a dog-cat-rat or the Devil it was all right and well treated—housed—petted—fed—fondled &c &c." The boys were entitled to their love of animals; Mr. Lincoln had it to a remarkable degree. He loved his horses which took him on the long, lonely journeys across the prairies when he was out on the circuit, and "old Buck" and "old Bob" have come down in history. As Mrs. Lincoln said, cats were his "hobby." One of his favorite ways of relaxing was to get down on the floor and play with the current cat or kitten, petting it and talking to it for a long time in complete enjoyment. But a neighbor remembered how Robert used to harness the cats, and any cat lover knows that is grounds for feline indignation. The same neighbor recalled that Bob and another boy used to "harness up" a dog (apparently to a little wagon) and go into the woods to get roots. The kind of root is not specified; perhaps the Lincoln family wanted sassafras tea.

The days fell into a pleasant pattern of small-town life for the growing family. The boys had many playmates living near and the gang could usually be found playing in this or that home or yard where the mother looked after her own and the neighbors' children indiscriminately. Sometimes it was the Lincoln back yard; sometimes it was at Mrs. Sprigg's or over at the Melvins'. After the Melvin family moved to the neighborhood with five sons, their house was such a popular place that Mr. Lincoln used to stop in sometimes on his way home from the office and inquire, "Are my boys here?" He would tactfully detach them from whatever important project they were engaged in, not always without difficulty, and shepherd them home.

There is a pleasant account of his collecting Tad at Mrs. Sprigg's. He would enter at the back door, in the informal way of close neighbors, and solemnly ask, "Where is that bad boy?" "Mith Spwigg," as Tad called her in his appealing lisp, would promptly enter into the spirit of the thing and reply, "I do not think he is so very bad. You are surely mistaken, Mr. Lincoln."

Mr. Lincoln would meditate on this idea a bit and then say, "Perhaps you are right, Mrs. Sprigg. Tad's really not very bad, but I don't want him to become unwelcome over here and I want to keep track of his whereabouts." Mrs. Sprigg would then silently indicate where Tad was hiding, usually under a bed, and Mr. Lincoln would get down on the floor and drag him out, probably to the accompaniment of squeals and childish giggles, hoist him to his shoulder, and carry him home in triumph. This little drama was so popular with Tad there had to be a number of repeat performances.

There were delightful days in summer when Mr. Lincoln would gather up some of the neighborhood boys along with his own, pile them in his "calash," a roomy kind of carriage, and drive them out to the Sangamon River for a picnic and fishing. He would play games with them, tell them stories, and have as good a time as any of them. Various recollections show that he enjoyed a game of marbles or blind man's buff as much as any child, and he was excellent at spinning a top.

Sometimes the outings were on foot. James Gourley, a good neighbor who lived around the corner on Jackson Street, so that his yard adjoined the Lincoln back yard, remembered that "Lincoln would take his children and would walk out on the rail way out in the country—would talk to them—explain things carefully—particularly."

The Lincolns had what might be called a milk alliance with Mr. Gourley. For a time they bought their milk from him, but three sons consumed a lot of milk and the four Gourley boys even more, so finally Mr. Lincoln bought his own cow, which was pastured east of the homes with the Gourley cow. It became the duty of the Gourley boys and Bob Lincoln to drive the cows back and forth at milking time, and when it was not convenient for them to do so, Mr. Lincoln himself often did it. It creates quite a peaceful rural scene to think of Mr. Lincoln or the boys walking along the overgrown country paths with the cows before them, a lowing-herd-winding-slowly-o'er-the-lea atmosphere.

On a certain glorified day when a circus came to Springfield, Mr. Lincoln was seen on the street carrying a small child with one arm, his free hand guiding another, and a whole troop of happy youngsters following closely, bound for the circus parade. In this recollection appears the last faint gesture of discipline: when his sons would not behave, he would ostentatiously break a switch off a shrub or tree, but somehow it was never used.

Across Eighth Street from the Lincolns lived the Solomon Wheelocks, whose teen-age daughter Ardelia ran in and out of the

Lincoln home almost as freely as she did her own. She later left some close-up and engaging recollections of the Lincoln boys. "Delie," as Mr. Lincoln called her, was helping Mrs. Lincoln get dressed one evening for a party at the Jesse Dubois' down the street when in came Willie and Tad from a candy pull smeared with molasses taffy from head to foot. They naturally wanted to know why their mother was putting on her yellow satin dress over the big hoop skirts, and when they heard about the party they decided they wanted to go too. Mrs. Lincoln said they could not go. (The plan was for them to stay at home with Robert as baby sitter.) The two little boys began to kick and scream in protest, which brought Mr. Lincoln to the scene at once.

"This will never do," he protested. "Mary, if you will let the boys go, I will take care of them."

"Why, Father, you know that is no place for boys to be. When people give a party like that it is no place for children." Willie and Tad stopped yelling to listen hopefully.

Mr. Lincoln said he would take them in the back way and leave them in the kitchen. He then talked to the boys about being good and keeping their promises and Delie and Robert began to clean them up and get them dressed. In the hurry and excitement Tad's small pants were put on hind side before. (Delie must have been responsible for this; Robert would have known better.) Tad set up a howl again because, as he said, he "couldn't walk good." But his father waved his hand disapprovingly, saying, "Remember, now, remember," and Tad evidently felt it was not safe to press the point. When the little boys were presentable (aside from the slight irregularity in Tad's appearance), Mr. Lincoln took them ahead in order to leave them in the kitchen and Robert hastily got ready to follow with his mother. Somehow the kitchen idea did not work out and the entire Lincoln family attended the dignified reception. Springfield had another choice incident to talk about on the general subject of the outrageous way in which the Lincolns were bringing up their children.

Going to a party at the Lincolns' dressed in one's best clothes was a positive hazard. Mr. Herndon wrote how "Tad would dash into the room with a bacon ham in his hands swinging it . . . among silks— gold—tinsels & lace" and how "the ladies and gentlemen would give Tad a wide birth parting to let him through." Mr. Lincoln, Herndon went on, would chide the boy for it mildly, "but he would fail to see disgust on the faces of those present and annoyed at Tad."

Such a resourceful, interesting, and comforting father as Mr. Lincoln was sorely missed when he was away from home. And he was out of town traveling on the judicial circuit approximately half of the time, three months in spring and three months in the fall with only occasional week ends when he could get back. During his absence Mrs. Lincoln had to take the place of both father and mother. No one could have been more loving and sympathetic than she was, but she did not have the resources of a balanced personality that Mr. Lincoln had and she could not give her children the sense of security which his presence brought. She did not have a sense of security herself. It was her nature to be cheerful and gay but, being nervous and excitable, it was hard for her to meet responsibility. At night when the little family was alone in the house and outside all was dark along the unlighted streets and inside candles and oil lamps cast long grotesque shadows, Mary Lincoln was afraid. Mr. Lincoln used to pay a neighbor boy five cents a night to sleep in the house while he was away, but that brought her little reassurance.

The Lincoln boys learned that their mother was often ill with terrible headaches and that when she was angry or frightened she was apt to go into hysterics, saying and doing things she was afterwards sorry for. If Mr. Lincoln was at home he would explain that Mother was not well and perhaps take the boys off for a while until she was better. This weakness or illness did not affect the devotion of the father or that of Willie and Tad; there is abundant evidence they loved their mother dearly. But one wonders if the less demonstrative and more thin-skinned Robert was not humiliated at his mother's shortcomings. There is no doubt that the emotional instability of Mary Lincoln was an unfortunate factor in the growing up of her sons. Tad as a little boy was like her in his tendency to fly off the handle on slight provocation, and Mr. Lincoln, deeply loving both, understood well that the only way to deal with them in such outbursts was through gentleness and affection. In the long run, two of her sons were to have their lives profoundly influenced by the mother's afflictions.

CHAPTER 5

"Me and Father"

THE GROWING up of these American boys, of course, involved going to school. Both Mr. and Mrs. Lincoln set the highest value on education. The father had obtained his the hard way; in his backwoods rearing he had been known to walk miles for the treasure of a single book to read. The mother in her love of literature had taken what might be termed a sort of postgraduate course after she had finished at the fashionable school in Lexington which girls of established families attended. It probably was a worry to them that Robert showed no such interest and enterprise, but in their complete indulgence of all the children they were not likely to use pressure in the matter.

Robert frankly admitted his inadequate scholarship at Springfield in the account of his education which he wrote when he was twenty-one. After telling of his attending Mr. Esterbrook's Academy (referred to as a "pay school" by one who was his classmate there), he continued: "At this time [1853] there had been founded at Springfield an Institution of Learning called the 'Illinois State University,' at which I was placed and remained until the summer of 1859." (This institution is not to be confused with the University of Illinois; it was never tax supported and later became Concordia College, a theological seminary.) Robert described it somewhat disparagingly: "This 'University' had, I believe, four instructors, Dr. W. M. Reynolds being the President. The government was very easy, and we did just what pleased us, study consuming only a very small portion of our time. The Classes were divided as at College; and when I left I was about to enter the Senior Class."

It was really no more than a preparatory school, but it had students who were inclined to make better use of its instruction than Robert. Among them was a red-cheeked, black-eyed young fellow with a sparkling gift of expression, to whom the assignments for study were very easy. He had come from Pittsfield, Illinois, just to attend this school. His name was John Hay and he was nearly five years older than Robert. They thus began in Springfield a friendship and association that would have many unusual aspects down the long strange years ahead of them.

By the time Robert was ready to enter the senior class he had begun to realize, as a youth often does, that he was wasting time and to make serious plans for himself. "I became aware," he said, "that I could never get an education in that way. . . ." His awakening, as frequently happens, was to be assisted by a hard knock, a salutary blow to a normally inflated teen-age pride.

"Illinois State University" offered its freshmen Latin grammar and when Bob started that, his father, with the eager reaching out for all kinds of knowledge which he never lost, studied the language with him. A neighbor boy remembered Mr. Lincoln declining Latin nouns aloud as he went about his home duties. Doubtless he got fun out of it and did it with more boyish enthusiasm than Bob. The father may also have been trying in his gentle way to get his boy interested in his studies, or it may have been an attempt at companionship with the son who seems not to have recognized that paternal camaraderie so loved by Willie and Tad and by other children in Springfield.

One can only speculate as to the causes of Robert's standoffishness. It may have been adolescence or he may have shared the Todd feeling of superiority to his lowly born father. He was probably jealous of the younger boys and resentful of the way in which they were indulged and apparently much more loved by the parents. Perhaps all these factors contributed. At any rate, it seems almost incomprehensible, knowing the richness and warmth of the personality which Lincoln gave out to all around him, to find Robert, when he was not quite twenty-two, writing a letter in which he practically said he had never known his father intimately. The son had been asked for details of Lincoln's early life and this was the colorless answer: "My Father's life was of a kind which gave me but little opportunity to learn the details of his early career. During my childhood & early youth he was almost constantly away from home, attending courts or making political speeches—"

Perhaps he resented the fact that his father spent more time on the judicial circuit than the other lawyers. Mr. Lincoln made the complete round of the towns, which was not really necessary and which very few did. Mrs. Lincoln herself is said to have resented this prolonged absence. Robert continued his account by saying that he went away to school when he was sixteen and after that the opportunity for intimacy with his father did not occur. Any boy in the neighborhood, if asked about Mr. Lincoln, could have given a more satisfactory answer than that.

It is true that by the time he was twenty-two Robert's complex against giving out any personal information had been greatly aggravated by circumstances painful to him. It is also quite possible that he did not wish the unsatisfactory relationship between his father and himself brought to light. He had awakened further by that time and his constrained words might faintly suggest regret.

If Robert's growing years gave his parents some anxiety and puzzlement, Willie's gave them pure joy. He was his father over again both in magnetic personality and in his gifts and tastes. A few years later an astute sixteen-year-old girl, Julia Taft, was to describe him as "the most lovable boy I ever knew, bright, sensible, sweet-tempered and gentle-mannered."

He attended a private school, as Robert had, Miss Corcoran's school, and there was no need for Miss Corcoran to apply the slipper. Willie delighted in the study of books, just as his parents had. He was to write a poem when he was less than eleven years old, which doubtless gave a thrill of happy surmise to Abraham and Mary Lincoln, who delighted so much in poetry, and themselves knew the pleasure of composing verses. Willie formed a contrast in this to Robert, who said later he had not known his father ever wrote any poems. The oldest son in time would come to write most effectively and with a clarity akin to that of his father, but one doubts if he ever had that feeling for the word that is so beautifully and poetically right that one finds in Lincoln's writings.

But with Willie his father could get that special joy that comes to a parent when he recognizes that his child is mentally like him. Lincoln said himself that Willie's mind worked like his. He said it at breakfast one morning after the family had moved to Washington. Tad, who was about eight at the time, had had his sensitive feelings hurt by an unintentional slight and he was in tears. His father took the little fellow in his arms, pressed him close, kissed him, and tried to console him, but still the tears flowed.

The two younger boys were so devoted to each other it was almost as hard for Willie to witness Tad's tears as it was for Mr. Lincoln. He looked on sorrowfully at their father's failure to bring Tad out of his woe, then lapsed into an absorbed silence which lasted for ten or fifteen minutes. He was evidently trying hard to think of some way he could cheer Tad up. Mr. Lincoln was watching Willie and making sure that no one disturbed his mental concentration. Finally Willie clasped both hands together, shut his teeth over his lower lip, and looked up into his father's face with a smile. Mr. Lincoln had been waiting for this. "There!" he exclaimed. "You have it now, my boy, have you not?" Then turning to a guest who was at the breakfast table he explained, "I know every step of the process by which that boy arrived at his satisfactory solution of the question before him, as it is by just such slow methods I attain results."

This child and his father were interested in the same things. The title of a notable lecture which Mr. Lincoln gave in the late eighteen fifties, "Discoveries and Inventions," mentions two topics which he found fascinating. The particular invention which was having a booming development during that decade was the railroads. The country had become railroad conscious, thrilled with the wonder of this grand new system of transportation. Mr. Lincoln, while away on the circuit, could get home more often at the week ends because railroads were so much speedier than stagecoach or river boat. Willie, born at the beginning of this railroad decade, thrived in this atmosphere of interest and wonder. Railroads fascinated the little boy even as they did his father.

One can safely guess it did not take long for the makers of toys to perceive the possibilities in producing toy trains. It is known that Willie had a toy train when he was in Washington. One has excellent basis for picturing the father down on the floor with Willie and Tad, all equally absorbed in operating the quaint little engine and cars.

Willie even developed a fancy for drawing up railroad timetables, and by the time he was ten or eleven he could conduct an imaginary train from Chicago to New York with perfect precision. This involved a considerable use of figures, and here again the middle son was like his father in having a natural taste for mathematics. Lincoln said that he as a matter of self-education studied and "nearly mastered the Six-books of Euclid" after he became a member of Congress. Interest in mathematics was also one of the few things which the eldest son had in common with his father. Robert had a marked facility at figures and it was a quality of his mind to enjoy figuring. The time would come in his life when he would use astronomical calculations as a recreation.

The love of trains undoubtedly added glamour to a trip Willie took in 1859. Mr. Lincoln had to try a case in Chicago in early June and he took Willie along. One can imagine the shining wonder in the child's eyes as the engine tooted and the cars whizzed along at the amazing speed of perhaps thirty miles an hour. Then there was the adventure of staying at a big hotel (the Tremont House). Willie put the glowing feeling of that new experience into a letter which he wrote to his friend Henry Remann on June 6. Miss Corcoran's school had done well; Willie at eight and a half years was a good letter writer. "This town is a very beautiful place," he said happily. "Me and father have a nice little room to ourselves." That itself was a special treat and one can imagine Mr. Lincoln playfully pointing out the special features of the room as Willie further describes it: "We have two little pitcher on a washstand. The smallest one for me the largest one for father. We have two little towels on a top of both pitchers. The smallest one for me, the largest one for father."

With the same foresight, just as if it knew that it would be occupied by a tall father and little son, the room had provided itself with "two little beds" and "two little wash basin" in large and small sizes.

The two were having a wonderful time and in eager, unspoiled interest they were, one suspects, approximately the same age. "Me and father" had gone to "two theatres the other night," wrote Willie, and he also mentioned an "exhibition on wednesday before last." Abraham and Mary Lincoln were both greatly interested in dramatic performances of all kinds; here was a son who instinctively shared that interest. Again a letter of Robert's in later years shows he had not shared that type of companionship: "Personally I never attended a play with my father. . . ."

Another letter written by Willie around this period exists but owing to its prolonged contact with a piece of candy, apparently chocolate, it is badly stained and the date is obliterated. It is possible, however, to make out that Willie wrote it in Springfield in April, that he said it was Sunday and the roads were drying up. Conceivably there could be a relation between these two statements; his father was usually out on the circuit in April and the matter of the roads drying up might affect his getting home at the week end. This letter concludes with much good sense: "I have not any more to say so I must bring my letter to an end." Then under the signature "Wm W. Lincoln" he playfully wrote, "The end," a whimsical twist that somehow suggests his father.

One long-delayed recollection mentions Tad as also attending what must have been Miss Corcoran's school. It could not have been for long, however, as he was not yet eight when the Lincolns left Springfield, and there is certainly no evidence that he had learned anything of reading and writing at that time. His father would not let him be pushed in his schooling. It became Tad's policy to evade school, and one wonders whether the other children had laughed at his first attempts to learn his letters (which would have been comical with his impediment of speech) and whether this teasing was a factor in his distaste for books. Robert had had his crossed eye to contend with; Tad had his lisp. It probably added to the appeal of his personality for older people as it heightened the effect of his droll sayings, but children are often cruel in their ridicule and mocking. It was remembered that he once said to his cousin John Grimsley, "I love you, Johnny, because you are nice to me and don't tease me." When Tad went through the process of losing his baby teeth, that comical stage of a little boy's toothless smile, his second teeth came in crooked, which did not help matters any.

The "tadpole" baby had, however, grown into a happy little fellow who was as lovable as he was exasperating. He was quick-tempered and difficult to deal with; he was also, with his quaint little ways and fancies, completely engaging. Above all, he was a warmly affectionate child, surely a joy to the parents who were themselves persons of deep affection.

Taddie would burst into the room where his father was sitting, looking for something, and having found it, he would throw himself on his father "like a small thunderbolt," give him a wild, fierce hug, and then rush from the room before his father could put out a hand to detain him. The hand was very apt to be put out, no matter what Mr. Lincoln was doing, for he loved to have the boy within his reach and touch.

As with little Eddie, Tad's tenderness would break forth when he saw anything pitiful; he had a quick and intuitive sympathy for others' hurts. Along with the little boy's warm heart went also a tender conscience. He could be counted on to be absolutely truthful. Each of these three Lincoln sons had a conscience, according to the light of his own personality; each had in the bedrock of his character a strong moral sense that promised integrity for his mature years.

A serious illness in 1859 may have been one reason why Tad had not been pushed in his schooling. A letter his mother wrote their friend, Mr. O. M. Hatch, tells the story. It was difficult for her to reach Mr. Lincoln quickly when he was away from home and she thought Mr. Hatch was going to Chicago and would see her husband that day and give him the urgent message. "If you . . . should meet Mr L—— there," wrote Mary Lincoln, "will you say to him, that our *dear little Taddie,* is quite sick. The Dr. thinks it may prove a *slight* attack of *lung* fever."

She was always nervous and overanxious when the children were sick, and since Eddie's death any serious illness was apt to make her frantic. She longed for her husband's calmness and strength: "I am feeling troubled & it would be a comfort to have him, *at home.* He passed a bad night. I do not like his symptoms, and will be glad, if he hurries home." It was several days before Mr. Lincoln could get home to give her that comfort. One does not know whether pneumonia developed or not, or other details. Tad recovered but he was not a robust child thereafter.

The mother did her part in teaching the children. She, of course, wanted them to grow up prepared to enter cultured circles of society. Her own training made this important to her. With her passionate devotion to her sons, and her love of books, poetry, and social graces, it was her joy to read to them, to help them memorize little verses, and to teach them children's dances. As so often, a bit of evidence creates a picture: the bright-faced mother, who danced so well herself, gaily showing her sons how to do the steps and making a game of training the awkward boyish feet into more graceful movements. But the evidence itself has come down in the scornful words of Mr. Herndon, who did not approve of Mrs. Lincoln any more than he did of the boys at the law office. Here is his description of her devoted effort: "It was the habit—custom of Mrs Lincoln when any big man or woman visited her house to dress up and trot out Bob—Willie or Tad and get them to monkey around—talk—dance—speek—quote poetry &c &c. Then she would become enthusiastic & eloquent over the children much to the annoyance of the visitor. . . ."

Mrs. Lincoln's half sister, Emilie Todd, visited Springfield the winter of 1854–1855. She was eighteen at that time and must have seemed like an older sister to Bob, who had seen much of her that year he spent in Lexington. She recorded how companionably they played checkers together. Emilie noticed how her sister Mary was training the boy who was going on twelve. When they went on long drives out on the prairie, and the ladies wished to alight in order to gather spring wild flowers, Bob would assist them out of the carriage in the gentlemanly way his mother had taught him. A lady needed help in those days to maneuver her hoop skirts to the ground without loss of grace.

Emilie remembered too how Mrs. Lincoln read the poems and novels of Sir Walter Scott to her sons—with some very tangible results. One day they heard a commotion outside and running to a window, saw a medieval jousting taking place. Bob and one of his playmates, using fence palings for lances, were hard at it and the young Lincoln was heroically proclaiming: "This rock shall fly from its firm base as soon as I."

Robert also retained his memories of that visit. Years later he recalled how "very beautiful" Emilie appeared to his admiring young eyes.

A Springfield friend remembered later that the Lincoln children attended Sunday School at the First Presbyterian Church, to which their mother belonged and which their father attended. Tad had been baptized in that church on his second birthday. The Lincolns were very fond of the pastor, Dr. James Smith, who often came to their home. It is possible this has some relation to the fact that Willie said he wanted to be a preacher when he grew up. Little Julia Sprigg recalled how she and the Lincoln boys used to play church together and Mrs. Lincoln would join them in their games. Willie not only could write a good letter by the end of the eighteen fifties; he was good at making little speeches. One likes to imagine him gravely delivering a sermon to a small and equally grave congregation composed of his mother, Julia Sprigg, and Tad.

Mrs. Lincoln in her mother's adoration later wrote that as to talents "my darling sons were perfect in that respect . . ." Willie seemed to be the child of greatest promise. But he was no goody-goody; he delighted in pranks as much as the others. It is a pleasure to record that when the Lincoln boys reached that episode of experimentation which is an expected part of the growing up of boys, it was Willie who obtained four fat cigars, rounded up Tad and two of the Dubois sons, and led them behind a barn where the four proceeded to find out some facts of life about smoking. Fred Dubois did full justice to the sequel: "A sicker lot of boys there never was." The sounds of woe brought a neighbor and then the two mothers, Mrs. Lincoln and Mrs. Dubois, who administered what aid they could and did not scold but were very sympathetic.

The social training Mary Lincoln tried to give her children was needed especially by Bob in the latter part of the frivolous fifties. Springfield, like Robert himself, was having a sort of adolescence, was growing, and putting on grown-up airs. When the legislature was in session, there were parties practically every evening, some of them generously planned to include all of the family circle of those invited. The result was they were described as perfect "squeezes." The governor sent out a thousand invitations for one party, giving half of the house to the older folk and half to the young people for dancing. The following evening all of the children were invited. Bob tried to dance, with the result that next day he and his cousin, John Stuart, Jr., were hunting up a dancing master. Bob was having many new experiences, some of them perhaps connected with his father's razor and quaint little shaving mirror.

Robert joined a military company named the Springfield Cadets. He was "4th Corporal." Membership involved military drilling, for one of the heaviest duties of this organization consisted of marching in parades. The uniform was most satisfactory and becoming to any young male: "a dark blue coat, made after the fashion of the United States uniform," and resplendent with gold lace, white pants, and a glazed cap. To belong had distinct social advantages, as a note in the *Illinois State Journal* on July 3, 1858, indicates: "The Springfield Cadets return their sincere thanks to Gen. John Cook for the elegant entertainment and other courtesies received at his residence on Thursday evening. . . ." Various other newspaper references tell of their activities, a parade on Washington's birthday, a "grand Military Festival" with Bob's father, the Hon. A. Lincoln, serving on the committee on arrangements.

The receptions and dinners which the Lincolns themselves gave afforded excellent social training for their sons. By 1857 the cottage on Eighth Street had been made into a two-story house and refurbished within and without, with the result that their party to entertain the legislature in February that year had a setting in which Mrs. Lincoln took considerable pride. About five hundred were invited, she said, but owing to "an unlucky rain" and the counterattraction of a wedding in Jacksonville, only three hundred came. A newly found recollection of one of the legislators, Harry G. Little, brings the scene in the dining room—and the host—into close focus: "A long table was stretched nearly the whole length of the room, while above the table was a succession of shelves growing narrower upward. On these shelves the edibles were placed, and the guests . . . were left to help themselves, the waiters serving only coffee. Mr. Lincoln passed around among his guests in his genial way, with a friendly word for each. I remember that he said to me, 'Do they give you anything to eat here?'" Mr. Little said that people had more fun at the Lincoln parties than at the governor's or the extremely fashionable homes. The Lincoln boys were meeting prominent visitors, learning the ways of society, and hearing much talk of politics and the current topics that were exciting the lively interest of Springfield. They were growing up in a stimulating atmosphere.

Mrs. Lincoln, who delighted in friends, festivities, and children, also entertained for her little sons. Their birthdays were properly celebrated. Today one can see an invitation in her smooth handwriting which reads: "Willie Lincoln will be pleased to see you, Wednesday Afternoon at 3 O'clock." This was written on December 22; the event was a somewhat late celebration of his birthday. His mother told a friend about such a party: "Some 50 or 60 boys & girls attended the gala," she wrote, and remarked in the same paragraph, perhaps a bit wearily, that her boys were *"disposed* to be noisy."

In 1858 the Lincoln family had lots of excitement. There was a possibility they might go to Washington again: "Father" was the Republican candidate for the United States Senate. His Democratic opponent was Stephen A. Douglas and the two had a series of debates at various towns in Illinois. Each town made a colorful spectacle of the event with tremendous fanfare. There was no debate at Springfield, but when Lincoln came home on September 25, a great crowd came to his house that evening to serenade him. One can imagine the wide-eyed excitement of Willie and Tad at the deafening cheers for "Father" and the enthusiastic manner in which the uninhibited little fellows joined in.

When the last debate was held at Alton, a special train with excursion rates was got up at Springfield and a large delegation attended complete with a band. Mrs. Lincoln was on that trip and Robert went with the Springfield Cadets. With that curious unawareness of his parents that was characteristic of him at this time he could not remember later that his mother had been present. While she was away, Tad stayed with the Wheelocks across the street. The long-suffering Delie Wheelock later made the restrained remark that he was restless and very determined—and left the rest to the imagination.

Robert was much concerned around that time with his own affairs. By his own statement he was realizing that he was not getting in Springfield the education he wanted. By 1859 he was wondering what he should do with himself. He thought he would like to leave Illinois and go East. John Hay had gone from "Illinois State University" to Providence, Rhode Island, taken his entrance examinations, and entered Brown University without difficulty. Robert said that at the end of his junior year in the Springfield institution "I . . . resolved to enter Harvard College, imagining that there would be no trouble in doing so, in which idea, it is unnecessary to say, I was very much mistaken."

People have sometimes expressed wonder that Lincoln sent his son to Harvard, which did not seem exactly the logical choice for the prairie lawyer to make. The answer is that it was not the father's decision but the son's. Robert said that he resolved to go there himself. Later when he told his father that he wanted to study law at Harvard, Lincoln, knowing his eldest son's temperament through and through, made the brief comment: "If you do, you should learn more than I ever did, but you will never have so good a time." "That," said Robert, "is the only advice I had from my father as to my career."

Robert then made up his mind, in 1859, to go East to Harvard. He was to receive a salutary hard knock when he got there and was to meet it with the substantial good qualities that underlay his prickly temperament. He departed in the summer and his going left an empty place at the Lincoln table. This affectionate family missed him terribly. Bob had shown more serious purpose of late and was getting a bit more companionable. After all, he was only sixteen and Abraham and Mary Lincoln doubtless had their anxiety about his going so far away when he was so young.

His mother's feelings were reflected in her letters. She wrote a friend on August 28: "I am feeling quite lonely, as *Bob,* left for College, in *Boston,* a few days since, and it almost appears, as if light & mirth, had departed with him." She added wistfully that she would not see him for ten months unless she took a trip East next spring to visit him.

Telling her friend about a journey she took that fall, Mrs. Lincoln again mentioned the subject: "I miss Bob, so much, that I do not feel settled down, as much as I used to & find myself going on trips quite frequently." But her usual buoyancy lifted her mood. She loved to travel and might go East next summer to see her son. "Bob & myself expect to be somewhat of travellers."

Bob, arriving in Massachusetts, found he was not destined to go to "College, in *Boston,*" yet.

CHAPTER 6

"Our Eldest Boy, Bob . . .
Promises Very Well"

FULL of the cocksureness of youth Robert, in the summer of 1859, made the journey East to Cambridge, Massachusetts. He carried with him a letter of introduction to the president of Harvard which his father had procured for him from Stephen A. Douglas. Mr. Douglas presented him as the son of his friend Abraham Lincoln, "with whom I have lately been canvassing the state of Illinois." President Walker had never heard of Abraham Lincoln before and perhaps only one or two of his faculty had.

Robert took his entrance examinations and failed ignominiously in fifteen out of sixteen subjects. As he put it five years later: "On being examined I had the honor to receive a fabulous number of conditions which precluded my admission." It was a severe blow and a testing of his grit. But Robert, like both of his parents, was not easily diverted from his purposes. "I was resolved not to retire beaten," he wrote, "and, acting under the advice of President Walker, I entered the well-known Academy of Exeter, N. H."

There his self-confidence was further deflated, as he freely admitted several years later when he had got a truer perspective on his own importance: "I went to Exeter, hoping to enter the Class preparing to enter College, the next July, as Sophomores. The worthy Principal, Dr. Soule, soon convinced me of the vanity of my aspirations and I was obliged to enter the Subfreshman Class."

Robert's education, academic and otherwise, had begun in earnest. He was thrown with a group of boys from well-to-do families in the East, where Illinois was looked down on by many as wild and uncivilized. It almost seems as if Harvard College itself took no chances with students from less enlightened states; Robert's bond for the payment of his college dues had to be signed by a citizen of the good State of Massachusetts. Judge Julius Rockwell, who had known Robert's father in Congress and was a brother-in-law of Lincoln's friend David Davis, fulfilled this requirement.

The young Illinoisan was on his own now. If he did not make himself agreeable, he would be lonely. He also had to buckle down to studying in earnest, as his classmates were apt to be much better prepared than he was. Getting away from home was probably the best thing that could have happened to him; it put him in a situation calculated to rub off his sharp corners. He later, with acquired insight, referred to his stay at Exeter as "a very valuable year to myself."

He had at least one friend with whom he could talk about home, George Latham, with whom he had played at Springfield. George was also a student at Exeter and the two roomed at the same brick house occupied by Mrs. S. B. Clarke. And Robert did make many new friends. One of his classmates, Marshall S. Snow, remembered him as a very popular young fellow, gentlemanly, quiet in manner, with a certain dignity of his own, and a "good dresser." "He was very popular with the girls of the town . . ." said Mr. Snow, which one suspects was something new, as the girls in Springfield had not been too enthusiastic about Bob. His great improvement was destined to create something of a sensation among them when he returned to Springfield. Mr. Snow also said he was "a very good fellow" and was always ready for a good time and clean fun.

But while this satisfactory development was going on, Bob's parents were much concerned about the welfare of their son so far from home. The beginning of his academic career in the East had not been calculated to build up their confidence in him. His father wanted to visit him and see for himself how his son was getting along in his studies, but the expense of the trip was an obstacle. Mr. Lincoln had frequently mentioned his financial limitations prior to this time and now he had a son off at college, always an expensive matter for fathers, especially when the son is a "good dresser."

Robert told a friend later that his father wrote him in January 1860 that he had just won a case and as soon as his client made payment he would come to Exeter. A week or so later the money-worried man wrote expressing his disappointment that the client had not been able to make payment and that the trip would have to be postponed for lack of funds. Then came a third letter saying some men in New York had asked him to speak to them and had offered the money for the trip. That speech so casually introduced as an incidental means for Bob's father to get to Exeter was the famous

Cooper Union address of February 27, 1860, which suddenly made the East aware of this Mr. Lincoln of Illinois and was a great factor in his nomination for President less than three months later.

Years afterward Robert often said with a smile that he was mainly responsible for his father's first nomination for President, that if he had not flunked his examinations at Harvard and if his father had not in consequence been so much worried about him that he wanted to come East to see him, it might not have happened. For both Robert and Mr. Lincoln that flunking proved remarkably beneficial.

Mr. Lincoln arrived in Exeter on Wednesday, February 29. His powerful speech in New York, which had dealt with the issue which was then shaking the nation apart—slavery—had attracted so much attention that he was overwhelmed with requests to speak elsewhere. He had agreed to talk at Concord and Manchester on Thursday and he was promptly met at Exeter by a committee which asked him to come to Dover on Friday. These invitations were a surprise, for, after all, his initial purpose in coming East had been to see Robert. He solved the problem by taking his son and George Latham, in whom he took a fatherly interest, along with him. Years later Robert wrote a letter telling of his father's visit and stating: "I was with him on this little New Hampshire tour."

On March 3 they returned to Exeter and two days later the *Exeter News-Letter* reported: "On Saturday evening last, A. Lincoln, the champion of the North West, addressed the Republicans of this town at the Town Hall, which was well filled with an enthusiastic audience, with a sprinkling of Ladies." Marshall S. Snow and another fellow student of Robert's, Albert Blair, later gave their recollections of that event. It began with a rather comic aspect. There were two speakers, Judge John C. Underwood of Virginia, very short and stout, and the tall, thin Mr. Lincoln. The contrast as they walked on the platform was amusing and it was equally so when they sat down. Judge Underwood's feet did not reach the floor and Mr. Lincoln had great difficulty arranging his long legs under and about his chair. Snow says there were whisperings among the students at the sight of Mr. Lincoln's odd figure, unruly hair, and rumpled appearance: "Isn't it too bad Bob's father is so homely? Don't you feel sorry for him?" But when Mr. Lincoln began to speak and the homely face lighted up in its characteristic way, he got hold of his audience and there was no more pity for Bob.

Father and son were thrown into a new companionship on that visit. Perhaps this was the closest they yet had come together. It may have helped a great deal that the spoiled Willie and Tad were not in the picture, constantly demanding their father's attention and indulgence. If Robert in Springfield had been a bit jealous and resentful of his father's attitude toward the younger children, the evidence suggests some excuse for it. But now Mr. Lincoln was centering his attention upon his eldest son. One likes to imagine the father's keen eyes noting Bob's growth and development of the last six months. He was pleased with what he saw, as a comment of his later that year would make evident. The two are reported to have slept together in Bob's room, and Sunday was a day which Mr. Lincoln devoted entirely to his son, meeting his friends and entering with zest into all his interests. Father and son attended church and afterward walked to Robert's lodging on Hemlock Square at the corner of High and Pleasant Streets, where they had Sunday dinner together.

Albert Blair told of a little gathering in Bob's room Sunday evening. His account creates a picture of a group of teen-age boys distributed in various attitudes about a boardinghouse bedchamber, their faces all turned toward the fatherly and magnetic Mr. Lincoln. Robert remembered that one of the boys, Henry Cluskey, had a banjo. Lincoln with boyish eagerness urged Henry to go to his room several blocks away to fetch it. This Henry did and played and sang, to Mr. Lincoln's great delight. In this enthusiasm he told Bob that he ought to have a banjo too. The boys were all drawn toward Bob's father.

Robert was to write later about a certain amusing foible of his headmaster, Gideon Lane Soule, at Exeter; perhaps he told his father about it. In the classroom Mr. Soule had a so-called "lottery" system of calling up his pupils in recitation. The little tickets bearing the names of those in the class were placed face downward in a tin box and, as Robert wrote, were "delicately picked out, one by one, with the moistened tip of his finger, and—laid aside until the name of the fellow he was after was reached."

In his autobiographical sketch Robert related an exciting adventure of his at Exeter, "a flight from Justice, who pursued me, in the shape of a policeman all over the flourishing village, for having, in company with others, committed sundry depredations on the property of various denizens." The sundry depredations consisted of making humorous changes of gates and signs in the nighttime, a prankishness which the tolerant Mr. Lincoln probably would have smiled at. But the New England citizens whose property was involved did not find it amusing and the majesty of the law was invoked. The upshot of the matter was that all the students concerned, except Robert, were called to the office of the justice of the peace next morning. Perhaps Robert, who was skilled in playing pranks, had managed to elude that policeman. But he went to the justice's office with his fellow pranksters and, according to a later account, stepped out and made a speech which would have done credit to the noble, stuffy little hero of a Horatio Alger story. He saw by the reading of the warrant, he said, that many of his school comrades were charged with committing offenses against good order "and the peace and dignity of this pleasant village." He continued: "I was in company with many of the parties mentioned in that warrant, and if they are guilty of the charges therein set forth, I am equally amenable before the law." (Robert, the future lawyer, did not admit actual guilt.) "I therefore ask, before proceedings commence, that this warrant shall be amended by having my name inserted with the rest of my comrades, for I do not desire any person to shoulder any responsibility rightfully belonging to myself."

This story appeared in the *New York Tribune* in the late eighteen seventies and the quotations from Robert can hardly be taken as verbatim. The account also referred to him as the President's son and leaves the impression that it was for that reason his name was omitted from the warrant. The incident could have happened after his father was nominated, but Robert left Exeter before his father was elected President, though it is true he went back for a visit about a month after that election. But the point of the story, that Robert was truthful, did not wish to evade responsibility, and did not desire special privileges, exemplifies a quality which he was to have through life. The conclusion of the episode can be given in Robert's own account: "Filthy lucre, also the root of all evil, proved a great blessing in the present case, and we all got off by paying damages."

Robert, at the end of his year at Exeter, was described by a gentleman whose good opinion was one greatly to be valued, Amos Tuck, distinguished citizen, trustee of Exeter Academy, and loyal friend and supporter of Abraham Lincoln. Mr. Tuck wrote David Davis on August 24, 1860, that Robert "has behaved himself as the son of Abraham Lincoln might be expected to do. He stands at the top of the ladder as a scholar, and is a singularly discreet, well behaved, brilliant and promising young man." His good sense was being severely tested by the attentions he was receiving, continued Mr. Tuck, "but he stands it all." It appears that Robert had again donned a uniform as he had with the Springfield Cadets; in Exeter, according to Mr. Tuck, he was "a member of our 'Wide Awakes'" and a few evenings before had been out "with the rest of the 'Boys' to attend the raising of a Lincoln and Hamlin Banner. . . ."

To go back several months, while the eldest son was studying at Exeter exciting events were taking place in Illinois. At noon on May 18 Willie and Tad in Springfield heard a strange sound for a quiet little town—the firing of a hundred guns. Some great news had come from the Republican convention meeting in Chicago: Father had been nominated for President of the United States. He came home from downtown right away to tell Mother about it, and the faces of both indicated to the little boys that it was something tremendously important. Tad at seven years was probably very hazy as to the nature of the honor, but the precocious nine-year-old Willie apparently understood quite a bit about it. He needed to know, for like his father he was going to be called on to make some speeches.

Neighbors and friends kept flocking to the house all the rest of the day and that evening a large crowd collected in front of it and Father made a speech to them. From that time on the days were to go by like the torchlight parades with which the boys were to become so familiar: one flaring event was destined to follow another in rapid succession.

The very next evening the Lincoln home was in an excited state of preparation for a momentous event. Perhaps Willie and Tad heard in the distance the shouting of the crowd and the stirring marches played by the bands which met certain distinguished gentlemen at the depot "at 7½ o'clock" and escorted them to their hotel. They were the members of the official committee who would shortly come to the Lincoln home and ceremoniously inform Mr. Lincoln of his nomination. A small Illinois paper quaintly named the *Prairie Chicken* afterward mentioned that Willie and Tad "gleefully participated in the unwonted excitement" on this occasion and added: ". . . among the most noticeable features, was the appearance of the two little sons (carefully imbued by parental hands with the whitest of pantaloons)." A later issue expressed editorial anguish over the use of the word "imbued." There is no doubt Mary Lincoln considered her boys an ornament and asset and dressed them up for special occasions. Perhaps she thought it would do no harm for the committee to see what fine children the candidate had. At all events, Willie and Tad, complete with white pantaloons, were on the front steps when the tall-hatted gentlemen of the delegation approached. Whether their mother placed them there by design or whether they stationed themselves there so as not to miss anything cannot be determined. They politely greeted the visitors.

"Are you Mr. Lincoln's son?" asked Mr. Evarts of New York addressing Willie. "Yes, sir," was the answer. "Then let's shake hands," said Mr. Evarts, and all the gentlemen cordially shook hands with Willie. Tad, who was standing neglected by the gatepost, felt he was not getting his share of attention and remarked loudly and pointedly, "I'm a Lincoln, too." The men laughed, elaborately shook his hand also, rang the doorbell, and were received into the house.

Inside, a dignified and historic event followed, Mr. Lincoln's official notification of his nomination. The names of the little boys do not appear in the accounts of that ceremonial; perhaps they stayed outside to watch Springfield's celebration. Down the streets all the houses were illuminated from top to bottom, bonfires blazed, and there was the continual burst of rockets. The pageantry of the political campaign had begun; the little town in the coming months was to be intoxicated with excitement.

All the endless demands of the new prominence did not diminish the Lincolns' attention to their children. Shortly after the convention a friend of theirs, Mark W. Delahay, came to Springfield bringing two convention flags, and one of the little boys got the idea in his head that the smallest flag was for him. The gentleman left town with both flags and the child was "inconsolable." Mrs. Lincoln, to whom the wishes of the children were as all important as they were to Mr. Lincoln, wrote to Mr. Delahay explaining that the boy thought the flag had been given to him and asked him to return it, adding: "I feel it is as necessary to keep one's word with a child, as with a grown person."

Willie and Tad, with that spontaneous enthusiasm which seemed lacking in Robert, entered with gusto into the campaign for electing their father. They promptly adopted the slogan "Vote for Old Abe." Willie would stand on the terrace of the Lincoln home (which made an ideal platform) and urge the passers-by to vote for Old Abe. To all the Springfield children it was a thrilling experience to have their loved Mr. Lincoln become so famous all at once. Since the grown people were constantly parading, ending up if possible with a speech from Mr. Lincoln, the boys of the neighborhood would have their own parades and end up by calling for "a speech from Willie." He would proudly respond and it is to be suspected that his manner and gestures were modeled on those of his father. One would give much to know if he told some of his father's stories.

When crowds cheered Mr. Lincoln and assembled in front of his home, the shrill yells of Willie and Tad were always added to the loud hurrahs. Most thrilling of all to them must have been the torchlight parades in the evenings when long rows of dark bodies clad in oilskin coats and carrying aloft an endless line of flaring torches marched past leaving a trail of smoke and kerosene on the night air. Years later one of the Springfield boys said he could not smell the odor of a smoky kerosene lamp without a pang of longing for those thrilling days.

Reporters flocked to Springfield to interview Mr. Lincoln; artists came to do his portrait. Among the latter was Thomas Hicks, who painted Mr. Lincoln in the big room at the State House which had now become his headquarters. While the presidential candidate was busy at his desk there one day with his back toward the door and the artist was working at his canvas, Tad and one of his playmates slipped quietly in and began some investigations. Mr. Hicks could see them but Mr. Lincoln was unaware of their presence. As the artist told it: "The little fellows got among my paints. They took the brightest blue, yellow and red. Then they squeezed from a tube into their little palms, a lot of the red, and smeared it on the wall; then they took the blue and smeared that in another place, and afterward they smeared the yellow." The resulting "brilliant wall decoration" may well have been the only example of present-day abstract painting in the eighteen hundreds! The two boys, of course, got as much paint on themselves as on the wall, and it must have been the twinkle in Mr. Hicks's eyes that caused Mr. Lincoln finally to turn around to see what was going on. He merely said "in the mildest tone and with the greatest affection, 'Boys! boys! You mustn't meddle with Mr. Hicks's paints; now run home and have your faces and hands washed.'" One likes to imagine these little war-painted Indians running homeward through the streets of Springfield and the amusement of the passing neighbors.

Another painter, Alban Jasper Conant, did a portrait of Mr. Lincoln later that summer and remembered an incident about Tad. When the portrait was finished, Mr. Lincoln wanted his wife to come to the State House to see it, and when she arrived, Tad, with a playmate named Jim, was with her. Perhaps Jim had been Tad's fellow artist in decorating the wall before and the creative urge was again stirring within them. Mr. Conant noticed how "Tad was everywhere at once, being repeatedly recaptured by his mother, and waiting but for a favorable diversion to be off again." The artist also observed "with what interested pride Lincoln's eyes followed him about the room." While the Lincolns and Mr. Conant were talking, Tad found an unfinished portrait leaning against the wall and turned it around, saying, "Come here, Jim; here's another Old Abe." Mr. Conant, not being as well acquainted with the Lincoln offspring as were the people of Springfield, was somewhat shocked.

Early in this summer of great excitement Willie was taken ill. His activities in behalf of his father's election came to an abrupt halt; he had, as his father wrote, "a hard and tedious spell of scarlet-fever." The illness probably left the child much less robust than he was before; Robert seems to have been the son who had the best constitution. His father's letter written on July 4, 1860, stated that Willie was "not yet beyond all danger." But by July 24 he was active and lively again. Carl Schurz, who was in town and came to supper with the Lincolns that evening, reported to his wife: "Lincoln's boys are regular fellows. One of them insisted upon going barefoot." Since going barefoot was the usual order of the day for little boys in small towns, perhaps Willie was reasserting his right after the restrictions of his illness.

Another visitor came to dinner at the Lincolns' that July, a young man named Frank Fuller, a friend Robert had made in New England. Though Mr. Lincoln had not seen him before, he had communicated with him in an interesting connection. It seems that young Fuller had had much to do with a Fourth of July celebration at a place not far from Exeter. The plans called for music, strawberries, and speeches, and he wanted Bob, as the son of the Republican presidential candidate, to read the Declaration of Independence. Bob, who was never to have any taste for public appearances, said he would not do so without his father's consent. (One wonders whether this was a case of stalling.) Fuller promptly sent a message to Lincoln asking him about it and received this hearty reply: "Tell Bob to read that immortal document every chance he has, and the bigger the crowd, the louder he must holler."

Bob then made his public appearance and he must have had to "holler" very loud indeed, for the crowd was immense. Posters advertising the event had been distributed to all the surrounding towns and New Englanders were enthusiastic about these patriotic occasions. Judging by what he wrote later, Bob did not enjoy speaking to "a vast sea of human faces"; he found it rather overwhelming.

He had written his family about Frank Fuller, so when that young man turned up in Springfield, Mr. Lincoln received him cordially and took him home to dinner. He was there "taken to the hearts and home of the charming family" with such warmth that afterward he thought of the occasion as a red-letter event. He had with him one of those posters advertising the Fourth of July festival, and after dinner he spread it out on the floor to the delight of Mrs. Lincoln and the two lads. It probably had Bob's name on it, and Willie and Tad climbed all over him in their interest and enthusiasm. Of course they wanted to know what their brother Bob had done to get on such an interesting poster.

Good news came from Robert that summer. To use his own words, which have a suggestion of justifiable pride: "After the commencement [at Exeter] in 1860, I was able to inform my father that I had succeeded in entering College without a Condition—quite a change from the previous year." Now he was going to Harvard. But his friend George Latham from Springfield had failed to make the grade. Lincoln, swamped with mail and busy as only a presidential candidate can be, took the time to write George a letter of encouragement. He well knew the danger for a young man in accepting failure instead of fighting to overcome it, and he did not want that to happen to one for whom he evidently had much affection. He began: "I have scarcely felt greater pain in my life than on learning yesterday from Bob's letter, that you had failed to enter Harvard University. And yet there is very little in it, if you will allow no feeling of *discouragement* to seize, and prey upon you. It is a *certain* truth, that you *can* enter, and graduate in, Harvard University; and having made the attempt, you *must* succeed in it. '*Must*' is the word."

Mr. Lincoln went on to say, as one much older than George, that he had found by severe experience "that you *can* not fail, if you resolutely determine, that you *will* not." In this temporary failure there was no evidence that George would not be yet a better scholar and a more successful man than those who had entered college more easily. The important thing was not to be discouraged but to go ahead and conquer the difficulties.

It comes to one's mind to wonder whether Mr. Lincoln had written such a letter to Robert the year before when he had flunked his entrance examinations to Harvard. At all events, Robert had made up his mind to succeed and had overcome his obstacles. One suspects this was a source of some pride to Mr. Lincoln. It glows faintly in the restrained lines he wrote his old friend Dr. Henry in July: "Our eldest boy, Bob, has been away from us nearly a year at school, and will enter Harvard University this month. He promises very well, considering we never controlled him much."

CHAPTER 7

"Aint You ... Tired of This Constant Uproar?"

AS THE election drew closer the excitement of the campaign in
Springfield increased. To Willie and Tad, who were untouched by the grave problems of a time when the nation was dividing, its pageantry must have seemed like one glorious Fourth of July
after another. Band playing, torchlight parades, processions of floats,
and hurrahs for "Old Abe" were all features calculated to delight
boys around ten and seven. One can imagine their shining eyes and
shrill yells on that day in August when what was perhaps the most
elaborate procession of all marched down Eighth Street past the Lincoln home, with music, banners, posters borne aloft, and fascinating
float after float. There were six thousand people in this procession,
according to the *New York Herald,* and it took two and a half hours
for it to pass Mr. Lincoln's residence. The campaign was playing up
his humble origin: one float represented the flatboat on which he
had traveled down the great Mississippi; another showed The Rail
Splitter at work.

Parades seem to have been the moving pictures of the middle
eighteen hundreds. It was a period of volunteer military companies
whose most important duties (as with the Springfield Cadets to
which Robert had belonged) were drilling and marching under the
public eye. The warmhearted Lincolns in 1860 took into their complete affection a young man who had organized such a company
into what became the famous Zouaves. Elmer Ephraim Ellsworth
came to Springfield and began to study law in the Lincoln and Herndon law office that fall; he also pitched in loyally to help in the presidential campaign. No personality could possibly have been more
appealing to the boys, though for that matter practically everyone
who came in contact with young Ellsworth was captivated. His biog-

rapher, Charles A. Ingraham, quotes a newspaper description of him: "A boyish figure, not exceeding five feet six inches in height, with well-formed, shapely limbs . . . a well-balanced head crowned with a wealth of dark brown hair that fell in careless, clinging curls about his neck, eyes of dark hazel that sparkled and flashed with excitement or melted with tenderness. . . ." Add to this a magnetic and chivalrous personality which created a feeling of well-being, enthusiasm, and gaiety in those it touched, put this romantic figure in a dashing uniform, watch him put his company of Zouaves through the most intricate drills with perfect precision, and what boy could resist him? The Zouaves themselves were irresistible in their picturesque uniforms modeled on those of the French Zouaves in the Crimean War: bright red cap adorned with gold braid, embroidered light blue shirt, dark blue jacket with orange and red trimmings, brass buttons, red sash, and loose red pantaloons gathered between knee and ankle into leather leggings. So much for the French model, but there was evidently some deviation from it among the American Zouaves. John Hay described what their young leader wore one evening: "He was dressed like his men, red cap, red shirt, grey breeches, grey jacket. In his belt, a sword, a very heavy revolver, and . . . an enormously large and bloodthirsty-looking bowie knife, more than a foot long in the blade. . . ."

Mr. Lincoln said of Ellsworth: "He is the greatest little man I ever met." He was somewhat like a gay young King Arthur, and his Zouaves were his Knights of the Round Table. He had taken his company on a tour in the East in the summer of 1860 and arrived with them in Springfield about the middle of August, where they were met at the station by the Springfield Grays with the Union Silver Band. Surely Mr. Lincoln and his boys were among the three thousand people who flocked to the vacant lot on South Sixth Street to see them put on the exhibition drills with which they had captured the imagination of every city they had visited.

Ellsworth became an intimate of the Lincoln family and the adoring Willie and Tad doubtless climbed all over him in their usual fashion when he came to the home. The bright skein of his life in the weeks ahead would be interwoven with the fortunes of the Lincolns; he was to share their widening interests, their enthusiasms, and even the boys' measles!

In the midst of the excitement and prominence the Lincolns tried always to keep the lives of their little boys normal and happy. Mr. Joseph Medill late that summer called at the State House to see Mr. Lincoln and for once found the big room empty of visitors except for

Willie and Tad. They had a top and Mr. Lincoln had just finished winding the string around it in the way that would give it the greatest force when it was whirled off on the floor. He explained that he was having a little season of relaxation with the boys.

There is no way of knowing how much Willie and Tad were aware of the wild night that followed the news of their father's election on November 6. Springfield was delirious with joy. The State House and homes were brilliantly illuminated and all night long the streets were filled with singing, yelling, shouting crowds. Guns were being fired and young men, old men, and even clergymen were throwing up their hats and dancing around the public square. It was an appropriate launching of the new and tumultuous life ahead for the Lincoln family. The little boys took the excitement in joyous stride; they were probably the only ones to whom it brought unalloyed pleasure. To Tad the fact that an admirer sent his father a pigtail whistle was probably as important as any public event following the election. A visitor at the home found him blowing blasts on the new toy that rendered conversation difficult, not to say painful.

The eldest son at Harvard was getting his own share of public attention and liking it less and less. One evening shortly after the election a large body of students called upon him to congratulate him on the success of his father. Early in October he made a trip to the White Mountains, where an enthusiastic demonstration was made over his arrival. By this time he had received from the public a nickname that he was soon to resent and loathe. The visit of the Prince of Wales, later Edward VII, to the United States, traveling incognito as Baron Renfrew, was still fresh in the public mind and with the campaign playing up Lincoln as The Rail Splitter, the result was inevitable: Robert was dubbed the Prince of Rails.

A reception was given for the Prince of Rails on his visit to the White Mountains; in humorous vein a procession was formed to escort the "Prince" and speeches were made, to which he gave a happy reply. Robert now had a certain hilarity and gaiety among companions of his own age and had developed quite a popular sense of humor. The *Illinois State Journal*, reporting this incident, remarked: "They say that for story telling and wit he is a chip of the original rail."

But two months later he appeared very definitely speech shy. Just how violent was his aversion to public speaking appears in a letter which he wrote "Dear Mother" on the second day of December. He and a fellow student had gone from Cambridge to Exeter for a brief holiday. He told his mother in detail of their "constant round of dissipation": dinners, teas, and parties, matters in which she was always interested. He named a friend who would soon pass through Springfield: "So look out for him." The readiness of his parents to welcome cordially and entertain anyone he sent to them is apparent in his telling also of two "nice fellows" from St. Louis "who are going to the inauguration after vacation is over and I have invited them to stop at our house on their road." Robert, though not a hail-fellow-well-met sort of person, was a loyal and thoughtful friend to those he knew well, and these two young men "have been with me for the last year."

The son's letter continued: "I see by the papers that you have been to Chicago." The parents had taken this trip in the latter part of November and a strenuous round of crowds, handshaking, sight-seeing, and hurrahing it had been. Mrs. Lincoln's buoyant spirit rose to meet such occasions and Mr. Lincoln was an artist in dealing with people individually and in mass, but Robert viewed all the ado with a disapproving eye: "Aint you *beginning* to get a little tired of this constant uproar?" he asked. The "aint" was, of course, used for comic effect.

The final passage of the letter reveals a great deal between the lines. Robert was getting the first diluted taste of what was to become a concentrated and bitter brew. To one of his reticent and retiring temperament the difficult position in which a President's son is always placed, with its impossible demands and public misrepresentations, was to become almost intolerable. The passage also suggests that he was easily annoyed and took his annoyances seriously.

"You will remember I wrote to Father about a fellow who is boring me considerably—" the letter continued. "He capped the climax lately." It seems there was "a Republican levee and supper" planned and this individual, who was probably the aggressive type, realized the publicity value of having the son of the President-elect attend. Robert anticipated what would happen if he went and did not go. But on the evening of the occasion, "about 9½" o'clock, two boys came to his room with an admission ticket "on the back of which this fellow had written, asking me to come over as they were calling for me—" Robert said he wrote a note excusing himself and continued: "He must be the biggest fool in the world not to know that I did not want to go over, when if I did, I would be expected to make a speech! Just phancy my phelinks mounted on the rostrum, holding 'a vast sea of human faces' etc. I stop overwhelmed." ("Phancy the phelinks" was apparently one of those catch phrases which suddenly invade conversations for a period and then vanish from the language.

One finds it in newspapers of the time.) The letter is signed "Yours affectionately, R. T. Lincoln."

Robert had mentioned the approaching vacation of the two "nice fellows" and had also said in his letter: "We have only about six weeks more before going home." That meant he would come to Springfield in January 1861. His mother made a trip to New York that month to buy some new clothes for her impending role as First Lady and Robert joined her in that city to return with her. She had not seen him for a year and a half and she could note, as his father had done, how much he had grown and improved. Always ready to appreciate any good qualities in her children to the point of glorification, she was delighted with her grown-up, well-tailored, and well-mannered eldest son. They returned to Springfield on the evening of January 25, where they were met at the train by Mr. Lincoln, who had gone to the railroad depot in cold and snow for three successive nights in his eagerness to receive them. That reunion and the tumultuous greeting Bob received from the little boys bring up a pleasant picture; it is always a very special event in a family circle when the first one to leave it comes home from college.

A friend of Mr. Lincoln's, Mr. Joseph Gillespie, stayed overnight at the Lincoln home shortly after Bob returned and remembered him as a grave and studious boy. Mr. Gillespie recalled that the eldest brother, when the subject of hanging up stockings at the recent Christmas was mentioned, was careful not to disturb the illusions of Willie and Tad as to the one who had filled those stockings. While they were speaking of Christmas Bob remarked to the visitor that his father had received a Christmas gift in a letter. The enclosure was an ominous sign of the way in which the nation was breaking up and heading toward civil war, a copy of the ordinance of secession adopted by South Carolina in December. It undoubtedly added much to the worn look on Mr. Lincoln's face and the loss of weight which his friends were noting at the time, but Gillespie thought the father did not wish Bob to know its grave import, for he hurriedly said: "'Oh, yes, Gillespie, I forgot to tell you that some kind friend in South Carolina sent me a printed copy of the ordinance they adopted a few days before Christmas, and I was telling Bob here,' he continued, affectionately laying his hand on the boy's head, 'that it must have been intended for a Christmas gift.'"

The arrival of Bob Lincoln, now an elegant young man from Harvard and the son of the incoming President, naturally created a flutter among the girls of the excited little town. As his mother had, he evidently had done some shopping and doubtless already was wearing the impressive stovepipe hat that was to adorn him on the journey to the inauguration. The correspondent of the *New York Herald* reported an amusing street scene: "'Bob,' the heir apparent to the President-elect, has been the observed of all the observing Springfield girls today. He walked the streets this morning [January 26] bringing up the rear of the 'old man.' The effect of a residence within the improving influences of genteel, well dressed and well behaved Boston is plainly noticeable in his outward appearance, the comparative elegance of which certainly presents a striking contrast to the loose, careless, awkward rigging of his Presidential father."

Thanks to an old diary in the Illinois State Historical Library, one knows the name of at least one Springfield girl who attracted the attention of the young man from Harvard. Nineteen-year-old Anna Ridgely recorded in this diary on Monday, February 4, 1861, that she "went with Bob Lincoln" to a reading that evening. Under the date of Saturday, February 9, she wrote: "Bob Lincoln called to bid us all good bye. . . ." Anna probably noticed that he had changed for the better, as there was a regular chorus of remarks to that effect on all sides. The word invariably chosen to describe him was "improved," which implies there had been considerable room for improvement before. Mrs. James Conkling, mother of Bob's good friend Clinton Conkling, wrote him on February 12: "The young ladies say that Bob has greatly improved, and that he is much more gentlemanly. . . ." Mrs. Lincoln was to write of him less than a year and a half later: "He has grown & improved more than any one you ever saw." Exeter and Harvard had done much for Robert, but it will be seen that he still had some foibles associated with the age of seventeen.

All efforts in the first few weeks of 1861 were directed toward the departure of the Lincolns for Washington. Provision must be made for the current pets. There was Fido, a rough-coated, yellowish, not very handsome dog of uncertain ancestry, but much loved by the boys. They undoubtedly begged to take him to Washington and it must have taken Mr. Lincoln's most consummate statesmanship to convince them to the contrary, but it was finally arranged that the John E. Roll family, which had two boys of the right age, would take care of him. With so much picturemaking in the air, Willie and Tad must have thought an important member of the family like Fido should be photographed too. At all events, a Springfield photographer took the pictures, Fido looking very patient and as if anxious to do what was required in this strange performance.

The furniture must be advertised for sale, and the house rented. But Mr. and Mrs. Lincoln wanted to give a final reception to their

Springfield friends before closing the door of their home behind
them. Mrs. Conkling wrote her son Clinton about it: "And such a
crowd, I seldom, or ever saw at a private house. It took about twenty
minutes to get in the hall door. And then it required no little management to make your way out." Her next words bring the young man
from Harvard into focus: "Bob figured quite largely. While I was
standing near Mr. L. he came up, and in his humorous style, gave
his hand to his father, saying: 'Good evening *Mr. Lincoln!*' In reply
his father gave him a gentle slap in the face."

The next day, February 7, the family left the house that had been
home for seventeen years and moved to the Chenery House for the
few remaining days. This hotel boasted of the new gas lighting that
Springfield had acquired in the eighteen fifties, and it is said that
Willie blew out the gas jets. When his father explained to him
that he must not do that, he answered that his mother let him blow
out the lamps at home. One can picture Mrs. Lincoln patiently holding a lamp at the proper position for a little boy's pleasure in
blowing out the flame.

Bob was to accompany his father when he left Springfield, but
the first plan was for Mrs. Lincoln with Willie and Tad to come to
Washington later. In the inflamed state of the nation violence on
the journey of the President-elect was feared. But the more Mrs. Lincoln heard about this danger, the more she wanted to go with her
husband, and a difference of opinion arose in the family. Once Mr.
Lincoln made up his mind, however, nobody could change it, so it
was only Bob who boarded the train with his father that rainy morning of February 11 when Mr. Lincoln said good-by to his friends
and neighbors in Springfield.

They were all assembled at the little depot of the Great Western
Railroad to shake his hand for the last time. As Mr. Lincoln stood on
the train platform looking out over the crowd and thinking of all
that living in Springfield had meant to him, it was family life and
neighborliness that stood out, in the tremulous words of his farewell
address, as the things that mattered most. "To this place, and the
kindness of these people, I owe everything. . . . Here my children
have been born, and one is buried."

Willie and Tad and their mother stood in that crowd. As the train
pulled out, its flags and streamers beginning to come to life under
its increasing motion, the cheers of the two little sons were said to be
the loudest of all.

In what happened next there is at least the possibility that
"Mother" gave "Father" a surprise. Mrs. Conkling, writing a letter the

following day in which she described Lincoln's farewell, said: "Mrs. Lincoln was not to leave for some days after his departure, but a dispatch from Gen Scott, determined her to leave the evening of the same day. The General thought it would be safer for him to be surrounded by his family." That settled the argument for Mary Lincoln; if their presence contributed to his safety, she and the little boys would just catch up with Father and take the trip with him. One can be quite sure Willie and Tad were enthusiastically in favor of the plan. They could join his train at Indianapolis. Whether Mr. Lincoln knew of this decision until after they had started and he could do nothing about it is an interesting question. In a remark he made on the journey after Mrs. Lincoln had joined him, there is a suggestion that he thought of the episode with a twinkle in his eye. An article very valuable to him was lost on that trip, to his great consternation, and he said to his friend Ward H. Lamon: "I feel a good deal as the old member of the Methodist Church did when he lost his wife at the camp-meeting, and went up to an old elder of the church and asked him if he could tell him whereabouts in hell his wife was. In fact, I am in a worse fix than my Methodist friend; for if it were nothing but a wife that was missing, mine would be sure to pop up serenely somewhere."

One who was traveling on the same train that took Mrs. Lincoln and the little boys to Indianapolis remembered how tense she was and how she repeatedly asked the conductor to telegraph ahead to make certain she would connect with the presidential train. It was a close thing; she and the little boys were scarcely aboard when Lincoln's train moved out. The joy of Willie and Tad at being united with Father (and that on his birthday, February 12, 1861) can be imagined. But this whole interesting family incident failed utterly to register on Robert, who was acting very seventeenish on that journey. He later denied that his mother and little brothers had joined his father at Indianapolis. His thoughts were centered on his own activities.

It was Robert who lost the valuable article, his father's "gripsack" containing his Inaugural Address, whose contents were a matter of the utmost secrecy. Mr. Lincoln on arriving at a certain city put the bag in Robert's charge without telling him what it contained. (Accounts differ as to what city it was.) Robert, being welcomed by a group of young men, disposed of the bag and went off for a good time with "the boys." Mr. Lincoln discovered that the address was missing, and finally Robert was located.

According to one account, in answer to his father's urgent questioning Robert replied "with bored and injured virtue" that he had handed the bag to a hotel clerk. Lincoln continued his questions and there was evidently sharp feeling between father and son. Ward Hill Lamon, who was with Mr. Lincoln at the time, said he had never seen him "so much annoyed, so much perplexed, and for a time so angry." Lamon, who was a very close friend of Lincoln's, added: "He seldom manifested a spirit of anger toward his children—this was the nearest approach to it I had ever witnessed." Lincoln and Lamon finally made a search in the pile of baggage at the hotel and after some disappointments at last located the little old-fashioned black gripsack with the missing papers. Needless to say, Bob was relieved of any further responsibility for the bag.

Bob was "figuring largely" on the whole trip, having an exhilarating time in certain respects and being very much bored in others. Along with his touch of Eastern polish seems to have come a feeling of superiority, which often resulted in his being bored, a not unusual phase in the development of the later teens. At Indianapolis, after Mr. Lincoln had made a speech from the balcony of the Bates House, there were loud cries for the Prince of Rails. Robert responded with a reluctant wave of the hand and his father saved the situation by saying that "his boy, Bob, hadn't got in the way of making speeches." The *New York Herald* remarked: "Bob was almost as much annoyed as his father by the persistency with which the curious pointed out and loudly gave vent to their expressions respecting the Prince of Rails."

Bob had companions near his own age in the group on the train. There were George Latham, now a student at Yale, and brilliant John Hay, not yet twenty-three, who perhaps still had traces of those phases of growing up with which Robert was affected. Hay was to assist John G. Nicolay, Lincoln's secretary, who of course was of the group. There was the bright presence of Elmer Ellsworth of the Zouaves, whom the Lincolns regarded almost as another son.

Among the older members of the party was Dr. William Wallace, the Lincoln family physician and the uncle for whom Willie had been named. He was a stout gentleman, but honors for portliness would have gone to two other friends of the Lincolns who were present: David Davis and Ward Hill Lamon. (In years ahead both would touch Robert's life closely; the first he would consider a blessing and the second very like a curse.) It is pleasant to imagine all these interesting figures grouped around Mr. Lincoln and his wife against the gay and patriotic background of the presidential car. It was decorated with flags and red, white, and blue festoons hung from the molding, while its walls were covered with crimson plush and heavy blue silk studded with silver stars. Willie and Tad, of course, were everywhere at once and there is mention of a "nurse" whose duty it was to look after them and protect them (and those in their vicinity) from destruction.

The engine of the train, which with its flaring smokestack and pointed cowcatcher looked like the prehistoric ancestor of the present-day streamliner, was gay with banners. The countryside held carnival at its passing: flags were waved all along the way, every town was decorated, and thousands of people crowded the stations to greet its arrival. To Mr. Lincoln that journey of nearly two weeks was a cruel strain, but to the two little sons it was an exciting adventure.

Newspapers seized eagerly on little stories about the presidential offspring. The *New York Herald* reported that one of the little boys [probably Tad] delighted much of the way in asking strangers, "Do you want to see Old Abe?" and then pointing out someone else. Willie and Tad for the most part took the public attention unselfconsciously, but Tad rebelled once at being exhibited. On February 20 the *New York Times* reported how the crowd at Poughkeepsie warmly welcomed Mrs. Lincoln, who stood at a car window of the train, and then a voice called out, "Where are the children? Show us the children." Mrs. Lincoln called Robert to the window and he was greeted with a rousing cheer. "Have you any more on board?" yelled the crowd. "Yes, here's another," Mrs. Lincoln called back cheerfully and turned to get her youngest. Tad would have none of this and promptly flattened himself on the floor of the car, laughing at the fun, and his mother had to signal the people that the "pet of the family" objected to being put on exhibition.

When the Lincolns stopped overnight at Cincinnati, there was a huge reception and endless handshaking for the President-elect in the evening. The hour was late when he finally returned to his room, but it is said he found a fretful little boy [Tad] waiting for his father to put him to bed. Lincoln took him lovingly in his arms, carried him into the adjoining room, gently undressed him, and laid him down. This had evidently been the custom at home and it was to be continued in the White House.

The question of food on the journey was not always well managed and at one town, through some misunderstanding among the committee of arrangements, no provision had been made for dinner for the presidential party. Therefore, when two baskets full of cakes appeared shortly after twelve o'clock, the rejoicing was very great.

As the *New York Herald* reported it: "A rush, headed by Bob, who swooped upon his prey with a yell of delight, was made, and the contents disposed of in a twinkling."

Robert frequently presented the picture of an exuberant college freshman. At Cincinnati the Republican youths of the city plied him with "sparkling Catawba," but it was recorded that he had no hangover the next day. It was a period of much intoxication and his mother was to worry about Bob in this respect. She had a horror of drinking; the life of one of her brothers was ruined by this weakness. Her worry was needless, however; when Robert would come out of his phases of growing up, it would be found that the bedrock of his character was sound and firm and he too had contempt for drunkenness.

The long journey with its ups and downs and excitement came to an end on February 23 and the Lincoln family was established at Willard's Hotel in Washington. But there was no end to the "uproar"; it seemed rather to increase until it reached that vast climax of ceremonial, the inauguration. On March 4, before a great crowd in front of the Capitol, Mr. Lincoln delivered the immortal First Inaugural that Bob had so nearly lost. Afterwards the family was driven through the tumultuous streets to the great white mansion at 1600 Pennsylvania Avenue which was now to take the place of home.

The pomp and circumstance gave no thrill to Robert. On March 5 the *New York Herald* reported: "Bob, the Prince of Rails, starts for Cambridge tomorrow. He is sick of Washington and glad to get back to his college."

Even patient Willie was very soon to say, "I wish they wouldn't stare at us so. Wasn't there ever a President who had children?"

CHAPTER 8

"Let the Children Have
a Good Time"

THERE was a large family group of "Mother's" relatives at the
White House following the inauguration. Various aunts, uncles,
and cousins of the boys had come from Springfield for the event,
among them Aunt Lizzie Edwards and Cousin Elizabeth Todd
Grimsley. Cousin Lizzie was to stay for six months and later tell
many intimate things that happened back of the pillars of the White
House during that time. She recorded how on March 5 the family
group went on a tour to inspect their new quarters and added:
". . . this was most faithfully done by the irrepressible 'Tad' and ob-
servant Willie, from dome to basement, and every servant interviewed by these same young gentlemen, from Edward, the door
keeper . . . to the maids and scullions."

The boys were probably sizing up the possibilities for fun and
pranks in their new abode and shrewdly determining which of the
servants might be of use in their enterprises. The ambition of Willie
and Tad at this time, the thing to which they were devoting their
tireless young energies, seems to have been to play one practical
joke or prank after another. This had been true in Springfield, as the
random recollections of certain indignant citizens have revealed, but
now that they were the President's sons, the searchlight of publicity
which is always turned on the White House family showed up every
antic in high relief and there were many somewhat startled observ-
ers to write them down. Eighteen sixty-one was a year of frolic for
Willie and Tad, though the Civil War, which began in April, was to
paint some black streaks on the bright-colored pattern of their lives.

One strongly suspects that the Lincoln sons would not have been
so mischievous if their father had not laughed at their tricks and
thought them smart. They adored him and he practically applauded

every caper their inventive minds could think up. Even as early as 1847, when Robert was only four, that annoyed fellow passenger on the train to Lexington had noted with amazement that the father "aided and abetted" him in his mischief and beamed proudly, when what was called for, in the passenger's opinion, was a good spanking for the brat. Willie and Tad, in inspecting their new home, were surveying the background of their future endeavors.

One windy day in March, shortly after the inauguration, they were in the conservatory, which joined the White House on the west side, watching the goldfish in the water-lily tank, when three visitors came into the room. Willie and Tad, looking up, saw two promising boys about their ages and a small, pleasing, sixteen-year-old girl. They were the children of Judge and Mrs. Horatio Nelson Taft: "Bud" (Horatio Nelson Taft, Jr.), who was a year older than Willie, and "Holly" (Halsey Cook Taft), who was about the age of Tad. The girl was their sister Julia. Mrs. Lincoln had met their mother the day before and learning of Bud and Holly had said, "Send them around to-morrow, please, Mrs. Taft; Willie and Tad are so lonely and everything is so strange to them here in Washington." Julia had brought them over. Seeing Willie and Tad gazing at the goldfish, her first impression had been: "Such nice, quiet, shy boys." This impression lasted about five minutes, when all four boys disappeared. At dark her little brothers turned up at home so untidy they seemed completely unrelated to the well-groomed lads she had taken to the White House that morning. They reported they had had "the best time" and Mr. Lincoln had "jounced" them on his lap and told them stories.

From then on through the rest of the year the four boys were inseparable and Julia was usually sent along with them with instructions to see that "those young rascals don't tear down the White House." She faithfully recorded what went on in her diary and later, as Julia Taft Bayne, wrote *Tad Lincoln's Father*, a priceless intimate report on the Lincoln family. The parents of Bud and Holly Taft had the typical Victorian attitude that children should be kept strictly in their place, but their boys readily adopted the seeming theory of Willie and Tad that one of their missions in life was to make things lively and interesting for the grown-ups around them.

Bud and Willie were the more quiet and thoughtful pair who sometimes showed a bit of restraint. They seem to have been somewhat alike and to have had a special understanding of each other. Mr. Lincoln took a great liking to Bud. Holly and Tad were the completely irresponsible and harum-scarum couple, the very two, for example, to whom it seemed an excellent idea to take Tad's toy cannon and bombard the room where the President was meeting with his Cabinet. No doubt the serious and bearded gentlemen around the table needed something to liven them up! Some of them with settled notions on child rearing probably received a severe jolt, but the only physical casualty at the bombardment was Holly, who pinched his finger. The meeting of the statesmen was suspended while the President left the room to restore quiet.

It was Holly and Tad who threw the family into a dither by disappearing one morning immediately after breakfast and failing to return by afternoon. The Taft boys had spent the night at the White House, as they often did, and Willie and Bud were playing more or less harmlessly on its flat roof, but there was no trace of the two younger boys. Servants were sent out in all directions to search for them and anxiety grew. It was after dark when a gentleman brought them back in his carriage, to the enormous relief of the parents.

The two little boys doubtless got a great thrill out of relating their adventures. They had gone to the Capitol, where, as Tad nonchalantly explained, "a man who knew Pa gave us some dinner in the restaurant." Then they decided to see how far down in the Capitol they could go. "We went down steps pretty near to China," Holly contributed, "and . . . Tad dared me to explore around and we did and got lost." Tad said there were rats and it was "awful dark," and the two at last began to call for help. Finally a man working in the subbasement heard them and led them out.

Tad's resourceful mind found other ways of throwing the White House into a dither. In an early exploration of the garret he and Willie discovered the center of the White House bell system. Tad, like his father, loved to investigate the mechanics of any contrivance and was very good at it. He soon found how to work the bells and the result was that bedlam broke out on the second floor of the White House: the secretaries, John Nicolay and John Hay, were rushing to the President's office with visions of a sudden national emergency or presidential ire; old Edward, the doorkeeper, was hurrying up the stairs; everyone was running somewhere to answer the violent ringing. The bells, as another secretary, William Stoddard, said, seemed "bewitched." Investigation disclosed Willie and Tad in the garret, Tad, of course, being the one who was seated by the "yoke" of the bell system, "tugging hard and bringing out at once all the jangle" there was in the mansion. Both boys were in high glee.

It was the young secretary Stoddard who noted that shortly after

Willie and Tad acquired new pocketknives, the top of a table in the northeast room upstairs suddenly was cut into what suggested a war map. It was Stoddard also who reported that the little boys got into a fight in which Tad the aggressor tried to make a war map of Willie.

The White House attic had rich possibilities of entertainment other than the bell system. It contained a large bin of visiting cards, many of them with very distinguished and historic names, though that fact did not interest Willie, Tad, Bud, and Holly, who came seeking diversion. The Lincoln boys missed the snows in which they had played back in Illinois, and it occurred to one of the four that they could pretend the cards were snow and play snowstorm. That called for a sled, and the attic fortunately was full of promising materials for inventive minds. The boys took an old chair minus a seat, nailed barrel staves to it for runners, and then originated an excellent use for a copy of the *Congressional Record*—they made a seat of it. They dragged this unique object around and exhibited it as a snow sled, and threw the cards up and played that it was snowing. They could not make snowballs of the cards, but they could and did stuff them down each other's backs, which had evidently been another gratifying use for snow in Springfield.

The entertainment and wrecking activities of the four boys had to be suspended for a while in the latter part of March. Willie and Tad broke out with the measles. What is more, they gave the disease to Elmer Ellsworth, who was like a member of the family at the White House and, according to Elizabeth Todd Grimsley's observation, "a great pet" of the Lincolns. It was humiliating for the dashing young Zouave to get a child's disease, and a severe case at that. Shortly after he recovered, the training of his Zouaves no longer was intended merely for parades but had a far grimmer purpose—by the middle of April the nation had plunged into civil war.

At its outbreak Julia told the boys of an old Negro woman who claimed prophetic powers. She had seen a comet blazing in the skies and had called it a great fire sword that meant war was coming. Its handle, she said, was toward the North and the point toward the South and that meant the North was going to take that sword and cut the South's heart out. Tad told his father about it and asked, "Do you think that's what it means, Pa?" Mr. Lincoln, whose deep-lined face looked suddenly older, answered gravely, "I hope not, Tad."

The boys found many things that war did mean. It meant that the streets of Washington were quickly filled with soldiers. It meant their burdened father had to give time to what Tad called "plaguey old generals." Willie and Tad visited with their father and mother the military camps that sprang up on all sides and watched the regiments that marched in review down Pennsylvania Avenue past the White House. When the New York Seventh came in April, a newspaper item noted that the "President's two little sons" each had "a Union badge adorning his jacket." Though the generals were "plaguey" in taking up their father's time, the boys, in a suddenly awakened and ardent patriotism, loved the "good soldiers" who were fighting for the Union. Their toys and play soon ran to war themes, their desires to guns and forts and uniforms. And to their loved Elmer Ellsworth the war meant brightly and darkly more than any of these things.

In the country's surge of enlisting and gearing for war Ellsworth went to New York in April to recruit a regiment from the fire department of the city. With the brilliance of his personality combined with the appeal of the brilliant uniform, success was overwhelming. When the "Fire Zouaves," as they were called, left the city, there were great festivities, with speeches, parades, and band playing. It is delightful to find this regiment the subject of a letter which Willie Lincoln wrote on May 3 to Henry Remann, the same Springfield friend to whom he had written the "Me and father" letter in 1859. The first sentence, with its Southern "you all" (which one might expect of a boy both of whose parents had been born in Kentucky) and its grammatical error, is especially appealing.

"Dear henry," began Willie, "I am sorry I have not wrote to you at all, since I left you all." He told Henry how "Colonel, E. E. Elsworth had gone to New York and organized a regiment—divided into companys, and brought them here, & to be sworn in—I don't know when." One finds that Willie did not neglect to write to Robert: "I told my brother bob in my last letter that there was at least ten thousand soldiers stationed at the capitol building."

Writing was too laborious a matter for a ten-year-old to give all the vivid details of what was happening at the Capitol. Ellsworth's regiment was quartered there in the south wing and its historic timbers doubtless were shocked with the rollicking horseplay that was going on. The Fire Zouaves gleefully organized their own House of Representatives, elected a speaker and other officers, went into session, dissolved the Union, and reconstructed it. They did other off-the-record things, including hanging from the outer edges of the unfinished dome, to the horror of passing citizens, knocking down sentinels, and walking the parapets of the Capitol with rifles on shoulder. The date that Willie had not been able to give was May 7, when the "Little Colonel," as he was called, formed his regiment in a hollow square on the open space east of the Capitol to be sworn in. A great crowd assembled to watch that bright scene: these spirited young men in their gorgeously colored uniforms taking the oath of loyalty to the nation whose Capitol rose behind them. Mr. Lincoln's tall hat towered above others in the crowd and Tad was with him. That much is known; it is to be hoped that Willie and the Taft boys and Julia were somewhere in the throng.

Under the date of May 19, 1861, Julia wrote in her diary: "Heard a fine sermon at camp to-day. . . . The soldiers sang 'I would not Live Alway' so heartily we could hardly hear the band. Col. Ellsworth escorted me home." What a picture the pair must have made: the gallant Zouave officer and the prim Victorian girl whom Mr. Lincoln described as "a small, slim thing with curls and a white dress and a blue sash . . ."

On May 23 Julia with her brothers and Willie and Tad went to the camp of Colonel Ellsworth's Fire Zouaves to see their gymnastic drill. She said he called them his monkeys and their agility made the name very appropriate. As they left he stood at the corner, "very bright and handsome," waving his red cap and calling, "Come again." But there were to be no more "agains" for the young soldier. The next day Mrs. Lincoln, overcome with sorrow, told Julia about the tragedy.

A Confederate flag had hung that day over the Marshall House, a hotel in Alexandria, Virginia, just across from Washington. The "Little Colonel" with an escort of his men had gone there, climbed to the roof, and torn the enemy flag down with his own hands. As he descended the stairs, still holding the flag, he was shot by the proprietor of the hotel, who in turn was immediately shot by one of Ellsworth's own men. The beloved young leader of the Zouaves was dead.

His funeral was held in the great East Room of the White House. The Lincolns were deeply grieved and Mrs. Lincoln was unable to control her emotions. During the service Julia Taft was horrified to see Tad and Holly perch themselves on the back of a chair regardless of the fact it was occupied by the redoubtable figure of General Winfield Scott, commonly called old "Fuss and Feathers." (It was perhaps their first funeral and little boys are too short to see what goes on when they sit decorously.) When the time came for General Scott to rise, of course the chair tilted, but some members of his staff caught the youngsters as they fell.

Julia wanted to tell the President of the gay visit she and the boys had had with Colonel Ellsworth the day before his death, but she refrained when she heard that Mr. Lincoln wept at the mere mention of the young man's name. The Confederate flag which he had torn down, stained with his blood, was given to Mrs. Lincoln. She put the tragic relic away, but later Tad found it and had some bright ideas as to pranks with it. Perhaps he never knew its story; as far as possible the Lincolns protected the children from sadness and the dreadfulness of war. Julia often heard Mrs. Lincoln say with a smile as the four boys rushed devastatingly through the room, "Let the children have a good time."

But war inevitably colored every activity. About the time it began it affected, in rather dramatic fashion, the church services which Willie and Tad attended with Julia Taft. Many of the members were in sympathy with the South and secession, and when the minister would pray for the President of the United States, they would rise and leave ostentatiously, banging the pew doors loudly behind them. The boys were delighted with this spirited interruption to the monotony of the long prayer. It was one reason they went to the Fourth Presbyterian Church with Julia instead of the New York Avenue Presbyterian Church with their father and mother; Julia's church was, as Willie explained to his mother, "lots livelier."

But the liveliness came to an abrupt end after a young lieutenant with a file of soldiers appeared before the congregation one Sunday morning and announced in businesslike tones that by order of the Provost Marshal anyone disturbing the service or leaving before it was over would be arrested and taken to the guardhouse. Tad, who always wanted action and plenty of it, was much disappointed with the lack of spirit of the secessionists in not resisting the lieutenant. "If I was Secesh," he said, "I wouldn't let him stop me banging pew doors."

Willie and Tad went to Sunday School and church for very different reasons. Willie, who had said he wanted to be a preacher when he grew up, was very conscientious, especially with regard to the Sabbath. Sunday behavior in that day was hedged about with very strict rules; anything that remotely suggested recreation was frowned upon by the orthodox. Once on a Sunday Willie sat down at the piano in the Red Room when visitors were present and strummed out a popular air. Good "Cousin Lizzie" Grimsley reproved him at the first opportunity: "No one is without example, and as your father's son, I would remember the Sabbath day to keep it holy." Willie solemnly promised he would and Cousin Lizzie said that he kept his word. Thereafter during her stay at the White House, when the Lincolns went for a Sunday drive, Willie would stay at home with her. She said he went to church both as a matter of conscience and because he loved it.

Neither reason carried any weight with the lighthearted Tad. He went mainly because he did not want to be separated from Willie and probably hoping he could get some diversion out of it, creating it himself, if need be. At church he usually sat on the floor of the pew and played with whatever he had in his pocket. Once, his supply of entertainment running low, he borrowed a knife from a young officer who sat in the pew and then promptly cut his finger. Julia, who was supposed to look after him, had to sacrifice her best embroidered handkerchief to bind it up. Utterly exasperated she hissed, "I will never take you to church again, Thomas Lincoln." She knew he hated to be called Thomas. He promptly got even by saying out loud, to her horror, "Just you keep your eyes on Willie, sitting there good as pie."

The proper Julia told Tad how one must be very quiet and still in church. "See the Lieutenant, how still he sits," she whispered, and Tad, who liked to argue, answered, "I bet he wouldn't sit so still if a bee stung him." Julia insisted that he would. Tad later referred the question to his father: "Do you think he would sit so still, Pa, if a bee was stinging him?" The President said yes, he thought he would, and his face went grave, as if he was thinking of worse things than bee stings which the soldiers must endure.

Tad argued with his father over the reason why he had to go to Sunday School. He evidently felt he had no call to visit a place with such uncomfortable standards of behavior. His father answered seriously, "Every educated person should know something about the Bible and the Bible stories, Tad." Mrs. Lincoln was very anxious that the boys should attend, and to the unfortunate Julia fell the task of teaching them their Sunday School lessons. Even Willie thought there were a lot of "hard words" in them, but he and Bud buckled down to the task of learning what was required. Tad and Holly wriggled and could not be made to concentrate.

Julia gave an example which showed how things went. The mention of the moral law reminded Tad of a new word he had encountered; a boy in Lafayette Square had said he and Willie were mudsills. The term implied they belonged to a low stratum of society, but the boys did not know that. It did not sound good to Tad, however, and he wanted to punch the boy, but Willie and Bud restrained him, saying with recently acquired wisdom that it would get into the papers.

The boy in Lafayette Square had expressed an opinion very prevalent in Washington. Presenting Lincoln in the campaign as The Rail Splitter was all right for getting votes among the people, but snobbish persons in the East, and there were a lot of them, looked down their noses at these Lincolns from the "uncivilized" state of Illinois and expected to find them crude and vulgar. One rather enjoys thinking of the impact which the uninhibited and highly original Lincoln boys produced on some of these stuffy Easterners.

In the first place, Willie and Tad looked and were dressed exactly like what they were: bright, active, democratic little American boys from a prairie town. They were not even aware of the question of style in their clothes; Robert was the only son who had developed fastidiousness in dress. A lady journalist gave a description of them which shows how they appeared to critical Washington eyes. "The younger Lincoln boys were homely," she said, "but intelligent in appearance." She thought their clothes were homely too. Willie, when she saw him, "had on a gray and very baggy suit of clothes, and his style was altogether different from that of the curled darlings of fashionable mothers; but there was a glow of intelligence and feeling on his face which made him peculiarly interesting and caused strangers to speak of him as a fine little fellow." Tad about this time she described as "rather a grotesque looking little fellow, in his gray trapdoor pants, made, in true country style, to button to a waist—and very baggy they were; but his face was bright and honest." Then comes the interesting observation: "Mr. Lincoln's two youngest boys, Willie and Taddy, resembled him strikingly."

Willie and Tad were far removed from the stiff little prigs who appeared in the fashionable Currier & Ives prints. They seemed, like their father, untouched by the Victorian period, but that period was putting its mark on the more conventional Robert. The little boys used language that was natural and vivid but not always grammatical. They were not sensitive about the fact that their father had split rails. Julia Taft told how Tad went around her home one day singing, "Old Abe Lincoln, a rail splitter was he. . . ." Willie asked Mrs. Taft if it was "real disrespectful to Pa" for Tad to sing that song, and she thought it was. Tad said, "Everybody in the world knows Pa used to split rails," and kicked the chair in his resentment at being reproved. He was not used to reproof.

Many in Washington came to the point of view held by the White House gardener, Mr. Watt, when he discovered that Tad had eaten up all the strawberries which he had been carefully forcing for a state dinner. Julia found him in a rage over it and threatening to tell Mrs. Lincoln about it. Julia remarked that Willie had already told his mother what Tad had done and she added, as a gentle hint that such reporting would accomplish nothing, "He is Madam's son, remember." The gardener exploded into a three-word description of Tad: "the Madam's wildcat."

In the spring of 1861 Mrs. Lincoln went to New York to buy some new furnishings for the White House. She asked Mrs. Taft to let Bud and Holly stay with Willie and Tad while she was away so that they would not be too lonely and also, one suspects, so that the careworn President would have lively company at meals. The Lincoln boys came to the Taft home to fetch their playmates, and the lady journalist who had described them so critically would have thought more than ever that they presented an unstylish appearance, for they arrived in a pouring rain under a dilapidated umbrella which they had borrowed from the cook. As they left, lugging the satchel with Bud's and Holly's clothes, Tad called back, "You bet we're going to have a good time."

There can be no doubt that they did. Several days later when Julia came over with clean "blouses" for her little brothers, she found all the servants and White House staff grinning broadly. The boys, she was told, were in the attic. When she had climbed the stairs, she came upon a most lively scene. Tad rushed at her shouting excitedly, "Come quick, Julie. We're having a circus. I've got to be blacked up and Willie can't get his dress on and Bud's bonnet won't fit." Behind a curtain made of two sheets pinned together was a motley audience of soldiers, servants, and anybody else, black or white, who could muster up the five cents which was the admission charge. There was no snobbery in Willie or Tad.

Julia kept the "program" of the circus which Willie himself had printed. It gives much interesting information. Several of the boys' friends were in the cast, especially one Billy Sanders and one Joe Corkhead. Tad was to play the part of "The Black Statue" in "III.Part," and when Julia arrived, he was flourishing a bottle of shoe polish which he intended to use as make-up. She took it away from him and made him up with burnt cork instead. Bud and Willie were to be lovely Victorian ladies in the show and each one was struggling into a dress belonging to Mrs. Lincoln. Julia pinned up the train of Willie's dress and the surplus folds of Bud's and straightened the latter's bonnet. She then by request bedaubed the "ladies" of the cast liberally with "Bloom of Youth."

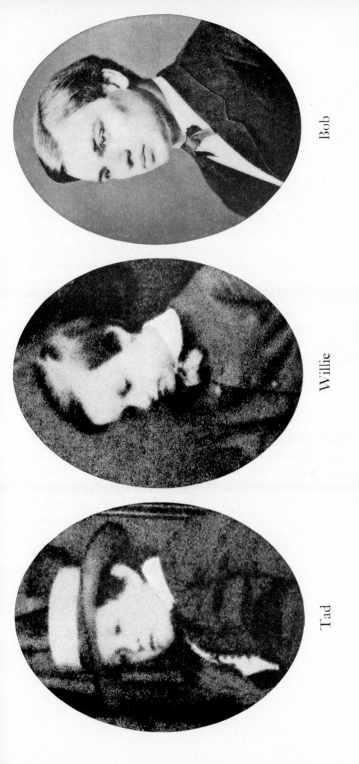

Tad

Willie

Bob

Lincoln's Sons

Tad, Willie, and Robert as they looked about the time the Lincoln family went to Washington in 1861. The photograph of Robert is from the National Archives, the other two by courtesy of the Abraham Lincoln Association.

Birthplaces of Lincoln's Sons

Above, the Globe Tavern, where Robert was born. This picture was taken in 1865. *Below*, the Lincoln home on Eighth Street, birthplace of Eddie, Willie, and Tad. Mr. Lincoln and Willie are standing in the yard. This picture was taken in 1860.

Taddie

An early ambrotype of Willie

Important Members of the Springfield Household

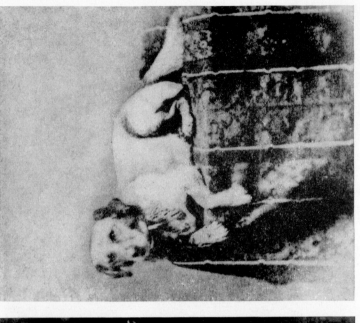

Mrs. Lincoln with Willie and Tad

Fido, the Lincoln dog

More Important Members of the Springfield Household

The show opened patriotically with a rousing rendition of "Hail Columbia" by the entire "troupe." Billy Sanders and Tad Lincoln then sang "The Star-Spangled Banner." Loyal Unionism having thus been demonstrated, there followed a duet of "Dixie Land" by Joe Corkhead and Bud Taft, Bud doubtless an irresistible Southern belle in Mrs. Lincoln's white morning gown and a stylish bonnet. Willie, in a voluminous lilac silk of his mother's, cut very décolleté, probably stirred deep emotions in the audience when he joined in a duet of "Home Sweet Home." Both Lincoln boys evidently could sing, which was an accomplishment their father did not have. Tad had been practicing "Old Abe Lincoln Came out of the Wilderness" for the show but was apparently talked out of it, for it does not appear on the program.

The doings in the attic all seemed very improper to Julia and she escaped as soon as she could. On the way down she met John Hay rushing up and looking very angry about something. He evidently, like Robert, did not approve of the way the Lincolns were bringing up their younger sons. "Have those boys got the President's spectacles?" he asked. Having just seen them on Tad's nose Julia replied that she thought they had.

A moment or two later as she went on down she heard Tad calling, "Julie, come back! Make Holly go and get us some spectacles." Hay had taken "Pa's" away from Tad and he remembered that an old gentleman who was visiting the Taft home had two pairs. "Make Holly go get one of 'em." The disgusted Julia walked on without replying. In the lower hall she met Mr. Lincoln on his way up to the attic to attend the performance. She heard later that he laughed at the boys' jokes and enjoyed it all hugely; in his words they were having "a great time up there." Tad's prediction had come true: they had a great time during the whole visit.

The Taft boys' shirts, or "blouses," as they were called, got mixed with those of the Lincoln boys and some were left at the White House. This proved very convenient one day when Mrs. Lincoln (under enthusiastic urging from the boys, no doubt) let them attend a state dinner. She put fresh blouses on them and let them sit near the foot of the table. It was a gorgeous scene with glittering ambassadors "all tied up with gold cords," as Tad said. "Pa looked pretty plain with his black suit," added Willie, "but Ma was dressed up, you bet."

The President liked nothing better than to romp with the four boys, but Willie would sometimes say mournfully, "Pa don't have time to play with us now." Julia described two appealing scenes. One was Mr. Lincoln sitting in a big chair telling stories to the boys. Willie was on one knee, Bud on the other, Holly on the arm of the chair, and Tad perched on the back. When Julia entered, a long arm reached out and drew her into the circle. The stories, she remembered, were exciting tales of hunters, settlers, and Indians.

The second scene gave Julia quite a shock. Hearing a terrific racket in another room and thinking that she had better investigate what the boys were up to, she turned the doorknob to behold the President flat on the floor with the four boys trying to hold him down. Willie and Bud were holding down his arms while Holly and Tad were sprawling over his legs. Tad regarded Julia as in the nature of a reinforcement and shouted, "Julie, come quick and sit on his stomach." Mr. Lincoln's twinkle and wide grin showed he was enjoying it all tremendously. Julia could only step back and close the door.

Julia's propriety and primness stirred in Mr. Lincoln a desire for gentle teasing. When he spied her serious young head with every hair arranged properly and every curl in its place, he just had to put his hand on that too-tidy hair and muss it up. A rapid rotation of those long fingers accomplished a most thorough mussing, which, as Julia said, "seemed to please him better than it did me." Willie and Tad, especially Tad, had this same love of teasing; in fact, they inherited it from both father and mother.

Tad found the Confederate flag that had been given to Mrs. Lincoln, the one Ellsworth had torn down at the cost of his life. It offered wonderful possibilities for teasing "Pa," not to mention some others. One day when Washington was celebrating a military victory with the Union flag flying at every house, Tad planted this rebel flag in front of the Taft home. That was no joke for wartime, but a scandalized neighbor came to tell Mrs. Taft before trouble resulted.

An even more propitious occasion for mischief came when "Father" stood at the front of the White House reviewing some troops who were marching by on Pennsylvania Avenue. The President was standing in great dignity with the flag of the Union in his hands, and the horrified onlookers saw his little son right behind him waving the Confederate flag. The resulting commotion must have convinced Tad that this was a very successful idea. Mr. Lincoln turned to see what was the matter, gathered boy and flag both in his arms, and turned them over to an orderly who carried them away from the public gaze.

It must have been quite a scene—that small gleeful figure with its impudent motions in contrast to the measured steps of the parading soldiers and the dignity of the presidential flag-bearer. The two flags were symbolic of the divided country; the four children who frolicked in the White House that year were small dancing figures on a stage with a grim backdrop of civil war.

CHAPTER 9

Young Ideas Shooting in
Various Directions

SOLDIERS were always parading along Pennsylvania Avenue; in fact, soldiers were everywhere. At the beginning of the war they had been in the White House itself. After the President had called for seventy-five thousand troops on April 15, there had been a period of intense anxiety for fear the Confederates would attack Washington before the Union forces could reach it, and "Frontier Guards" camped in the East Room and corridors of the Executive Mansion. Of course Willie and Tad made friends with the soldiers under their own roof; the responsive little fellows were naturally very popular with the soldiery.

Even the President in those days of agonized waiting for the Union troops to bring protection looked out of the window with drawn face and repeated the words which were on everyone's lips: "Why don't they come! Why don't they come!"

When finally the Seventh New York arrived on April 25 and marched past the White House with band playing and flags flying, the excited boys, watching with their mother and Cousin Elizabeth Grimsley, saw the two women wiping away their tears. Adult tears are impressive and somehow terrible to children. Willie and Tad felt they must do their part in defending Washington. With public buildings barricaded all around and the Capitol looking like an armed fort, the boys busily began to take over the matter of safeguarding the White House.

With the co-operation of Bud and Holly Taft they constructed a fort on its roof. When Julia Taft was called upon to inspect it, to her sixteen-year-old sophistication it appeared to consist of a small log representing a cannon and a few rifles that had long since ceased to function. But Tad at least was sure of its threat to the enemy.

"Let 'em come," he said proudly, "Willie and I are ready for 'em." The flat roof at times also served as an excellent man-of-war and from its deck the boys peered hopefully through an old spyglass for signs of "enemy cruisers."

The most strenuous endeavors of Willie, Bud, Holly, and Tad were concerned with raising a soldier company of boys. On September 30 Willie wrote his friend Henry Remann about these efforts. As in his letter to Henry in May, military matters predominate. There is a gay and spirited quality to this letter, a touch of humor, and a clear conciseness of statement that all suggest the writing of Mr. Lincoln in embryo. The letter unfolds a tale of disappointments and frustrations ending in ultimate triumph through perseverance.

Willie began: "Dear Henry, The last letter you sent to me, arrived in due time, which was on Saturday. My companions and I are raising a battalion." He explained that in June he had joined another boy in trying to get up a regiment: "We failed however, and I then attempted to muster a Company. That soon broke up." The next development was that some boy told him that he commanded a battalion, "and my Company and I at once joined, believing that he spoke the truth, but we found out that was not the case." Then came the climactic statement which closed the letter with a flourish: "Disappointed in every way we set to work and raised one, which is in a high state of efficiency and discipline."

They had gathered up all the boys they could get to enlist, and Julia Taft said the company was called "Mrs. Lincoln's Zouaves." It was a foregone conclusion that they would choose to be Zouaves with the memory of the gallant young Colonel Ellsworth fresh in their minds. And then there was that irresistible red, blue, and gold uniform. Not many of the company had uniforms, but one can be quite sure that they were provided for Willie and Tad. Tad gave Julia Taft a picture of himself taken in what appears to be this uniform. He holds a gun and looks very belligerent, and one wishes the picture were in color with red cap, short blue jacket trimmed in gold braid, baggy red pantaloons, and Tad's dark eyes flashing defiance.

Willie was colonel, Bud major, Holly captain, and Tad, who liked a noisy part, was drum major. President and Mrs. Lincoln gave them a flag and reviewed them with great ceremony, just as they did other heroic troops who were defending the Union. But in spite of that "high state of efficiency and discipline" of which Willie had boasted, there were a number of desertions and finally only the four officers were left. Willie, like his father, was having trouble getting the military to do what was wanted.

Reviewing troops was one of the presidential duties and the Lincoln boys apparently considered it one of theirs. Their father delighted to take them with him when he visited the camps for review and his manner of doing it was sometimes frowned upon. Among the multitudinous letters of advice on how to run things which were constantly pouring in on Mr. Lincoln was one which remarked in critical tone: "And when you are passing lines of soldiers, reviewing them, afoot, they say you take your boys along, and straddle off as if you were cutting across lots. . . . For God's sake consult somebody, some military man, as to what you ought to do on these occasions in military presence."

Mr. Lincoln was not likely to take this advice very seriously, but once when he did want to leave the boys behind, the headstrong youngsters took matters in their own hands. He was to review some troops at a camp across the Potomac and as it was a cold, windy day and the boys had colds, Mrs. Lincoln had forbidden them to go along. The resourceful "codgers," however, had some money left from the circus and they made their own arrangements. So it happened that at the review, as the President and other dignitaries passed solemnly and ceremoniously down the line of soldiers, just after them came a rickety, mule-drawn cart driven by a small, grinning Negro and containing Willie, Bud, Holly, and Tad, each stiffly holding a battered sword at salute.

Visiting the camps was one of the greatest pleasures of the boys, though Julia Taft noted that they grew tired of the constant attention they received as sons of the President. Sometimes they went with their mother and "Cousin Lizzie" Grimsley to take good things to the soldiers or to assist in christening a camp. The one named for their mother, "Camp Mary Lincoln," was the favorite with Willie and Tad, the one for which they saved the choicest gifts. Tad especially delighted in carrying presents to "his good soldiers," fruit, and other food, books, papers, and sometimes flowers he obtained by raids on the White House conservatory, to the renewed ire of Major Watt, the gardener.

Once Tad with the best of intentions took to camp and distributed a supply of religious tracts. The soldiers laughed heartily and told him they had plenty of paper to start fires with and they would rather have posies. Tad, like Robert, was very sensitive to being made ridiculous; he wept at such misunderstanding and ingratitude and his father had great difficulty consoling his "little man." It was a long time before he would visit that camp again.

The Lincoln boys, like all White House children, received many gifts. The Sanitary Commission in New York sent Tad a handsome soldier doll which he named Jack. It was dressed in the favorite Zouave uniform and must have been a very appealing toy. But Jack seems to have had a most unregenerate character: the boys frequently had to hold court-martial over him, finding him guilty of such things as sleeping at his post or desertion, and sentencing him to be shot at sunrise. The execution, however, would take place immediately, Tad with his cannon playing the part of the firing squad.

The dishonored soldier would then be buried inappropriately with full military honors and the place chosen for burial was among Major Watt's newly planted rosebushes. Julia Taft, who tells the story, was in Mrs. Lincoln's room one day when a strange and dreadful sound came through the window from the White House grounds without. "What is that noise, Julia?" Mrs. Lincoln asked the girl.

"It is probably the 'dead march,'" Julia answered. "I suppose the boys are burying Jack again."

Mrs. Lincoln asked Julia to go quick and tell the boys not to dig among the roses because it would kill them. Julia knew they had been told this several times before, but she was obedient, if the boys were not, and she went outdoors to deliver the message. She found the band which was playing the excruciating "dead march" consisted of a broken-down fiddle, a dented horn, a paper over a comb, and Tad's drum. About the time she reached the spot, the gardener, Major Watt, arrived, looking like a man who had had about all he could take. Out of his desperation came inspiration. He suggested that the boys get Jack pardoned.

This fine idea won instant approval all around. "Come on, Bud," said Tad enthusiastically. "We'll get Pa to fix up a pardon." Julia tried to prevent the four from bothering the President but they clattered noisily upstairs toward his office on the second floor. When she followed them, she found John Hay in the waiting room trying to head them off. This produced such an indignant protest that Mr. Lincoln in the inner office heard it and opened the door. He smiled down at the youngsters and asked what was the matter. Tad dodged around John Hay and threw himself on his father explaining what was wanted.

Mr. Lincoln began to enjoy himself. He told Tad it was not usual to grant pardons without some sort of hearing and invited them in to tell him why Jack deserved a pardon.

John Hay gave up "with a disgusted snort" and stepped aside to let the little group follow Mr. Lincoln into his private office. There he seated himself in a judicial pose and told Tad to state his case.

Tad delivered his argument in a rush of words: almost every day they tried Jack for being a spy or deserter or something and then they shot him and buried him and Julie said it spoiled his clothes and Major Watt said it dug up his roses so they thought they would get Pa to fix up a pardon.

The President considered these facts with due gravity and then told Tad he thought he had made a case. It was a good law, he said, that no man shall twice be put in jeopardy of his life for the same offense. Since Jack had been shot and buried a dozen times, he was entitled to a pardon. Turning to his desk, on which so many pardons were to be signed, he wrote on his official paper: "The Doll Jack is pardoned by order of the President. A. Lincoln."

John Hay bundled Julia and the boys out of the door with scant ceremony. He evidently felt, like the gardener, that he had had about all he could take from those boys.

Sad to relate, Jack's pardon did not cause him to reform. In less than a week he was proved guilty of being a spy again. The boys thought it wise to have a change of venue this time and he was hanged from a tree in the Taft garden.

As the pressure of the war bore in more heavily upon their father and mother and all around them, the martial aspect of the play of the children increased. They turned a vacant room in the attic at the Taft home into an "old Capitol Prison" and incarcerated the Taft cat and a neighbor's dog as prisoners of war. (The prisoners made such vociferous protests that Mrs. Taft released them.) They would hunt the praying mantises on the Taft grapevines and set them to fighting each other, which they did with such ferocity there was seldom a survivor. The boys dug a rifle pit in the Taft garden and once Tad and Holly found a loaded gun at the Tafts' and fired it out of the window, to the great jeopardy of the colored washerwoman in the yard next door.

Perhaps the feverish activity of the boys was to some extent due to the upset and unrest that war brings to every individual, old or young. The White House, the storm center of the conflict, was not a normal or wholesome place for growing children. Tad, a nervous child to begin with, undoubtedly suffered from this environment, but it seems to have had the effect of making the thoughtful Willie mature more rapidly. The war front came very close at times, bringing fear and terror to the people in Washington. One day in July of that first year there were strange, ominous sounds in the air and pale, strained faces on the streets. Willie, his eyes wide with questioning, exclaimed excitedly, "Pa says there's a battle in Virginia; that's big cannons going off that sounds like slamming doors." The Battle of Bull Run was in progress.

There were high hopes of Union success at first; then came the news of defeat and Washington was in a panic of fear that it would itself be the next target of those cannon. Ambulances rumbled along the streets bringing the wounded; the boys saw soldiers who had looked so grand and invincible on parade limping along, some with empty sleeves or bandaged heads. General Scott raised the question as to whether the boys and their mother should be sent North out of danger. Mrs. Lincoln refused to leave her husband's side in this crisis. One may be sure the spirited lads concurred in the decision not to run away and leave Father.

As always in wartime, people tried to go on with normal activities and pleasures as much as was possible within the war effort and sense of depression. On Wednesday and Saturday afternoons the Marine Band gave serenades on the White House lawn to which the public was invited. A special tent was erected for their shelter; one finds from a receipted bill that it took 508 yards of blue and white "Duck" for its making. A band and a tent both are magnets for small boys; Willie and Tad were undoubtedly popular figures at these concerts. Tad liked his music full of blood and thunder. It is remembered that once at a private concert in the White House he and his father called for the song "Ship on Fire," which begins with a tremendous thunderstorm, while passengers and crew kneel and pray for deliverance, and ends with the ship bursting into flames. It must have been a highly satisfactory production to Tad.

On Easter Monday that first year the lawn at the rear of the White House was a gay scene of children and baskets and bright-colored eggs rolling down the gentle slope. The first child to get his egg to the bottom without the shell being broken was proclaimed the winner. Bud and Holly Taft came, each with his basket of eggs, and Julia, as usual, was with them as a sort of chaperone. She remembered how "hugely" Willie and Tad enjoyed the occasion and how disgusted everyone was when it was discovered that one boy was using a colored china egg. He and his egg were promptly evicted. The episode gave Tad an idea; he remarked that next year he would get him an egg made of cast iron.

Family life was perfectly normal in one way—the boys caught the usual children's diseases. It had been measles for Willie and Tad in March; it was mumps for Bob in July. On the seventeenth of that month he telegraphed his father: "I have the mumps. Home in a few days. Not sick at all." Perhaps related to this was another telegram sent in July (day of month not given) to the Cambridge, Massachusetts, telegraph office which read: "Mrs Lincoln is very much alarmed, has her trunks packed to leave. Did you receive message for Robert T Lincoln of this morning. Why no answer." Though unsigned, this telegram evidently came from the White House and it suggests that Robert had failed to reply to one sent to him. Devoted mother that she was, Mrs. Lincoln was quick to get alarmed at the slightest hint of anything wrong with one of her children.

Robert at Harvard was not being neglected by the rest of the family. His father did not have time to write much except checks for him but Willie wrote and, fluent letter writer that she was, Mrs. Lincoln undoubtedly did. No letters of hers to Robert at this time are known to exist, however; unfortunately, Robert was not one to preserve personal letters.

His mother frequently went to Boston to see her eldest son, and was constantly planning for him. She and "Cousin Lizzie" Grimsley spent a couple of days with Robert sometime that spring or summer of 1861, having a most delightful time and meeting, as Mrs. Grimsley wrote, "many of the most distinguished men of Boston and Harvard."

Distinguished visitors came to Washington too and were officially entertained. In August Willie and Tad saw a real prince and very princely he looked at the formal dinner President and Mrs. Lincoln gave for him, for he was in full dress with many decorations and had a broad crimson sash across his breast. He was the French Prince Napoleon and during his stay he had a brief, pleasing contact with Willie. The incident was witnessed by Nathaniel P. Willis, a well-known writer, editor, and friend of the Lincolns whose poetry was much admired by Mrs. Lincoln. Willie was on the sidewalk one day when Secretary Seward drove into the White House grounds with Prince Napoleon and two of his suite in the carriage. Secretary Seward (who, like others of the Cabinet, had evidently grown fond of Willie) in a mock-heroic manner took off his hat, and Prince Napoleon did the same, all making a ceremonious salute to the small boy on the sidewalk who was the President's son. Willie was not the least embarrassed with this homage; he drew himself up to his full height, gracefully took off his cap, and bowed down to the very ground "like a little ambassador." Then when the carriage had passed, he unconcernedly resumed his play. It took more than a prince to shake the composure of this sturdy Westerner.

Willie's richly endowed and well-balanced nature was developing beautifully in spite of the disturbed setting in which he was placed. The bright-faced boy was very popular with the friends of his father and mother, more so than the unpredictable Tad. Mr. Willis had a great affection for him. He said Willie had an endearing way of always seeking him out in a crowd of visitors to shake his hand and make some pleasant remark. It was the same gift of making friends by genuine interest and good will that his father had. In his magnetism, responsiveness, and tincture of fun he "faithfully resembled his father," said Mr. Willis and added a bit of description which contains a fundamental element of that resemblance: "With all the splendor that was around this little fellow in his new home, he was so bravely and beautifully *himself*—and that only!" Willie had, wrote Mr. Willis, "a fearless and kindly frankness, willing that everything should be as different as it pleased, but resting unmoved in his own conscious single heartedness."

Shortly after Prince Napoleon's visit Willie and Tad had a journey northward with their mother. Washington, as always, was extremely hot in summer and diseases now controlled by sanitation and medical knowledge raged unchecked in the eighteen sixties. Mrs. Lincoln, who suffered from the widespread chills and fever, had to get away for a while. She wrote her plan to a former Springfield neighbor, Mrs. John Shearer, whom she urged to join her in a trip to Long Branch, a resort on the New Jersey coast. To the motherly Mrs. Lincoln her neighbor's children were always welcome. "Bring your boys with you," she said to Mrs. Shearer, "it will be more pleasant all around. I am going to take my boys, with me, with a servant man, who will take charge of your children also."

One wishes for the recollections of this unnamed man who watched over Willie and Tad at Long Branch. It was the boys' first close acquaintance with the ocean, though they possibly had seen it when they had come through New York the February before. Perhaps they went sea bathing. Tad could not know that in a little over seven years he would be crossing that mighty ocean. Mrs. Shearer did not bring her sons, but it was quite a party nevertheless; Cousin Elizabeth Grimsley and John Hay went with them from Washington and Bob joined them at Long Branch. There was much entertainment for the President's family, including the inspection of a new lifesaving station, which doubtless, being a thing of action, interested the boys very much.

But something—sea bathing or sea breezes perhaps—gave Tad a severe cold and the return from the holiday was delayed on that account. The recurring illnesses of the boys were a constant source of anxiety to the parents.

Following this expedition Willie was honored with a namesake.

Mrs. Shearer had a son born about two months later and named him William Lincoln Shearer. She was drawn to Willie, whom she had known in Springfield, and Mrs. Lincoln had suggested that if the coming baby proved to be a boy, he should be named for the son who was undoubtedly her favorite.

The boys, of course, needed to go to school. Julia Taft recorded that in the fall of 1861 Mrs. Lincoln engaged a tutor and had a desk and blackboard put into the end of the state dining room, which was on the southwest corner of the first floor in the White House. Bud and Holly Taft had their lessons with Willie and Tad, the two older boys doing well, but it comes as no surprise that the younger ones were, as Julia said, "a little unruly."

It seems likely that the Lincoln boys had had a tutor before this in Washington, if one may judge by the great improvement in Willie's letters. A comparison of his letter to Henry Remann in May with that of September 30 shows remarkable strides in capitalization, grammar, and facility of expression. Willie's mind was becoming amazingly mature. He was comprehending some of the history that was being enacted around him and was quietly collecting "memoranda" (probably clippings) on important events. The following year his father would find this collection and show it to his old friend, Senator Orville H. Browning, who would write in his diary what it contained. There was an account of the inauguration of Richard Yates as governor of Illinois. History was so close to Willie he could see it in personal terms; Governor Yates was a friend of his father's, probably of Willie himself, and how well the boy remembered the Governor's Mansion in Springfield just a short walk from home. There were records of his father's inauguration and dates of battles and deaths of distinguished persons.

Perhaps Willie's collection contained a poem written by himself. A certain death on the battlefield in the fall of 1861 cut deep into the hearts of the Lincoln family. It was on October 21 that a passerby, looking curiously at some figures on the White House lawn, as people always do, saw Mr. Lincoln seated on the ground with his back against a tree and close by, stretched out at full length, an officer with whom he was in earnest conversation. It was a golden October day with the trees in the full blaze of their autumn coloring. The prone figure was a handsome one and one also very dear to the eyes of the Lincolns. It was Colonel Edward D. Baker, for whom, long ago, they had named their second son Eddie. Near the two men Willie Lincoln was playing in the red and gold of the fallen leaves.

Finally, the conference ended, the two men arose. Colonel Baker lifted Willie, whom he had known since he was a baby, into his arms and tenderly kissed him; then he mounted his horse and rode away to the west. Mr. Lincoln, who knew he was going into battle, followed that riding figure with shadowed eyes until it disappeared. The next day Colonel Baker was killed in action at the battle of Ball's Bluff. The news overwhelmed the President with grief, the whole family sorrowed, and thoughtful Willie was moved to write a poem about the fallen hero. Its style is now as out of date as hoop skirts but was in keeping with the poetic standards and attitudes of the day. The effect this literary endeavor produced on the poetry-loving and doting parents can well be imagined; perhaps it was their encouragement that prompted Willie to write a brief note to the editor of the *Washington National Republican:* "Dear Sir: I enclose you my first attempt at poetry. Yours truly, William W. Lincoln."

The editor thought the lines "quite creditable, as a first effort, for one so young," and published them in his paper on November 4, 1861.

> There was no patriot like Baker,
> So noble and so true;
> He fell as a soldier on the field,
> His face to the sky of blue.
>
> His voice is silent in the hall,
> Which oft his presence grac'd,
> No more he'll hear the loud acclaim,
> Which rang from place to place.
>
> No squeamish notions filled his breast,
> *The Union* was his theme,
> *"No surrender and no compromise,"*
> His day thought and night's dream.
>
> His country has *her* part to play,
> To'rds those he has left behind,
> His widow and his children all—
> She must always keep in mind.

Willie must have been the delight of his tutors. But Tad drove them to despair. He seemed to have an allergy to lessons. "He had a very bad opinion of books," wrote John Hay later, "and no opinion of discipline. . . ." If Tad sized up a tutor as one who would be serviceable in any important project of his (such as hitching up the pet goats to a chair), it was well and good, but if the benighted pedagogue thought the study of grammar a more desirable pursuit than flying a kite, for example, Tad would have none of him. Both John Hay and Noah Brooks (a delightful newspaperman who became a close friend of the Lincolns in their second year at Washington) agreed that Tad was very shrewd in sizing up the tutors. Many of them did not stay long enough to reach an understanding of him, said Mr. Brooks, "but he knew them before they had been one day in the house."

A close-up view of Tad's method of resisting any attempt to teach him was given by Mrs. Elizabeth Keckley, a mulatto woman who first came to the White House to be Mrs. Lincoln's dressmaker and then evolved into a kind of maid and companion. Tad, whose speech impediment seems to have included the use of a *y* for an *l*, called her "Yib." Mrs. Keckley described an incident that showed how Tad devoted more energy and ingenuity to evading a lesson than would have been required to master it. This incident occurred later when Mrs. Lincoln attempted to teach Tad something herself.

The lesson began with a book containing a picture with the word "ape" beneath it. Tad spelled out a-p-e and his mother asked what the word was. Tad, looking at the picture, insisted that "a-p-e" spelled "monkey." His mother, of course, did not accept that answer and a prolonged argument followed. Tad said he knew the picture of a monkey when he saw it, that he had seen lots of them in the streets with organ-grinders, and he knew more about monkeys than his mother because she never went out to see them when they came by. He appealed to "Yib," who also held firmly to the theory that "a-p-e" spelled "ape." Tad got more and more argumentative and excited; it was impossible to pin him down to the simple spelling of the word. He also had other methods of evading the issue, such as an important and pressing project, or a place he must go; one has considerable sympathy for his tutors. "To teach the young idea how to shoot" in Tad's case was a frustrating business; the idea always "shot" in the wrong direction.

Tad was keen and apt enough in subjects that interested him. Even when he "could scarcely read," said Noah Brooks, "he knew much about the cost of things, the details of trade, the principles of mechanics, and the habits of animals, all of which showed the activity of his mind and the odd turn of his thoughts." (He was one of those children whom animals instinctively love. Though he gave his pets strenuous treatment at times, they recognized his affection for them and his fundamental kindness.) Both Mr. Hay and Mr. Brooks agreed that he had singularly accurate ideas in practical matters, yet the imaginative turn of his mind was one of his most endearing traits.

Tad's slowness to learn worried his mother, though she had every confidence in what she called "his *natural* brightness." But his indulgent father upheld the youngest in his resistance to lessons: "Let him run," he would say, "there's time enough yet for him to learn his letters and get poky. Bob was just such a little rascal, and now he is a very decent boy."

Yes, Bob was still improving. Eighteen the summer of 1861, he had grown into a nice-looking young man who was perhaps a head taller than his plump little mother. He was of an age now to be her escort on trips (no proper lady of the time cared to travel without a masculine escort to protect her), and he had gone with her and Cousin Elizabeth Grimsley as far as Niagara Falls on the latter's way back to Springfield. (Lest there be anxiety about Cousin Elizabeth, it should be quickly added that a male cousin of hers escorted her the rest of the way.)

Bob and his mother both loved to travel. Though their personalities were very different and he did not see events and people in sparkling colors as she did, they had many tastes and traits in common. The mutual tastes made for congeniality between them but the mutual traits did not. Both had nervous temperaments and were easily upset. Both were inclined to see their own point of view so strongly that it was hard to see that of the other person. Both had tempers and were extremely thin-skinned. These qualities sometimes made adjustments difficult for them and neither would be able, as time would show, to understand the other in a crisis where their views and desires differed.

But in that first year at Washington the parents seem to have felt very good about the way Bob was developing. His mother went to Boston again in November to visit him. She found the cultural atmosphere of that city very congenial; she had a taste for intellectual and well-educated people. Both parents were concerned about the son who was off at college, but the mother was the only one who could get away to go and see how he was doing.

By Robert's own account he was finding life at Harvard "very pleasant." "I have studied enough to satisfy myself," he wrote about the time he graduated, "without being a 'dig.'" He was taking part in various campus activities and, in his sophomore year, he said, "I was a member of the 'Institute of 1770,' and was 'Editor' for one Term." The "Institute" was a social club for sophomores which still retained in the eighteen sixties something of its original purpose, the promotion of public speaking. Robert also confided to his brief autobiography that in his sophomore year he belonged to a "Secret Society." "At the beginning of the second Term of Junior Year," he added, "I became a member of the 'Hasty Pudding Club,' and was Vice-President, first Term Senior." The principal activity of the famous Hasty Pudding Club at that time was the production of dramatic skits and farces.

In other words, his college career was having all the normal interests that were conducive to a well-rounded development. Friendships are a valuable part of college years and Robert was enjoying the companionship of a picked group of young men his own age, which was good for a personality that tended to be somewhat shy and unadjusted. "I have chummed during the whole of my course with Fred° P. Anderson of Cincinnati," he wrote, "occupying during Freshman Year, rooms at Pasco's corner of Main & Linden Sts—Sophomore & Junior Years, Stoughton 22—Senior Year, Hollis 25." Frederick P. Anderson came from a family of distinguished record and his uncle was the Major Robert Anderson who had been in command at Fort Sumter when the Confederates opened fire on it in April 1861. Two telegrams from the Lincoln family in Washington bear evidence of the close friendship between him and Robert.

Mr. Lincoln once wrote: "The better part of one's life consists of his friendships." Robert had a gift for friendship too. He did not draw people to him as his father did, but once he made friends and they came to understand that certain facets of his personality had to be handled with tact, they found friendship with him very rewarding.

At Harvard he was keeping up some of his boyhood friendships. Two of the Springfield boys with whom he had grown up were at Yale, George Latham and Clinton Conkling. The roots of his friendship with "Clint" went back to the parents; Clinton's mother, Mercy Levering Conkling, had been the dearest friend of Bob's mother when they were girls and were being courted in Springfield, Mercy by James C. Conkling and Mary Todd by Abraham Lincoln. Clinton's remarkably fine letters to his parents contain a number of items about Bob Lincoln, even though they were at different schools in the East.

"I get a letter from Bob Lincoln about every two weeks," wrote Clinton to his mother in December 1861. "He is a good correspondent." There was much contriving between the two boys that year for visiting each other; in June "Clint" mentioned expecting Bob to come to New Haven, in December he spoke of Bob's repeated invitations to him to visit Boston. One of Clinton's letters tells of his visiting Bob several years later. They had the common problems of the boy from the West at college in the East: "I never knew what the word 'study' meant until I came here," wrote Clinton.

Robert's studies in his first two years at Harvard included Greek, Latin, mathematics, chemistry, religious instruction, elocution, rhetoric, themes and composition, one term of history and one of botany. He was, as he said, not a "dig" but had a satisfactory rating, and when he would finally graduate, would be thirty-second in a class of about a hundred.

If Mr. Lincoln in 1861 remembered what he had written in 1846, that he feared Bob might be "one of the little rare-ripe sort, that are smarter at about five than ever after," he would have had to take it back. His correct statement in that letter was that Bob "is quite smart enough." Bob was demonstrating that he was a great deal smarter than he was at five, and he would continue to demonstrate it in unmistakable terms the rest of his days. He knew what he wanted out of life and he was preparing himself to achieve those things—they just happened not to be the things his father had wanted to achieve in his.

Bob came home for Christmas in December 1861; once more the family circle was complete. Again one can picture the Lincolns sitting around the table, this time in the family dining room at the front of the White House toward the west. The eyes of the parents could look upon their sons and take stock of them with loving satisfaction. Robert was developing and was indisputably "a very decent boy." Any father would take pride in such an upright and fine-looking son who was well thought of and liked and was getting along so well at Harvard.

Taddie, the little sprite going on nine, would have brought an indulgent tenderness to the eyes of his parents. With his appealing lisp, his crooked teeth, his mischief, and his firm resistance to lessons, he was the "little troublesome *sunshine*" of both father and mother. No one could deny the troublesomeness, but his quaint, original, happy, and affectionate ways made life immeasurably brighter for his parents.

As to Willie, everything was just right about him. He had his eleventh birthday just before Christmas, but intellectually he was developed far beyond that age. He was the sort of child people imagine their children will be, before they have any. Abraham and

Mary Lincoln could speculate on his future in terms of thrilling possibilities; with his talents Willie might become almost anything, a great writer or minister, perhaps, or a great statesman. It could have made life worthwhile to the parents just to look forward to Willie growing up. And Mary Lincoln, who was struggling with an ever increasing sense of insecurity under the strain of the war, had often said that Willie "would be the hope and stay of her old age."

In spite of war, intolerable burdens, and public abuse, it was still a real Christmas for President and Mrs. Lincoln; its essence lay in the fact that their sons were around them. Three years later, looking back to their enjoyment of Willie, his mother wrote: "We were having *so much bliss.*"

CHAPTER 10

Mourning in the White House

IT MUST have been recognized that the President and his little boys loved animals, for Willie and Tad were constantly receiving presents of pets of all kinds, dogs, rabbits, goats, and best of all, ponies. Any regrets over Fido left at Springfield surely were quickly crowded out. Willie seems to have had a new pony early in 1862, and though that was a winter of notoriously bad weather, rainy, cold, and muddy, so that it became a game to count the few sunny days, he insisted on going riding every day. Both boys were spirited little horsemen; it creates a pleasing picture to imagine their small straight figures and delighted faces on ponyback. John Hay said that Tad rode fearlessly when he was still so small that his legs stuck out horizontally from the saddle.

Whether it was from exposure or because he caught one of the infections that constantly floated around unsanitary and unscreened Washington, Willie became ill. Mrs. Lincoln had issued cards for a large party to be held on February 5 and it was a question whether to cancel the invitations. The illness was a fluctuating one; some days Willie would seem better, then he would be worse again; but the physicians assured his mother that it was safe to go ahead with the reception. The ailment had been diagnosed as "bilious fever," a term which in those days of medical ignorance might cover a number of diseases. Dr. W. A. Evans, who in the nineteen thirties wrote a valuable book on Mrs. Lincoln from the physician's viewpoint, suggested that Willie might have had "an acute malarial infection." One also finds the illness referred to as typhoid.

When the evening of the reception arrived, the parents went through it as in a nightmare; Willie had suddenly grown much worse. The loved child lay tossing with pain and fever upstairs in an ornate bedchamber whose regal purple draperies looped back with gold cords seemed as out of place as the revelry below. Tad, too, had become ill and the mother had been up for two nights tending her sick children.

Mrs. Lincoln was well qualified as a White House hostess and wished to fill her position becomingly. Stung by the constant gossip that the Lincolns were crude Westerners from uncivilized Illinois, the First Lady had planned the reception as a model of splendor in a time when entertainments were almost incredibly elaborate. A New York caterer had charge and the tables were decorated with masterpieces of ornamental confectionery, the war theme predominating. There was the steamer *Union*, armed and proudly bearing the "Stars and Stripes"; there was also a model of Fort Sumter done in sugar.

To the gay music of the Marine Band in the corridor, President and Mrs. Lincoln, stationed in the glittering East Room, had to greet a crowd of five hundred people, Cabinet members, senators, generals, justices of the Supreme Court, and others, saying to each the appropriate and gracious word, while all the while their hearts were racked with anxiety. Robert was home from Harvard and stood near his mother, who occasionally would slip away and go upstairs to stroke Willie's hot forehead and watch his labored breathing with sickening apprehension.

The newspapers reported the fluctuations of the disease: very ill on February 9 but improved on February 10. Then all hearts lightened on February 12; Willie was reported out of danger. What a birthday present that news was to his father. But the days dragged on and he grew worse again. No noisy romping of little boys was heard in the corridors now, but Willie asked for Bud Taft. There was understanding and affection between them and perhaps Bud's presence helped take away the strange, dreary feeling of the sickroom and made him feel less shut off from the happy normal days that they had so lately shared together.

By February 17 the newspapers announced that Willie was hopelessly ill. After that his mother stayed beside his bed night and day. Bud was there much of the time. The President would come in, stand looking at Willie, sometimes leaning over to smooth the light brown hair on the pillow, then go out without speaking. Once he came late at night and found Bud still there. Controlling his voice he said, "You ought to go to bed, Bud." Bud said simply, "If I go he will call for me." Later Mr. Lincoln found the little chum fast asleep at Willie's bedside, picked him up tenderly, and carried him off to bed.

On the morning of February 20 Willie held Bud's hand and seemed better. But the boyish hand relaxed its hold that afternoon as life slipped away, and at five o'clock Willie's eyes were closed forever.

Willie died on a Thursday; the funeral did not take place until the following Monday. The precious body was embalmed and put in a metal casket finished in rosewood and silver. Willie lay in state in the Green Room adjoining the East Room where the services would be held. The boy was beautiful in death, dressed as for the evening, his soft brown hair parted over the pale forehead, his eyes closed, his hands crossed on his breast, one hand holding a small bouquet of exquisite flowers.

The sight of that pale beloved face had thrown his mother into convulsions. She lay ill upstairs, in a state of collapse, at times giving way to paroxysms of cries and weeping. She was not able to be with Tad, who was desperately ill himself by this time and was not expected to recover. The blow seemed more than she, with her emotional instability and passionate maternity, could bear. Her husband feared for his wife's sanity.

His own grief was so overwhelming it took all the strength within him to go on. He too had looked on the face of his dead son, saying brokenly, ". . . he was too good for this earth . . . but then we loved him so." He had remembered to send for Bud to look at Willie for the last time. The faithful little comrade was so affected he had to be carried from the room and was ill for some days afterwards.

Death often brings an inventory of friends. There were so many who came to the Green Room to say a last good-by to the little boy they had all loved. Among them was the journalist, Mr. Nathaniel P. Willis. It was just before the funeral service; in the East Room people were already assembling and the casket was about to be closed. As Mr. Willis looked down with deep emotion on the still face that he had so often seen lighted up with boyish friendliness and affection, a message came from Mrs. Lincoln requesting that the bouquet in Willie's hand be saved for her.

The White House was festooned with black crepe. In the East Room the great mirrors which reflected those who had come to the funeral were heavily draped in mourning. The services were conducted by the Reverend Phineas D. Gurley, pastor of the New York Avenue Presbyterian Church, which President and Mrs. Lincoln attended. Officers in uniform and all of official Washington were there. Mr. Willis noted the quiver of Secretary Seward's austere features, the wetness of General McClellan's eyes as he bowed his head to the prayer. When the casket was removed from the Green Room to the hearse, there followed after the pallbearers a little group of children, the members of Willie's Sunday School class.

In the procession to Oak Hill Cemetery in Georgetown two white horses drew the hearse bearing the little boy who had known only happiness. But black horses drew the carriage in which sat the worn and grief-stricken President. His son Robert, Senator Lyman Trumbull, and Senator Browning rode with him. Nature herself had gone into a paroxysm this morning; there was a terrific storm which took off roofs and knocked down trees, chimneys, and steeples, and the wind was still very high. To the parents the storm and destruction may have seemed symbolic of the devastation in their own hearts. The casket was placed in a vault belonging to a friend of the Lincolns' (William Thomas Carroll, clerk of the Supreme Court), pending its ultimate removal to Illinois.

One day the little body would go home to Springfield, would make a strange, circuitous journey through a weeping nation. When Willie returned, he would not return alone.

After Willie's death things never again could be quite the same for Abraham and Mary Lincoln. Nor could they ever be the same to Tad. Upstairs in a chamber of the White House lay a small boy with a loving heart which had been cruelly hurt. He had thought life was all play, but that phase of his little boyhood was over. Desperately ill, he tossed upon his bed, at intervals, like his mother, breaking into wild, convulsive weeping. A nurse had been brought from one of the soldiers' hospitals in Washington to aid in caring for him, an understanding and comforting person, Mrs. Rebecca Pomroy. She found him sobbing about Willie, "who would never speak to him any more."

Tad, like Willie before him, had suddenly been shut off from a carefree, romping existence to be thrust into a painful world of doctors, nurses, medicine, and suffering. The adult faces around him brought no reassurance, as grown-up faces should do; they were sad and often tear-stained. During the small hours of the night when things seemed so strange, he could hear through the haze of fever and illness the low voices of those who were sitting up with him, often his father and Mrs. Pomroy, or his father and Senator Browning, and sometimes other friends. His father, who had always been able to offer comfort and make things right, could not do it now. The twinkle was all gone from his eyes; they seemed sunk in his face and were dark with anxiety as well as grief. Mr. Lincoln told Senator Browning that he feared Tad was going to die too.

The President himself looked like a man who was ill. It was Robert who on his brother's death sent an appeal for help back to Springfield; he wrote his Aunt Elizabeth Edwards "very imploringly" to come to Washington as soon as she could. She responded promptly and Senator Browning recorded in his diary that on the day after the funeral he "went in Prests carriage to Rail Road depot to meet Mrs. Edwards," who arrived on the nine o'clock train in the evening. Her letters written in March and April to her family back in Springfield picture the dark situation at the White House.

The gloom in the great mansion was so overwhelming Mrs. Edwards found it almost intolerable and constantly longed to get away from it and go back home. But she was glad, she said, "to aid in nursing the little sick Tad, who is very prostrated with his illness, and subdued with the loss, he evidently suffers from, yet permits no allusion to." Mrs. Edwards's letter was written on March 2, when, she added, Tad was considered out of danger "but still unable to sit up." His mother, the letter continued, had risen from her sickbed for the first time that morning and had put on a black dress of deep mourning; she had been but little with Tad, "being utterly unable to control her feelings."

Mr. Lincoln had to control his feelings; he had to carry on the heavy burden of the Presidency. On March 10, the day after the battle of the *Monitor* and the *Merrimac,* he was discussing grave questions with certain important men when John Hay came in and said something to him in a low tone. (The President's office and the Cabinet room were on the second floor to the east, and the family bedrooms were down the hall to the west, so the father at his place of business was not far removed from Tad's chamber.) Mr. Lincoln excused himself and went into the hallway, where Tad's nurse stood waiting. Apologetically she said to the President, "Mrs. Lincoln insists that I see you, sir. Tad won't take his medicine and the doctor left strict orders for me to give it to him regularly."

Mr. Lincoln followed her to the door of the sickroom. "You stay here," he said, "and I'll see what I can do." Then he entered Tad's room.

A few minutes later he came out with a smile. "It's all right now. Tad and I have fixed things up," he announced as he started back to the waiting statesmen. The nurse found Tad clutching a bank check which still exists as a collector's item. It read: *"Pay to* 'Tad' (when he is well enough to present)" five dollars and was signed "A. Lincoln."

(On another occasion Mr. Lincoln had to excuse himself from a conference with Benjamin B. French, Commissioner of Public Buildings, to give Tad his medicine. The President explained to Mr. French

that Tad refused to take it from anyone else, but the financial details,
if any, of this transaction were not revealed.)

On March 12 Mrs. Edwards's report to her daughter in Springfield
read: "Tad is still feeble, can merely walk a few steps at a time. He
deeply feels the loss of his loving brother." His mother, according
to her sister's letter, "still confines herself to her room, feeling very
sad and at times gives way to violent grief." Mrs. Edwards was somewhat critical of her sister Mary's "indulgence of such gloom"; she
did not understand that Mrs. Lincoln's lack of self-control was
pathological. It was also an age that made a ceremony and almost a
virtue of grieving. Mrs. Edwards concluded: "I had a letter from
Bob yesterday expressing his gratitude for my timely presence."

So Robert had returned to Harvard. He had evidently been with
his parents during the strain of Willie's illness and death. Robert had
affection underneath his somewhat constrained personality and was
very sensitive to hurt; he undoubtedly was deeply grieved over
the loss of his promising little brother. His turning to his Aunt Elizabeth in the hour of need may well be an indication of his closeness
to her and her viewpoints.

On April 9 Mrs. Edwards wrote again to her daughter Julia in
Springfield. Julia was the wife of Edward Lewis Baker, co-editor and
proprietor of the *Illinois State Journal,* and had a little son, Edward
Lewis, Jr., five years younger than Tad. Mrs. Edwards was sending
a trunk to Springfield containing shrubbery and other articles that
had been given to her. Among the things, she wrote, were "*two cars*
that belonged to Willie. Tad insisted upon sending them to Lewis,
saying he could not play with them again." The sight of Willie's
little train and other toys with all their memories hurt too much.

This is understandable. But Mrs. Lincoln was carrying the attitude
of avoiding those things that were associated with Willie to an un-
wholesome extent and Tad tended to follow her example. Though
she treasured keepsakes of Willie, such as the bouquet that had been
held in his hand in the casket, she would never again go into the
purple-draped room where he had died, or the Green Room where
his body had lain in state. She had written Mrs. Taft: "Please keep
the boys home the day of the funeral; it makes me feel worse to
see them." Never again was Tad to have the companionship of Bud
and Holly; that happy phase was over too.

Tad undoubtedly took from his mother the attitude that it made
him "feel worse" to see them. Julia Taft and her brothers were shortly
afterwards sent North to school, and Julia did not see Tad until about
two years later. She had come home to Washington and went with

a relative to one of Mrs. Lincoln's Saturday afternoon receptions in the winter of 1864. Mrs. Lincoln greeted her most affectionately and asked about her mother and all the family. But when Tad came in and saw Julia, he threw himself down on the floor in the midst of the guests, kicking and screaming until he had to be carried out. Mrs. Lincoln said to the girl, "You must excuse him, Julia. You know what he remembers." It was a painful scene for the sensitive Julia, who was never again to see Tad, nor to see Mrs. Lincoln, whom she really loved. If Tad was still in this state two years after his brother's death, the difficulty of helping him in the first weeks that followed it can well be imagined.

Of the four members of the family left after Willie's death, three had their lives and personalities changed by it. The father, in his agonizing desire to feel that Willie's spirit was still alive, in the end had his religious faith deepened. He, like the mother, treasured keepsakes of Willie. He would show visitors, as one of them said, a little "framed picture of Illinois" hanging over his mantel, telling them it was painted by his little boy who had died. He would sometimes dream that Willie was with him, alive and well again, and wake in the darkness to the terrible truth that it was only a dream.

The mother did not need to strengthen her faith in immortality; she took comfort in the thought that their "Angel boys" were united, that Willie and Eddie were together. But, as she wrote Mrs. Sprigg, at whose home in Springfield Willie had once played, "when I think over his short but happy childhood, how much comfort, he always was to me, and how fearfully, I always found my hopes concentrating on so good a boy as he was—when I can bring myself to realize that he has indeed passed away, my question to myself is, 'can life be endured?'" Mrs. Lincoln with her weakness of emotional instability was to break under the strain of the White House years and the death of Willie was a great factor in this breakdown. It caused a permanent impairment in her loving but ill-balanced nature. Attorney General Bates, who like other Cabinet members had a friendship with Willie and who had often delighted in giving the little boys candy and a glorious supply of marbles, wrote sadly in his diary on the day Willie died that he was "too much idolized by his parents." With Robert a self-sufficient young man at college, Tad was the only child left with them, and it followed, of course, that they could deny him nothing.

Tad's life as a little boy became less normal after Willie's death. He had occasional playmates, but he became more and more the companion of his father and of adults in general. Probably he had never slept in a room by himself; presumably he and Willie had occupied a room together. When his illness and the night watching of nurse, father, and friends had ended, a problem arose as to who should stay at night with the nervous and grieving child. Perhaps Tad had learned how good it was to have his father in the deep night hours when things seem more terrible; at any rate, his choice in the matter could easily be predicted and neither parent could say no to him. So this was probably the time that he began sleeping with his father.

The bond between them was stronger than ever and Tad was constantly with the President, whether his presence was appropriate to the occasion or not. Those who had to do business with Mr. Lincoln often had to take Tad on as excess baggage. A visitor who had come to ask a favor found the chief executive most willing to help: ". . . let us see what we can do," he said pleasantly and began to search for pen and paper to write an order. The visitor recorded that he was aided in this effort by little Tad, "who was present—and, I must say, somewhat troublesome—and toward whom his father manifested the most anxious and considerate affection." This was a common experience and one not always appreciated.

The overworked President frequently had to stay at his desk until late at night and Tad had his own ideas about going to bed alone. So it often happened that when Mr. Lincoln at last laid down his pen near midnight, he would find the boy asleep on the floor beside his desk or lying in front of the fireplace. He would pick him up tenderly, the dark tousled head settling trustfully upon his shoulder, and, dodging chandeliers and stooping under doorways, carry him off to undress him and put him to bed. It the father dreamed of Willie and woke to cruel realization, or if he lay awake from the pain of his loss, it was a comfort to him to have the warm limbs and living breath of this loved child beside him.

Tad was to show increasingly that he had inherited his father's instinctive understanding of the feelings of others. If those feelings involved hurt or pain, he was all sympathy. The little boy was, of course, turning to his father's love and strength for comfort, but perhaps his affectionate heart also sensed his father's need of him. He made up a special name of endearment by which he called his father. It is usually written "Papa-day," perhaps an attempt with his quaint impediment of speech to say "Papa dear." Julia Taft never heard him call his father anything except Pa (pronounced *Paw*), but she was not associated with him after Willie's death.

Tad also responded with intense affection to his mother's increased need for his love. He was always to do this. There was a certain buoyancy and valor of spirit in this nine-year-old boy. One catches a glimpse of it in what his mother wrote to Mrs. Sprigg the latter part of May in this year of mourning: "Dear little Taddie who was so devoted to his darling Brother, although as deeply afflicted as ourselves, bears up and teaches us a lesson, in enduring the stroke, to which we *must submit.*"

His mother almost invariably called him Taddie instead of Tad. His name in the next three years was to become known all over the country, for White House children are in a sense the nation's children. Kindly people felt sympathy for the little boy who had lost his brother and playmate and was now the only child in the great presidential mansion. Gifts of all kinds poured in, especially animals, until the livestock around the White House must have been the gardener's despair. That individual could hardly have appreciated a gentleman's gift of some white rabbits to Tad, but Mr. Lincoln did and had John Hay write a gracious letter of thanks which he signed, contrary to his usual practice, with his full name, Abraham Lincoln.

It is an evidence of change in Tad that after Willie's death people began to use new adjectives in speaking of him. Julia Taft in her detailed account of Tad during the first year in the White House wasted no words of commendation on him; she was politely restrained in what she said, but it was plain that she felt the correct word to describe him would be "exasperating." One suspects she would have opened her eyes wide if she had read the recollections of another frequent visitor at the White House, a young woman friend of the Lincolns, Mrs. James S. Delano. Mrs. Delano recalled Tad as "the kindest, brightest, most considerate child" she had ever known. Each of these young ladies presented evidence to substantiate her choice of adjectives.

Mrs. Delano, like Julia, attended an Easter egg rolling on the White House lawn. She saw Tad proudly show his father the two dozen eggs the cook had dyed for him. One dozen, he said, was for him and the other was for a little lame boy named Tommy whom he was looking after. Tommy's father had been killed in the war and his mother worked in the Treasury, and Tad was doing everything he could to make Tommy have a good time. He had a servant carry out a chair for the lame boy from which he could lean over and roll his eggs. He led his father to his protégé so that Tommy could have the thrill of shaking the hand of the President.

Mrs. Delano saw that incident. Her husband witnessed another scene indicative of Tad's tenderheartedness. The halls and corridors of the White House were nearly always crowded with people waiting to see the President: politicians, office seekers, and many who came to plead for help in the pitiful emergencies which the war had brought them. Tad apparently had a way of looking them over and taking the measures he thought fit.

He had a supreme contempt for office seekers in general, evidently sensing what a problem and drag they were to his father. With perhaps some thought of relieving his father of the pressure, he would circulate among them, get their stories, ask how long they had waited and how long they proposed to wait, and make an effort to get rid of them. To some he gave good advice; they better go home and chop wood for a living. He tried to send others away by volunteering to tell his father about them, if they would promise not to come again.

But it was a different story when someone came in genuine distress. Mr. Delano noticed in the crowd one day a poorly dressed woman who wiped tears from her sad face as she waited in the front hall downstairs. Tad noticed her too and went up to her to ask her what was the matter. She told him she had a son in the army who was ill and she wanted him sent home. Tad cried out in instant sympathy and championship. "You tell my father about him." The boy rushed upstairs to the Cabinet room, where the President was holding a meeting. Tad had no respect for Cabinet meetings, that has already been established; he would burst in, demanding that his complaints be attended to immediately. He told his father about the distressed mother. Mr. Lincoln answered, "My son, I cannot come now. You see that I am engaged."

"Well," cried Tad excitedly, "I'll bring the woman up to you." Mr. Lincoln arose, excused himself a moment, went outside and listened to the mother's story and signed the paper which would enable her to take her son home. Such stories of Tad's tenderness of heart were frequent as the war years brought more and more hardship to people. He would sometimes gather up hungry street urchins and take them to the White House kitchen to be fed. If the domestic staff protested, he would appeal to his father: "Isn't it *our* kitchen?" Of course the presidential decision was in favor of Tad and the urchins.

It must have meant much to Mr. Lincoln to see in this child his own great compassion. But this quality in no way interfered with Tad's pranks; he was as bent on mischief as ever. His Aunt Elizabeth Edwards undoubtedly felt considerable exasperation with him on one occasion in the spring of 1862, shortly before she returned home from her visit after Willie's death. She was a conscientious woman and had done what she could for the bereaved family. Seeing

Mr. Lincoln so worn out and grieved over the loss of his son, she asked him one day, hoping it would be a small diversion for him, to take a walk with her in Lafayette Square. He had not been there for a year, although it was just across Pennsylvania Avenue north of the White House. Tad went along; the little park with what he called the "tippy-toe" statue of General Andrew Jackson had probably been a familiar playground for him and Willie and the Taft boys, and he perhaps already knew the possibilities that lay in the fact that it had a fence around it with a gate which locked with a key. According to Mrs. Edwards's account she "made" Mr. Lincoln walk to the park; he may not have been too keen about this attempt to cheer him up, but he received an unexpected diversion from it which he greatly enjoyed. Tad locked the gate and hid the key. When his father told him to get the key, the boy only laughed teasingly. Mrs. Edwards remembered indignantly that Mr. Lincoln thought this prank "smart & shrewd" of Tad, but she, like Queen Victoria, was "not amused." Perhaps the President with his long legs clad in trousers could negotiate that fence better than the hoop-skirted Mrs. Edwards. She doubtless reported to the large assortment of relatives when she returned to Springfield that the Lincolns were spoiling Tad worse than ever.

Which was quite true. After Willie's death Tad became the absolute monarch of the presidential mansion. He had a certain imperiousness of manner and issued orders in a tone that left no doubt that he expected immediate obedience. Noah Brooks recorded that as he entered the White House one day he met a prominent man who remarked: "I have just had an interview with the tyrant of the White House." Now a great many people were calling President Lincoln a tyrant and worse during these war-inflamed years, but Mr. Brooks did not expect such a term from this particular quarter and looked much startled. The gentleman laughed at his expression and explained his little joke in one word: "Tad."

CHAPTER 11

Father and Son in Conflict

MRS. LINCOLN'S letter to Mrs. Sprigg in May of 1862 had indicated that she was looking forward to the coming of their eldest son: "Robert will be home from Cambridge in about 6 weeks and will spend his vacation with us." Then she commented on how he had "grown" and used the word that was applied to him so often in these years that it is amusing, "improved."

Robert's visit meant much to her. In this same letter she mentioned their summer plans: "The 1st of July, we go out to the 'Soldiers' Home,' a very charming place 2½ miles from the city, several hundred feet, above, our present situation, to pass the summer." There was a suitable house for them there and she, who had so loved excitement and society, now wanted seclusion in her sorrow. She wrote another friend from Soldiers' Home in July: "We are truly delighted with this retreat, the drives & walks around here are delightful. . . . Then too, our boy Robert is with us, whom you may remember. We consider it a 'pleasant time' for us, when his vacations roll round, he is very companionable, and I shall dread when he has to return to Cambridge."

His mother was finding Robert a comfort in her sorrow. He had become helpful too in attending to small matters for her, and whatever he did was done efficiently. A telegram he sent in her behalf to the proprietors of the Fifth Avenue Hotel in New York showed his precision. He gave full details of the date and hour of his mother's trip, asked that a carriage please be waiting for her on her arrival, and added specifically: "She prefers the rooms over the Ladies' Drawing room 2nd story."

Mr. Lincoln also looked forward to Robert's visits home, but he was so burdened he had little time for his eldest son. Robert himself wrote that after his father went to the White House, "any great intimacy between us became impossible—I scarcely ever had ten minutes' quiet talk with him during his Presidency, on account of

his constant devotion to business." If Robert reflected upon the fact
that his father always had time for Tad, even though it kept business
and statesmen waiting, and if he resented this, it is quite understandable. In another connection, however, Robert said that when
he was in Washington, he would once in a while find his father alone
in his office and would ask him questions, and they would discuss
current questions of war and politics. The thought arises that perhaps
this essentially shy son sometimes lingered near the office hoping
for just such an opportunity. Robert was keenly aware of what was
happening in the nation.

One thing which was happening led to a long-drawn conflict between father and son. Robert knew that he was being criticized as
an able-bodied young man who was not fighting for the country of
which his father was President. He was always, after the irresponsi-
bility of boyhood was over, very conscientious about doing what was
right and proper. He had intense patriotism, a quality that is fanned
to white heat in time of war; he was devoted to the Union cause; and,
in spite of his sympathy for his Southern relatives, he sternly regarded all Confederates as rebels and their war as a rebellion. He
wanted intensely to do what many of his friends at Harvard were
doing, go into the army. The *Boston Herald* had reported in May of
1861 that sixteen undergraduates had left Harvard for the war. In his
conspicuous position as the President's son such incidents were not
easy for Robert to take.

His father's political enemies would not fail to make capital of the
situation, accusing the son of cowardice, lack of patriotism, or
traitorous leanings toward the Confederate side. He probably received letters of abuse, just as his father and mother did. With his
extreme sensitiveness to criticism, these accusations would have been
intolerable. Stories made up of whole cloth were circulated about
him; he was accused of making half a million dollars in questionable
speculation during the war.

Even before war became an actuality he seems to have been interested in the army. A letter of Senator Lyman Trumbull in early
1861, arranging for him to look through the War Department, is perhaps an indication of the direction his thoughts were taking even
before his father was inaugurated. Another straw which shows the
way the wind was blowing is a book called *Cadet Life at West Point*
(now owned by the Lincoln National Life Foundation), which is
inscribed on the fly leaf "R. T. Lincoln, Harvard College, March
1862." Robert wanted very much to enter military service, and his
father objected to his doing so. It must have been a conflict of opinion

always in the background of Robert's visits to the White House until
1865. The President was in a cruel dilemma. He had reason to know
how he was being criticized because his son of military age was not
in the army; it was a political liability. He himself thought Robert
should go to war—it was what he would undoubtedly have done in
his son's place. But his wife, who was so impaired by Willie's death
that he feared for her reason, could not face up to the thought. Mrs.
Keckley, who added her own testimony that Robert was "very
anxious to quit school and enter the army," told of the determined
opposition of the mother. "We have lost one son," she would say to
her husband, "and his loss is as much as I can bear. . . ." Mr. Lincoln feared that this was literally true, that if Robert should be
exposed to danger or be killed, his wife, in her grieving and unstable
condition, would lose her sanity completely.

He would gently argue with her, trying to make her look at the
matter objectively, something she could not do if the question were
a personal and emotional one. He would point out to her that their
son was not more dear to them than the sons of other people were
to their mothers. "The services of every man who loves his country
are required in this war," he would say to her. "You should take a
liberal instead of a selfish view of the question, mother."

There must have been many such arguments between them.
Emilie Todd Helm, who visited the White House in 1863, reported
one which she overheard. When the President renewed the subject,
Mrs. Lincoln answered tremulously, "Of course, Mr. Lincoln, I know
that Robert's plea to go into the Army is manly and noble and I
want him to go, but oh! I am so frightened he may never come back
to us!" Mr. Lincoln reminded her that many a poor mother had made
this sacrifice and given up every son she had. Emilie left the room,
but it is safe to assume that the discussion ended with the shattered
woman going into a wild fit of weeping.

She received her own barrage of abuse about the matter and
sometimes very directly. Emilie Todd Helm witnessed such an incident. Senator Ira Harris was calling at the White House one evening and during the conversation he turned to Mrs. Lincoln and said
accusingly, "Why isn't Robert in the Army? He is old enough and
strong enough to serve his country. He should have gone to the front
some time ago." Mrs. Lincoln turned very pale and struggling to
keep her self-control, answered, "Robert is making his preparations
now to enter the Army, Senator Harris; he is not a shirker as you
seem to imply for he has been anxious to go for a long time. If fault
there be, it is mine, I have insisted that he should stay in college a

little longer as I think an educated man can serve his country with more intelligent purpose than an ignoramus." Senator Harris got up and said harshly, "I have only one son and he is fighting for his country."

If his mother received such a direct jab, it can be imagined how Robert was being needled from all sides. If he felt a great resentment toward both parents and particularly toward his father for giving in to his mother in the matter, that is easy to understand. Mr. Lincoln was in a position where he had to place either his wife or his son in an almost intolerable situation, and he chose to protect his wife. He could see how she was ailing and getting nearer and nearer the breaking point as time went on. It is doubtful whether Robert knew at this time that mental illness was involved in his mother's case, though he would realize it all too bitterly later. He probably felt that she was spoiled by Mr. Lincoln's indulgence. This was quite true, as Mrs. Lincoln herself freely admitted later, but Mr. Lincoln had a compassionate understanding of human weaknesses that did not come naturally to Robert. It took certain qualities of a physician or humanitarian to comprehend an afflicted personality like Mrs. Lincoln's and her first-born was not the type. Willie had understood his mother by instinct, Tad ultimately would, but one doubts whether Robert ever did. But if he was resentful toward both parents because of their opposition to his going to war, it was only natural. From his point of view he was not being treated fairly.

Yet Mr. and Mrs. Lincoln loved their eldest son dearly and in all other ways were doing everything they could for his happiness. But traits of personality and circumstances seemed to conspire to keep the father, especially, from coming close in congeniality to the son. Robert's own choice of going to Harvard was a force to increase the distance between them in that it gave him certain standards of the East which were somewhat less democratic than those of the West.

There was a sharp division in manners and social customs between East and West in the eighteen sixties. The recent rise of railroads and other means of communication had begun to break this down a little, but the Lincolns and others who came East encountered a feeling of superiority on the part of certain Easterners toward those who hailed from such a backwoods section of the country as Illinois. In the campaign of 1860 Republicans in Springfield had sung "Old Abe Lincoln Came out of the Wilderness" and gloried in its democracy, but there were doubtless people in New England who had no taste for such a song. Class distinctions figured more largely then than now; it was a stuffy age and stuffiest in the East. At Harvard Robert encountered Eastern attitudes in full strength and possibly absorbed some of them. His father, who was to be the great exponent of American democracy, seemed untouched by the class attitudes of his day. Mrs. Lincoln was essentially a Victorian woman, but in her complete devotion to her husband his views influenced her, and then she had a natural outgoing friendliness toward people. Robert seems to have fitted well into the atmosphere he found in the Harvard of the Victorian era, and that fact probably drove him further from his father's viewpoints. The perspective of the college years is a narrow one; time and a mature life usually broaden it. Robert's attitudes would change in many respects, but perhaps some of his qualities in later life, when he had lived on into the twentieth century, are explained by the fact he grew up in the Victorian age and accepted many of its standards.

The very subjects he was studying in 1862–1863 were subjects his self-educated father could not share with him. Robert was continuing his Greek, Latin, and chemistry. He had elected French, which was doubtless a great joy to his mother as she spoke and wrote that language well. One can almost imagine them practicing it together on her frequent visits to Boston. He was continuing his work in declamations, themes and rhetoric, and the following year would take a course in forensics. The days were gone when he would be overwhelmed on the rostrum by "a vast sea of human faces." He was being trained to write and speak effectively, though making speeches was evidently never to his taste. His own thorough education would show up to him the gaps in his father's, and he was at an age which was more apt to feel its own young superiority than to understand the pathos of that father's struggle to attain what was being handed to the son on a silver platter. This is the usual shortsightedness of youth. In his senior year he would again take up history, elect Italian, and would explore the mysteries of philosophy and political economy.

By Robert's own statement his father wrote him few letters while he was at college and these few were "with one or two exceptions letters enclosing money." (Perhaps once his father was late with the cash, or Robert did some unexpected shopping; at any rate, he sent a telegram from Philadelphia to the President's secretary, John G. Nicolay, which sounded very much like an SOS: "Send me a ten dollar bill to the Continental.") But on one occasion Mr. Lincoln sent his son a rather pointed rebuke. Friends at Harvard prevailed upon Robert to write his father in behalf of a certain candidate for the Cambridge post office. The President is said to have replied: "If you do not attend to your studies and let matters such as you write about alone I will take you away from college." It is possible to see both sides of this matter. Robert liked to do nice things for his friends and it seemed a small thing to ask. The President, however, could not make appointments on the basis of the personal wishes of members of his family. It was perhaps a sore point with him, as he was embarrassed during the war by pressure for special privilege from some of the Todd family connections. Robert was young and unaware of many factors involved and his father had to put a stop to his being used by office seekers. Robert wisely kept Mr. Lincoln's message and showed it to all who made similar requests.

Yet once in 1862 he apparently did influence an appointment. His father wrote Secretary Welles about a young man from Harvard who wished "to be an Asst. Paymaster in the Navy," adding, "The within shows that my son 'Bob' has a high opinion of him." The appointment was made.

An incident which happened when Tad was eleven brought into sharp focus Robert's disapproval and resentment of his father's indulgence of the younger son. The artist Francis B. Carpenter, who told the story, was sitting in John Nicolay's room about ten o'clock one evening when Robert came in "with a flushed face." "Well," he burst out, "I have just had a great row with the President of the United States." The flush was evidently one of anger; underneath his reserved exterior Robert was strongly emotional. Mr. Carpenter wanted to know the details and Robert gave them indignantly.

"Yes," he answered, "and very good cause there is for it, too." Then he explained that Tad had gone over to the War Department that day and Secretary of War Stanton, "for the fun of the thing," had given him an officer's commission. "On the strength of this," continued Robert, "what does 'Tad' do but go off and order a quantity of muskets sent to the house! Tonight he had the audacity to discharge the guard, and he then mustered all the gardeners and servants, gave them the guns, drilled them, and put them on duty in their place."

Robert said he had found this out about an hour before and "thinking it a great shame, as the men had been hard at work all day, I went to father with it; but instead of punishing 'Tad,' as I think he ought, he evidently looks upon it as a good joke, and won't do anything about it!" The former Springfield neighbors and many who came to the White House undoubtedly would have agreed with Robert one hundred per cent. Mr. Lincoln had no intention of letting the weary men watch all night; he was avoiding an issue with the high-strung Tad by waiting until he went to bed and then he had the reluctant recruits quietly dismissed. The White House went unguarded that night. Possibly the father thought it better that the men stand watch a little while longer than that the excitable Tad should get worked up at bedtime. But the result was that his eldest son, who was also high-strung, was considerably worked up; and there were probably many times when Robert felt indignation over such incidents and was equally helpless.

There were so many matters on which he could not see eye to eye with his father. There is no doubt that father and mother both felt strong parental affection for Robert and were very proud of the way he was developing. The telegrams of the Lincoln family, sent through the War Department and preserved today, often give considerable insight into their feelings toward one another. The concern Robert's parents felt for him is written into certain telegrams they sent him. As is often the case with sons off at college he did not always tell them all they wanted to know and perhaps at times neglected to write. "I send your draft to-day," wired his father once. "How are you now? Answer by telegraph at once."

Sometimes what he told them awakened anxiety. "Your letter makes us a little uneasy about your health," ran another telegram. "Telegraph us how you are. If you think it would help you, make us a visit." In the torrid summer of 1864 his mother wired Robert, who was at Saratoga, New York, and who, like herself, suffered greatly from heat: "It is very warm & dusty here. If agreeable to you, remain a week or ten days longer—on Monday will send you what is necessary."

The Lincolns welcomed Robert's friends to the White House and again a telegram throws a sidelight. Apparently Robert on a vacation early in 1864 was to have had his chum Frederick P. Anderson and one or more others with him in Washington but something prevented. Mrs. Lincoln wired Frederick's father, Larz Anderson, at Cincinnati: "It is a great disappointment, not having the young gentlemen, with us at this time—can they not, still come on?"

His mother continued to visit Robert at Cambridge throughout the White House years. Both parents looked forward, as has been seen, to the vacations which brought him from Cambridge to Washington. On one of these train journeys in 1863 or 1864 he narrowly escaped disaster. If he had told them about it and how a certain man had saved him from death or mutilation, their hearts would have been filled with gratitude for that man. With their interest in the theater they would have known the name of Robert's rescuer; it was the famous actor Edwin Booth, who had an actor brother, John Wilkes Booth.

Robert himself wrote an account of the incident later. He said it occurred late at night when passengers were buying their sleeping car reservations from the conductor who stood on the station platform at the entrance to the car. The platform was about the height of the car floor and between train and platform was a narrow space with a drop. The crowding pushed Robert across this opening against the train. "In this situation the train began to move," he wrote, "and by the motion I was twisted off my feet, and had dropped somewhat, with feet downward, into the open space and was personally helpless, when my coat collar was vigorously seized and I was quickly pulled up and out to a secure footing on the platform." Robert recognized the arresting and dramatic face with its great, dark, compelling eyes and thanked the actor by name. A Booth had saved the life of a Lincoln that day; it is a strange story in the light of later events.

But perhaps Robert did not tell this incident to his parents; he was one to keep things to himself. One does not know how much his resentment at their keeping him out of the army put him further apart from them. There were undoubtedly times when father and son found a congenial topic to talk about, but true sustained companionship between them apparently could not be achieved. This sometimes happens between a father and son of marked personalities —it is not necessarily the fault of either. There may also be inherent in the relation of father and son certain possibilities of antagonism. In spite of Mr. Lincoln's parental pride and affection and Robert's sense of filial obligation, they seem to have been too different in make-up for either to feel essential kinship with the other. There are cases of incompatibility where the chemistries of two personalities simply will not mix.

CHAPTER 12

"How Mr. Lincoln and Taddie Are"

To ONE who writes of the Lincoln sons there comes at times an almost passionate wish that the recollections of Tad might have been written and preserved. The scenes witnessed by his young eyes in 1863 would make a brilliant picture gallery of life in the Civil War Presidency. Tad would be ten years old on April 4 of that year, and surely no boy before or since ever had such a birthday event as was planned for him.

Christmas of 1862, the first Christmas after Willie's death, had probably been dismal enough, especially as it came so close to his birth date; had he lived, he would have been twelve that December 21. But January 1 of 1863 brought an event of great uplift, the issuing of President Lincoln's Emancipation Proclamation. Mrs. Lincoln's letters show her exultation of spirit, and Robert and Tad, who both left evidences of their sympathy for the colored race, probably shared, each in his own fashion, something of the thrill that swept over the Union.

But the first outstanding picture etched on Tad's memory would have been perhaps the scene in the White House on February 13, the day after his father's fifty-fourth birthday. As the hour of eight approached that evening, carriages were turning into the driveway that curved past the portico of the Executive Mansion. Gentlemen in tall hats and ladies in wide hoop skirts were arriving for an impromptu reception. President and Mrs. Lincoln were greeting their guests as usual in the great illuminated East Room and a special selection of officialdom was there dressed in its best: Cabinet members, generals, and senators, with their gorgeously appareled wives. Such brilliant receptions were routine, but there was something out of the ordinary about this one—an air of excited expectancy.

Suddenly there was a loud announcement and the guests of honor entered. Up the long drawing room came two doll-like figures, a well-proportioned little man approximately three feet in height, dressed in an elegant miniature wedding suit, and a resplendent little woman slightly shorter than he, clad in a white satin hoop-skirted wedding dress adorned with point lace, orange blossoms, and pearls. The train which trailed behind her was about twice as long as she was. The pair advanced toward the President and First Lady with "pigeon-like stateliness."

They were Mr. and Mrs. Charles Sherwood Stratton, but the public knew them as General and Mrs. Tom Thumb. Accounts of their wedding three days before in Grace Episcopal Church in New York had almost crowded current news of the Civil War off the first pages of the newspapers. They were the midget protégés of that great American showman Phineas T. Barnum and their romance, publicized by this superadvertiser, had seized on the imagination of the country. They had come to Washington and some of Mrs. Lincoln's friends had advised her to entertain them; hence this reception on short notice.

The pigmy couple advanced until they stood before President and Mrs. Lincoln. The little general, who was twenty-five at this time, had not yet reached his maximum height of three feet four inches. The contrast between him and the towering Mr. Lincoln must have put a strain on the self-control of the other guests. Lincoln, his rugged face kind and gentle, bent down and shook the tiny hands in turn, holding that of the bride with special wariness as if it were a bird's egg he was afraid of breaking. With his intuitive understanding he greeted and talked with the midgets as if they were as normal as other people.

Tad, of course, was much in evidence on this occasion and Robert happened to be home on his February vacation. He had entered his mother's room just as Mrs. Keckley finished robing her in a pink silk low-necked gown with flounced hoop skirt. Mrs. Lincoln asked Robert to attend the party. The eldest son was now approaching his senior year at Harvard and was evidently feeling somewhat superior. He put his mother in her place by answering loftily, "No, mother, I do not propose to assist in entertaining Tom Thumb. My notions of duty, perhaps are somewhat different from yours." One suspects that Mr. and Mrs. Lincoln more than once had the experience, not uncommon to parents, of being put in their places by their college-age son.

But Robert's curiosity must have got the better of him, or perhaps

John Hay persuaded him this was a sight not to be missed, for a lady journalist reported seeing the two of them at the reception, looking "clever, thoughtful and scholarly." (Bob and John might have approved the first adjective; they were at an age when they seemed to make special efforts to be "clever.") The lady also noticed how Tad, viewing the wee couple, became suddenly impressed with his own lordly inches and was a bit patronizing toward them, an attitude his father observed with an amused twinkle. But Tad's protective feeling came to the fore too, and when Mrs. Lincoln, mindful of the comfort of her small guests, arranged for them to take their refreshments off a chair, he eagerly superintended the preparations.

Later the little bride wrote her own description of this event, adding some interesting details: " . . . the President took our hands and led us to the sofa, lifting the General up and placed him at his left hand, while Mrs. Lincoln did the same service for me, placing me at her right. . . . Tad, the favorite son, stood beside his mother and gazing at me . . . whispered to his mother, 'Mother if you were a little woman like Mrs. Stratton you would look just like her.'" The tiny lady added that she heard others remark on the resemblance between herself and Mrs. Lincoln. A resplendent First Lady faced with a miniature living replica of herself made an unparalleled spectacle.

An event which occurred in April would have furnished a series of rare pictures. As Tad's tenth birthday approached, Mrs. Lincoln suggested that it be celebrated by a visit to the headquarters of the Army of the Potomac under the command of General Joseph Hooker in Virginia. The boy so loved seeing the soldiers and soldier life that nothing could have pleased him more, and it meant much to the morale of the army to have the President and his family visit the camps.

The celebration evidently was to have been held at the headquarters, but bad weather delayed the trip for several days and it was on April 4, the birthday itself, that the party boarded the President's little steamer, the *Carrie Martin,* at the Washington Navy Yard. Shortly after it pushed out into the Potomac River and started on its journey, a blinding snowstorm began and the only thing to do was anchor in a cove for the night.

That was quite all right with Tad. He promptly rigged up a fishing line and went to work in the furiously falling snow to catch fish for supper. He enthusiastically reported every bite to his father and mother and finally rushed into their presence excitedly exhibiting a small and unprepossessing fish. Noah Brooks, that excellent friend and reporter, accompanied the Lincolns on this trip and he recorded: ". . . we actually did have a smoking platter of fish for supper, much to the delight of Tad, who had marked the three fish of his own catching by cutting off their tails."

To a boy of Tad's tastes and happy buoyancy the journey must have had much enchantment. When they arrived at the raw little settlement of Aquia Creek with the snow still falling, the party boarded an ordinary freight car fitted up with rough plank benches, true wartime accommodations, but the car was decorated with flags and bunting. At General Hooker's headquarters the presidential party stayed in army hospital tents which were floored and furnished with camp bedsteads, surely a thrilling place for a boy to sleep. Then for some days one grand review followed another.

Tad was part of the brilliant cavalcade that rode from headquarters to the reviewing stand. Noah Brooks described it: General Hooker and President Lincoln in his tall hat rode at the head of the column, then came a great array of high-ranking officers in their impressive uniforms "and lesser functionaries innumerable." This long train was flanked by the showy uniforms of the "Philadelphia Lancers," who acted as the President's guard of honor on his visit. On the skirts of this procession rode that intrepid little horseman, Tad, with a handsome young soldier as his orderly. The boy was mounted on a small gray horse, his "short legs stuck out straight from his saddle," and his little gray riding cloak flew "in the gusty wind like the plume of Henry of Navarre."

The procession finally arrived at the appointed place and the review began. Noah Brooks described the stirring spectacle that Tad gazed upon: ". . . this immense body of cavalry, with banners waving, music crashing, and horses prancing, as the vast column came winding like a huge serpent over the hills past the reviewing party, and then stretching far away out of sight."

Other reviews followed and Tad enjoyed them tremendously. The soldiers would salute him as they passed and he was told he ought to doff his cap to them in return. Tad seemed to think this was thrusting an adult responsibility upon him. "Why," he answered, "that's the way General Hooker and Father do; but I'm only a boy."

The soldiers, of course, made much of the friendly and spirited lad and would often give him three cheers. Once a soldier called for three cheers for the next fight, adding, "and send along the greenbacks." The word "greenbacks" was new to Tad and he asked what was meant. It was explained to him that a shortage of greenbacks had caused the army men to go without pay recently. Tad knew Mr.

Chase was Secretary of the Treasury and indignantly demanded to know why he did not print some more greenbacks.

The visit to the army lasted five days and for Tad there was one fly in the ointment. On the day they had left Washington he had received a new pony for a birthday present and had had no time to get acquainted with it. He longed for that pony. It was all right during the excitement of the reviews in the daytime, but in the evenings, when he had nothing to do except hang around his father and mother, he began to beg to go home and to argue about it. Mr. Brooks remembered he told his father that soldiers did not like visitors and informed his mother that women were not wanted in the army! Finally his father, who well knew that Tad was susceptible to the financial approach, said, "Tad, I'll make a bargain with you. If you will agree not to say anything about going home until we are ready to go, I will give you that dollar you want so badly."

Tad accepted the terms of the bargain but still he pestered his parents about the matter. Finally, when the day of departure came and the party was waiting for the carriages to take them back to the *Carrie Martin*, Mr. Lincoln took a dollar bill out of his pocket and looking in the boy's eyes, said, "Now, Taddie, my son, do you think you have earned this?" Tad could not honestly defend himself, so he hung his head and said nothing. His father handed him the dollar, saying, "Well, my son, although I don't think you have kept your part of the bargain, I will keep mine, and you cannot reproach *me* with breaking faith, anyway."

Tad was destined to do more traveling in 1863. The strain of life at the White House was almost unbearable for everyone. Mrs. Lincoln, who was increasingly ailing, had to get away once in a while and she constantly tried to arrange little trips for her burdened husband. He had said at Hooker's headquarters one evening, "It is a great relief to get away from Washington and the politicians. But nothing touches the tired spot." The parents evidently thought it well to get Tad away from the storm center too and he liked to travel. The trips did not go well with lessons, but he was making little or no progress in his schooling anyway.

Incidentally, it looked as if Tad needed some of those carefully avoided lessons when he became a bit confused over the question of why all little boys were not nine years old just as he was in the early months of 1863. Mr. Leonard Swett visited the White House, had a talk with Tad, and wrote his own little son: "Tad is older than you. He is nine years old & the other day he wanted to know why you were not nine & when I told him you would be soon & would grow to be that old, he could not seem to understand it."

It is possible that one reason Mr. Lincoln did not force Tad to study was that he realized that the frail, high-strung boy was all too often ill and in a difficult environment for a child. His father may have felt that when the war was over and the family could return to a peaceful normal life, it would be time enough to pin Tad down to his studies.

The lad's traveling, usually with his mother, led to an exchange of letters and telegrams that are an intimate source of information to-day. Once Mrs. Lincoln even wrote about saving "Taddie's tooth" for his father. The parents kept constantly in touch when apart, sometimes sending more than one telegram a day, the main topic being their concern for each other and for their two sons. Mrs. Lincoln, accompanied by Tad, was in Philadelphia on June 9 when she received the following wire from her husband: "Think you better put 'Tad's' pistol away. I had an ugly dream about him."

Julia Taft had known of Tad's great longing for a revolver in his first year at the White House. Julia herself was a good shot with a pistol and Tad had borrowed her weapon one day, only to point it at Bud and pull the trigger. Fortunately it was unloaded. She disarmed him promptly and told him with emphasis that he was not fit to have a revolver. He implored her not to "tell Ma" about it, as he wanted her to give him a real revolver. And he gave Julia his "after-David" that he would never point a pistol at anyone again. Now two years later he had prevailed upon his benighted parents to let him have some such firearm and his father, rather understandably, was having bad dreams. Mrs. Lincoln evidently wired him they were all right, as two days later he sent this typical telegram to her: "Your three despatches received. I am very well; and am glad to know that you & 'Tad' are so."

By July 2 she and Tad were back and the Lincolns were again established at Soldiers' Home for the hot summer months. This was possibly the year when Mr. Benjamin B. French witnessed an appealing incident just as the family departed for their summer quarters. The carriage was at the door with Mrs. Lincoln and Tad in it when the President emerged from the White House to join them. Tad called out, "I have not got my cat." His father replied, "You shall have your cat," and went back into the house. After a few minutes the tall figure reappeared at the door with the cat nestled in his arms. The family cat was always Mr. Lincoln's pet too.

On the second of July Mrs. Lincoln, driving to the White House from Soldiers' Home, had a carriage accident in which she was thrown out and her head was injured. The Battle of Gettysburg was in progress at the time, but the President, even in this hour of terrific anxiety, still had the thoughtfulness to send a reassuring telegram to Robert at Cambridge on July 3: "Dont be uneasy. Your mother very slightly hurt by her fall." He knew Robert would read about the accident in the papers. The reassurance was premature, however; Mrs. Lincoln's wound became infected and she was dangerously ill for several weeks. On July 11 the President wired Robert, who had gone to New York, a brief command: "Come to Washington." Apparently the son failed to answer. Three days later his father wired again: "Why do I hear no more of you?" By that time Robert was nearing Washington.

Robert naturally supposed from his father's first telegram that his mother's injury was not serious. But he came in time to recognize that it was. Two years later he told his Aunt Emilie Todd Helm: "I think mother has never quite recovered from the effects of her fall." Then he paid a tribute to Mrs. Lincoln's courage in physical pain: "It is really astonishing what a brave front she manages to keep when we know she is suffering—most women would be in bed groaning, but not mother! She just straightens herself up a little more and says, 'It is better to laugh than be sighing.' " It is one of the few comments which he made about his mother that has survived and it is especially noteworthy in that it contains words of praise. After the tragic period later when this mother and son inescapably caused each other great mental anguish, Robert did not like to speak of her.

He had arrived in Washington on July 14, the very day his father sent the telegram of inquiry. That afternoon he went to his father's office at the hour when the President usually left off work to go out to Soldiers' Home. Apparently they were to go out together. This was shortly after the Battle of Gettysburg and Mr. Lincoln, as John Hay wrote in his diary, had been watching the progress of the army "with agonizing impatience." He was hoping passionately that General Meade would capture General Lee's army. Robert said he found his father "in much distress, his head leaning upon the desk in front of him, and when he raised his head there were evidences of tears upon his face."

Mr. Lincoln explained to his son that he had just received word that General Lee had escaped across the Potomac River. He felt that the enemy had been within Meade's grasp and had been allowed to escape. "If I had gone up there, I could have whipped them myself," he lamented. Robert would remember later what a burden and agony it was to be President.

The eldest son had an upsetting emotional experience that summer, one that is very common at the college age. He and John Hay evidently went around together socially and both had become keenly aware of the charms of a certain unnamed young lady, Bob especially so. On August 7 Hay wrote to John Nicolay, who had gone out of town: "Bob and his mother have gone to the white mountains." (The young individualist explained parenthetically that he did not care for that locality and therefore wrote it without capital letters.) "Bob was so shattered by the wedding of the idol of all of us, the bright particular *Teutonne,* that he rushed madly off to sympathize with nature in her sternest aspects. They will be gone some time."

Things which hurt his pride Robert took hard; the experience was evidently an unhappy one. And on top of that the newspapers were now referring to him as "Bob O'Lincoln," just as if he had not been humiliated enough by being called the Prince of Rails. He was not enjoying the role of President's son.

He, his mother, and Tad had gone to Mount Washington. The day after John Hay wrote his letter to Nicolay, Mr. Lincoln wrote one to his wife bringing her up to date on events in Washington. One item was bad news: "Tell dear Tad, poor 'Nanny Goat,' is lost; and Mrs. Cuthbert [the housekeeper] & I are in distress about it. The day you left Nanny was found resting herself, and chewing her little cud, on the middle of Tad's bed. But now she's gone! The gardener kept complaining that she destroyed the flowers, till it was concluded to bring her down to the White House. This was done, and the second day she had disappeared, and has not been heard of since. This is the last we know of poor 'Nanny.'"

The goats were very important personages at the White House and were much spoken of, though not always in terms of approval. There were to be more of them; a year later Mr. Lincoln was to write about "the goats." In addition to Nanny there had also been Nanko, and Mrs. Keckley told how Mr. Lincoln delighted to stand at a window and watch the goats jump and play on the White House lawn. Tad's idea was to hitch them to a little wagon, or if a wagon were not available, a chair would do. On one occasion a party of dignified ladies were in the East Room conversing in stately fashion when there was a violent clatter, a cry of "Get out of the way there!" and Tad, driving a team of goats hitched to a chair, catapulted into the room, drove once around it and then out again. There must have been great commotion among the hoop skirts and devastation of delicate Victorian nerves, and to cap it all the ladies were said to have been proper Bostonians!

Noah Brooks, who related this episode, remarked that Tad made so much noise and disturbance that ". . . one would suppose that there were at least six boys wherever he happened to be." His whoops could be heard as he galloped his pony toward the stable or put his "dog-team" through their paces on the south lawn of the White House.

A friend of Mr. Lincoln's, Leonard Swett, who visited the White House one day in February 1863, wrote his small son about one of Tad's dogs: "a very beautiful little dog" who "runs about the house . . . & barks & stands straight up on his hind feet & holds his fore feet up." Mr. Swett was quite captivated and thought him "a very cunning little fellow." It is possible this was the dog named Jip who always managed to be present at Mr. Lincoln's lunch and claimed his portion first and was caressed and petted through the whole meal. With such an irresistible method of begging, he probably got more lunch than Mr. Lincoln did.

Reassuring news came from Fido in Illinois in the year 1863. Mr. Lincoln's colored barber at Springfield, William Florville, usually called "Billy the Barber," wrote the President a neighborly letter in which he said: "Tell Taddy that his (and Willys) Dog is a live and Kicking doing well he stays mostly at John E. Rolls with his Boys who are about the size now that Tad & Willy were when they left for Washington."

Life was not all pets and play for Tad. He was with his father on all kinds of occasions, which resulted in his finding out a great deal about serious matters. To be under the influence and example of Abraham Lincoln meant learning very excellent rules by which to live. Time would show that Tad had absorbed some of these rules. Aside from books he was receiving a liberal education. He appreciated his father's humor. John Hay recorded in his diary that Tad laughed "enormously" whenever he saw his father's eyes begin to twinkle. One suspects that Tad was going to have a similar sense of humor himself when he grew older.

In spite of his prankishness he was developing a firm conscience on many questions. He came to share the views of his father and mother on temperance. They did not use wine or liquor and keenly disliked the prevalent drunkenness they saw around them. Temperance, of course, had its champions and crusaders, and perhaps a certain incident, reported in a newspaper in 1863, dramatized the cause somewhat for the ten-year-old boy.

Of course it was a presidential duty to receive all kinds of delegations. One day the Order of the Sons of Temperance staged an impressive parade and came marching to the White House to the music of the Marine Band. Among the features carried along in the procession was a fountain with a huge inscription: "Come ye to the waters." Equally in keeping with the taste of the times were three young ladies representing Love, Purity, and Fidelity. Love, Purity, and Fidelity each presented the President with a large bouquet, and having only two hands (and not caring for flowers anyway), Mr. Lincoln was at a loss how to hold them. Tad, who was present as usual, came to the rescue immediately and carried the bouquets off to his mother, whose love of flowers he shared.

This dramatization may have influenced Tad or it may not have, but sometime during those years in Washington he joined a temperance society. Never could he be induced to taste an alcoholic drink. Even though in the future he would spend nearly two years in Germany, where wine and beer drinking was common enough and not to drink was sometimes embarrassing, he never broke his rule.

Tad seems to have had much to do with flowers. When in May of 1863 General Hiram G. Berry was killed at Chancellorsville and his body was brought to Washington, it was Tad who took the President's flowers and wreath to be placed on the coffin. The harum-scarum boy could be trusted now for mannerly behavior, if the occasion demanded it. An English girl who attended a White House reception noticed that, while he placed himself on the stairs, and tried his best to upset the gravity of the servants, he would answer politely and with dignity if a guest spoke to him.

Once, in his desire to be helpful, Tad committed a *faux pas*. According to Ward Hill Lamon's recollection, the incident happened in 1864. There were four or five gentlemen who had been trying to see the President for a week, and he, for reasons of his own, had been trying just as hard to avoid them. Finally, after waiting for days in the lobby, the men were about to give up and leave. Tad overheard them talking about their disappointment at not "seeing old Abe" and at once began to talk with them, listened to their story, learned they were Kentuckians (which was evidently a good recommendation in his eyes), and told them to wait. Then he rushed into his father's office and asked him if he could introduce "some friends" to him. Of course Mr. Lincoln said yes; he was always ready to meet any friends of Tad's. Tad then ushered the gentlemen in with great dignity, asked the first one his name, introduced him, and requested him to introduce the others, a very courteous way of handling the situation. Mr. Lincoln dealt with the unwanted visitors as best as he could and delighted afterwards to tell the story. One day he asked Tad why he called those men his friends. "Well," said Tad, "I had seen them so often, and they looked so good and sorry, and said they were from Kentucky, that I thought they must be our friends." The father's hand caressed the boy. "That is right, my son," he said, "I would have the whole human race your friends and mine, if it were possible."

In September of 1863, seemingly because of much prevalent illness in Washington, Mrs. Lincoln took Tad on a trip again, this time to New York. On September 20 Mr. Lincoln reported on the situation: "I neither see nor hear anything of sickness here now; though there may be much without my knowing it. I wish you to stay, or come just as is most agreeable to yourself." Next day he sent another telegram, which seemed to indicate he was getting lonesome for his wife and son: "The air is so clear and cool, and apparantly healthy, that I would be glad for you to come. Nothing very particular, but I would be glad [to] see you and Tad." After a short unavoidable delay in which she wired him that "Taddie is well," mother and son returned.

In October the pistol motif reappears in the telegrams. On the sixteenth the President wired Thomas W. Sweney, assessor of Internal Revenue at Philadelphia: "Tad is teasing me to have you forward his pistol to him." Mr. Sweney was evidently a great friend of Tad's and sometimes purveyed to him various playthings he desired. He promptly replied to Mr. Lincoln: "Love to Tad. He shall have it tomorrow."

In November the boy was down with another illness which a newspaper referred to as "scarlatina." Otherwise he and his mother might well have gone with the President when he went to Gettysburg to make a speech at the dedication of a soldiers' cemetery. He was kept constantly informed of Tad's condition by telegraph while he was away. He departed on November 18, evidently before getting the physician's report for that day, and Mrs. Lincoln wired him as soon as she could: "The Dr. has just left. We hope dear Taddie is slightly better. Will send you a telegram in the morning." Taddie did get better but the President returned from making his Gettysburg

Address to develop a case of varioloid, a mild form of smallpox. With medical diagnosis so unreliable in that day the question has been raised as to whether Tad and his father really had the same disease.

In early December Mrs. Lincoln for some reason had to go to New York again. She often had to make an appearance at some public patriotic function. She was much worried about the two convalescents she had left at home and, though Mr. Lincoln faithfully wired her each day that all were doing well, she kept sending messages that embodied her anxiety. On December 6 she telegraphed her husband: "Do let me know immediately how Taddie and yourself are. I will be home Tuesday without fail; sooner if needed." Then, knowing he would not want to make her uneasy, she checked on him by sending a message the same day to a member of the White House staff: "Let me know immediately exactly how Mr. Lincoln and Taddie are."

There is much to be said for a narrative told in telegrams. Three more messages, all sent on December 7, complete this story of family affection and concern. At 10:30 that morning Mr. Lincoln sent this to his wife: "All doing well. Tad confidently expects you to-night. When will you come?" The answer came promptly: "Will leave here positively at 8 A.M. Tuesday morning. Have carriage waiting at depot in Washington at 6 P.M. Did Tad receive his book? Please answer." At seven o'clock that evening the husband replied: "Tad has received his book. The carriage will be ready at 6 P.M. tomorrow."

Upon Mrs. Lincoln's return a visitor came to the White House, a surprising visitor in that she belonged to the enemy, being the young widow of a Confederate officer who had been killed shortly before at the battle of Chickamauga. It was the loved "Little Sister" of Mrs. Lincoln, the boys' Aunt Emilie Todd Helm, her face pale and drawn with grief and the disaster war had brought her. With her was her small daughter Katherine, who was several years younger than Tad. The two little cousins had a dispute, which creates another scene that might well go into the picture gallery of the year 1863, one symbolic of the divided loyalties produced by the Civil War. Both children were seated on the floor in front of the fire one evening at the White House and Tad was politely showing his guest some photographs, a good old-fashioned way of entertaining visitors. Holding up one of his father he said, "This is the President." The little Confederate looked at the photograph, shook her head in quick denial, and tried to set Tad right by saying, "No, that is not the President, Mr. Davis is President." Tad in quick rising indignation shouted, "Hurrah for Abe Lincoln." The children had exactly the same portion of Todd blood, and the Todds could hold their own in a dispute, so Katherine yelled back, "Hurrah for Jeff Davis." The situation had reached the point where it required the skill of the master statesman, who took it in hand. Mr. Lincoln lifted the glaring antagonists to his lap, one on each knee, saying, "Well, Tad, you know who is your President, and I am your little cousin's Uncle Lincoln."

It was the middle of December that Aunt Emilie and Katherine left with a pass from the President that would enable them to go to the old home, Lexington, Kentucky. Christmas preparations were now in order at the White House. A friend had sent a fine live turkey with the request that it be used for the presidential Christmas dinner. Noah Brooks related what followed. Tad found the turkey, named it Jack, made a pet of it, and won its affection "as he did the affection of every living thing with which he came in contact." The boy began to teach the turkey to follow him around the White House grounds.

Just before Christmas one day when Mr. Lincoln was conferring with a member of his Cabinet, Tad burst into the room like a bombshell sobbing and crying with grief and a sense of outrage. The turkey was about to be killed for the Christmas dinner. Tad had managed to procure a stay of execution while he flew to lay the case before his father. Jack must not be killed, he sobbed, that would be wicked.

"But," said the President, "Jack was sent here to be killed and eaten for this very Christmas."

"I can't help it," cried Tad passionately. "He's a good turkey, and I don't want him killed." Mr. Lincoln reached for a card and wrote out a formal reprieve for Jack. Tad seized it joyfully and fled to set his pet at liberty. From that time on Jack became a character on the White House grounds and will enter again into this story.

Tad had visited the military camps with his father as usual that fall. Winter was a dismal time for the soldiers; with inadequate shelter and the lack of warm clothes the men were cold and homesick. On Christmas Eve of 1863, as Mr. Lincoln sat at his desk with the work which was never ended for him, Tad came in with his arms full of books, some of the Christmas presents he had just received. His face was lighted with a new idea. Excitedly he told his father that he wanted to send these books to the soldiers at camp.

"Do you remember how lonesome the men looked?" he asked. Mr. Lincoln held the sensitive little face against his own for a moment without speaking. Then he answered, "Yes, my son, send a big box. Ask mother for plenty of warm things, and tell Daniel to pack in all the good eatables he can, and let him mark the box 'From Tad Lincoln.'"

CHAPTER 13

"To Have Our Iowa Friend
at the Shindig"

ROBERT came home for his usual vacation early in 1864. He was
in Washington by Sunday, January 31, as Senator Browning
jotted down in his diary on that day: "At Church A.M. Mrs. Lincoln &
Robert drove me home." It undoubtedly meant much to Mrs. Lincoln
to have her first-born, this fine-looking senior from Harvard, escort
her to worship. He had, as she remarked to Mrs. David Davis about
that time, "a great deal of *Style* about him." Mrs. Davis commented
later that year that Robert had come to look "like both parents."
There was no doubt as to his likeness to the Todds, but there were
some slight resemblances to the Lincoln side of the house—at least
the dimple in the chin. And now that his voice had matured, it was
said to be strikingly like that of his father.

On February 11 Robert wrote an intriguing letter which can be
found today in the Nicolay Papers at the Library of Congress. It
seems a letter of rather heavy-structured humor. The circumstances
that called it forth must be a matter of conjecture. There is possibly a
grievance about Robert's having to return on foot (on Shank's mare)
from the National Hotel. The letter is to John G. Nicolay, who, as
the President's secretary, made various arrangements at the White
House; could Mr. Nicolay have refused or failed to send horses and
carriage to bring Robert home? Is it all humor or is there some resentment in the overelaborate lines?

*It is my opinion that the Equine Quadrupeds you have had the
honor to see me handle with such skill, had better have the benefit
of a little more exercise before they are put into practical trac-
tion of vehicles of pleasure. A man known as "Shanks" kindly
offers me the use of his mare to return from the National Hotel
on the evening of Feb. 11th 1864.*

I take the opportunity, Mr. Private Secretary, to renew to your

*Private Secretaryship the assurance of my most distinguished
consideration and I have the honor to be*

Mr. Private Secretary
Your Private Secretaryship's
Most Obedient Servant,

R. TODD LINCOLN

A month later Robert wrote another letter to Mr. Nicolay from Cambridge which also discloses something of his personality. He was approaching graduation now, the Harvard Commencement would be held on July 20, and he had been put on the Class Day Committee. "I am pretty busy with getting things in train for our class-day," he wrote. "It seems a good while ahead but there is a lot to do." Then comes the real reason for his writing the letter. It is also the first whisper of his romance with Mary Harlan, the daughter of Senator James Harlan of Iowa: "I should like very much if possible to have our Iowa friend at the shindig but do not know where a card would reach her about that time—June 4th. I wish you would ask her when you next see her and let me know." The *Teutonne* was long since forgotten; Robert had met the young woman he was destined to marry and had already, perhaps, fallen in love.

The letter contained one somewhat disgruntled note about his return to Cambridge: "I found to my utter disgust when I got here that I might have waited at W. two days longer instead of getting up at five o'clock in the morning." He added cryptically: "John Hay is getting to be a notorious person in this region. Let him beware."

One does not know whether the "Iowa friend" attended the "shindig" or not, but judging by results, Robert was engaged in courting her for the next several years. Coming to Washington now had a new attraction for him. Mary Eunice Harlan was eighteen on September 25, 1864, and was therefore three years younger than Robert. Owing to the idea of the time that it was "indelicate" to bandy a lady's name in print, it is difficult to get a full description of her, but she had the enthusiastic endorsement of two very particular ladies: of that sixteen-year-old soul of propriety, Julia Taft, and of the mother of the suitor in question, Mrs. Abraham Lincoln.

Mary Harlan had attended the same school as Julia, Madame Smith's exclusive French school at Number 223 G Street in Washington. It was a common saying that a girl had to know who her great-great-grandfathers were in order to enter this school. There, according to Julia, the young ladies were taught important matters of deportment, how to stand and sit in a ladylike manner, how to dance with a train and, dropping it at the end of the measure, give it a little backward kick to get it out of the way before sweeping gracefully to one's seat. Madame Smith drilled them in giving the court curtsy and initiated them into the mysteries of the receiving line, the rules of precedence in Washington society, and the proper forms of social correspondence. It would seem that the main textbooks were books of etiquette, but the girls also had courses in the "three R's," literature, and some other studies. French was spoken exclusively; if any girl was overheard using a word of English, she received a black mark in Madame's deportment book. It was a finishing school somewhat like that which Mrs. Lincoln herself had attended in Lexington, Kentucky.

Julia Taft recalled that Mary Harlan played the harp "divinely." It also lurked in her memory how once Mary told her to hush, saying, *"Taisez-vous, taisez-vous,"* to her when she whispered. But Julia had a great admiration for Mary Harlan, an admiration that seems to have been shared by all. No young lady could have been a more desirable choice for Robert.

Mrs. Lincoln was delighted. It has been said that she saw the lovely daughter of Senator Harlan at the opera one evening and remarked to her husband and Senator Sumner, "I should like Robert to marry just such a girl as that," and Mr. Lincoln thereupon observed to Mr. Sumner, "My wife is a great match-maker. She will make a match between Harlan's daughter and Bob; see if she don't." The story continues that Mrs. Lincoln sent a bouquet of flowers to Miss Harlan, a favorite friendly gesture of the First Lady's. Meanwhile, the young people had met at a dance at the National Hotel. Could this by a long chance have been the evening of February 11, when Robert walked home from the National Hotel on Shank's mare?

Mrs. Lincoln's niece quoted Mr. Lincoln as saying that his wife was "in love with Senator Harlan's little daughter." Robert's mother promoted the courtship in every way she could, and there was much she could do in such matters, inviting the Harlans for special occasions when Robert was at home, and otherwise throwing the young people together. Mary's father, Senator Harlan, was a good friend of Mr. Lincoln's, who made him Secretary of the Interior at the beginning of his second term. Robert had caused his parents much anxiety, but in the crucial matter of his choice of a wife he gave them both complete satisfaction. As for Robert himself, as for any young man who is still in the stages of developing, falling in love with a girl of fine personality and standards was probably the best thing that could have happened to him.

It is hard for a person living in a goldfish bowl like the White House to keep his romance from public notice, but Robert studied the matter of shunning publicity (he almost made it a fine art in the end) and few details of his courtship survive. Perhaps the Gideon Welles family helped out, as they certainly did later when the Lincolns were no longer in the White House. Edgar Welles, son of the Secretary of the Navy, was an intimate friend of Robert's, just as Mrs. Welles was of Mrs. Lincoln. At the time of Robert's marriage in the fall of 1868 Secretary Welles recorded in his diary: "Young Lincoln has made my house his home when in Washington during the days of courtship." One wonders whether the young people made the Welles home a meeting place during the Presidency. It is a surmise that inevitably calls to mind the secret meetings of Abraham Lincoln and Mary Todd at the Simeon Francis home in Springfield during their courtship, secret because of the opposition of Mary's family.

Bob came home for a visit prior to the Harvard Commencement. His mother had been on a trip and had joined him at Boston. The *New York Herald* reported that they arrived together on July 2 and the family at once moved out to Soldiers' Home for the summer. Bob and John Hay were running mates and their activities in early July can be followed very intimately (and with no editing inhibitions) in Hay's diary. The items present a close-up picture of two young men, in a mood of sophistication and disillusionment, restlessly seeking entertainment to combat the depression of war.

On the morning of July 5, John Hay recorded, he went to "the Canterbury" (the vaudeville theater) to get seats for the evening performance. He also had occasion to drop in at the National Theater to see a friend and meet up with "3 Canterbury girls," and "we had some Bourbon whiskey which the sprightly ladies drank like little men." Bob missed this adventure, but that evening he and John with two other men dined together and went to the Canterbury. There were evidently no ladies present, as the diarist continued: "The room was hot and we took off our coats & sat comfortably in the box. . . . The show was the Bushwhackers of the Potomac, filthy & not funny" except in one piece of burlesque. Hay's unflattering description of the play leaves no doubt it was low grade.

The war was pressing close upon everyone in Washington. In the second week in July the Confederate forces were so near that the sound of the cannon at Fort Stevens could be heard at the White House. It was feared that the enemy was about to enter the capital itself. Sunday night, July 10, as John Hay lay in bed at the White

House shortly after midnight, he was surprised to have Bob Lincoln
enter the room and get into bed with him. Secretary of War Stanton
had suddenly arranged for the Lincoln family to be brought in from
Soldiers' Home for better safety. That must have been an unnerving
carriage ride through the darkness for Mrs. Lincoln and Tad.

Fort Stevens was Washington's defense. President and Mrs. Lincoln visited the fort, and Mr. Lincoln was standing on the parapet
when a Confederate sharpshooter shot an army doctor who was
standing beside him. Mr. Lincoln was a man of unhurried movements; he did not get down from the parapet as quickly as was
expedient and the story goes that a young officer named Oliver
Wendell Holmes (later to become a justice of the Supreme Court
of the United States) called out to him, "Get down, you fool."

Whatever Captain Holmes said to the President, he met and companionably joined Robert Lincoln and John Hay when the two rode
out to the front two days later to investigate the encampment at
Crystal Spring. What a pity the photographer, Mathew B. Brady,
did not take a picture of these three strolling young men, so different
in personality, yet each destined to a remarkable future and national
reputation. "We went to F^t Stevens & had a good view from the
parapet of the battlefield of yesterday," wrote Hay. "Then went to
McCook's headquarters and drank lager beer." Hay's telling phrases
sketch the battle scene vividly—an orchard with the trees riddled
with musket fire, the dirty ragged prisoners, the rebel dead whom
the Union soldiers were preparing to bury. One connected with this
interment remarked sardonically to those who were to carry the
stretchers, "Chief mourners, to the rear as pall bears. Get out y^r
pocket handkerchers." Robert was seeing some grim realities of war.

Evidently the President had hoped to attend the graduation of his
eldest son. But that event came in the middle of what has been
called the dark summer of 1864, when in addition to the burden of
running the war and government Mr. Lincoln had to conduct his
campaign for re-election. He could not get away; on July 18, two days
before Commencement, Robert telegraphed to Cambridge: "The
President will not be at Commencement."

Robert himself made a statement of what happened after his graduation, a statement that could be interpreted as having much bitterness and resentment in it: "I returned from college in 1864 and one
day I saw my father for a few minutes. He said: 'Son, what are you
going to do now?' I said: 'As long as you object to my joining the
army, I am going back to Harvard to study law.'" Was that reference
to his father's objection meant to be a dig about the conflict between

them? His father's answer, already quoted, seemed to point out Robert's stiffness of personality and the difference in their attitudes. "If you do," replied Mr. Lincoln, "you should learn more than I ever did, but you will never have so good a time." The bitterness of Robert's final comment seems unmistakable: "That is the only advice I had from my father as to my career." If the eldest son felt cheated of the rich companionship and guidance that Tad was receiving in overflowing measure, it is understandable. Later evidence suggests that Robert, underneath, passionately wanted the warm approval of his father.

Robert entered Harvard Law School on September 5, 1864.

On February 9, 1864, Mr. Lincoln took Tad with him when he went to the familiar studio of Mathew B. Brady to sit for some photographs. As the photographer was preparing the glass plate Mr. Lincoln picked up an album of photographs from the table and began to show them to Tad. Mr. Brady, when he had finished his preparations, found them looking at the book together and took the picture. Years later Robert, telling this incident, called the result "one of the most characteristic and excellent portraits" of Mr. Lincoln. With the gentle and interested expression induced by Tad's loved presence it might well be labeled "Lincoln the Father." The picture disturbed the conscientious President in one respect: he was afraid people would think the book was the Bible and that he was "making believe read the Bible to Tad."

It was on the night of the following day, February 10, that a tragic event took place: the White House stables burned to the ground. Tad apparently did not see the terrifying scene, the high flames against the blackness of the night, the running figures, the fire engine that arrived too late. He fortunately did not hear the cries of the President's horses and of his own loved pony, which, along with the pony that had been Willie's, died in the fire. The current pet goats also perished. When Tad learned what had happened, he threw himself on the floor and could not be comforted. He, like his father, had the terrible vulnerability of his own tenderness and pity.

Robert, who was home at the time, may have witnessed the fire. At all events, he had one of his rare conversations with his father because of it. He came into the presidential office the next morning to say he had a point of law he wanted to submit for his father's opinion. One of the coachmen had had two or three hundred dollars in greenbacks in his room over the stables which of course had been destroyed. Robert said he and John Hay had been having an argument as to the liability of the government for its notes where it could be shown that they had been destroyed. Mr. Lincoln thought it over for a while and then delivered his lawyer's opinion. "The payment of a note presupposes its presentation to the maker of it," he said. He explained at length why the government was under no legal obligation in this case; "therefore, I don't see but that it is a dead loss for Jehu."

Needless to say, Tad's lost pony and goats were soon replaced by others. The parents gave the loved child everything he wanted. What Tad wanted in livestock were pets, and in playthings toy soldiers, flags, firearms and other weapons used in war. His father was certainly in a strategic position to satisfy these wishes, and certain documents show that he did so. He wrote a note to Captain John A. Dahlgren asking him to let Tad "have a little gun that he can not hurt himself with." The forthcoming miniature brass cannon was a model of Dahlgren's Boat Howitzer, perhaps a model used in designing it. (One may see it today in the Illinois State Historical Library.) The President wrote to Secretary of War Stanton: "Tad wants some flags. Can he be accommodated." To Secretary of the Navy Welles: "Let Master Tad have a Navy sword."

But one thing Cabinet members and officers were not supplying during the Civil War was toy soldiers—they were dealing in the live article. Mr. Lincoln and Tad had to find another source for little wooden captains and men, but they knew just where to go—to Stuntz's toyshop on New York Avenue.

The tall deliberate father, wrapped perhaps in his familiar gray shawl and wearing his high hat, would come out of the front door of the White House with his quick-motioned, excited little son. The two, usually hand in hand, would turn to the right on Pennsylvania Avenue, walk to Fifteenth Street, and head into New York Avenue. After they had gone about four blocks in all they would come to a quaint little toyshop. It seemed very small, being only two stories high and two windows wide, and with the ornate iron railing that ran around its second-story balcony it had an appealing old-world look. On the ground floor there was a double door and an enchanting show window full of bright toys of all kinds. Small children on the sidewalk outside stood on tiptoe or pulled themselves up by their fingers to see its treasures.

Inside was a long tunnel of a room whose shelves were piled high with everything a child could wish. To enter it was like going into a Christmas scene in toyland. Here Mr. Lincoln could watch Tad's illumined face and, throwing off his burdens for a moment, enter the uncomplicated world of a child's delight. The little shop stayed open in the evenings too; it would have been a wonderful place to visit after darkness fell and the lamps were lighted to reflect the color and glitter of the toys.

Back of the toyshop was a living room where sat Joseph Stuntz, the owner, who was an old soldier—and worshiper—of Napoleon's. He had been a color-bearer and had finally received in battle a wound in his foot which crippled him. After a life of adventure, he now sat in the little back room day after day, with the wounded foot propped up on a chair, carving all kinds of wonderful toys for children. Especially did he delight in making little wooden soldiers, officers, and men and their equipment of swords, guns, and cannon. Coming from France, he certainly must have carved and painted perfect miniature Zouaves with their red, blue, and gold uniforms. No one could have offered wares more to Tad's taste.

Mr. Lincoln and Tad seem to have made a habit of going to this shop in their increased companionship after Willie's death. Added to the Christmasy atmosphere of the shop itself was the attraction of talking to the old soldier in the back room and watching him carve the toys. Mr. Lincoln is said to have formed an attachment to the shut-in; with their warm sympathy it was inevitable that he and Tad should do so. And then Joseph Stuntz had so much he could tell two responsive listeners who both loved travel—stories of his being apprenticed to a cabinetmaker for the Tuileries when he was a boy and of learning to carve the great *N* of the empire and of fighting for his emperor. Though he went to Paris when very young, he had been born in the Tyrol. (One day Tad would go to the Tyrol himself and have a stirring war experience there.)

Joseph Stuntz was not the only old soldier of Napoleon's whom Tad had known. During the first year in the White House he and Willie with Bud and Holly had delighted in visiting an old Frenchman who lived across the street from the Tafts. He had been one of Napoleon's Old Guard and would tell them stories of the Napoleonic wars. Every time Napoleon's name was mentioned he would click his heels together and pull off the blue cap he wore. The boys made a game of asking questions in turn which involved Napoleon's name and then counting up afterwards which one had made him take off his cap the greatest number of times. "I made him pull off his old cap nine times," Tad bragged once, and Willie answered, "Yes, but you asked questions out of turn, Tad Lincoln, and that isn't fair."

Sometimes, perhaps just before Christmas, Mr. Lincoln would come to the Stuntz toyshop alone to pick out toys for Tad. He was quoted as saying: "I want to give him all the toys I did not have and all the toys that I would have given the boy who went away."

It is known that Mr. Lincoln would spin tops and play ball and marbles with children. It seems safe to picture him playing with the toy soldiers with Tad. If Tad had a mechanical toy, Mr. Lincoln was likely to be extremely interested and there was a drawback to this. Noah Brooks, speaking of Mr. Lincoln's eager curiosity, said: ". . . he would take one of his boys' toys to pieces, find out how it was made, and put it together again. 'Tad,' . . . on more than one occasion, had cause to bewail loudly, his father's curiosity."

The boy had inherited his father's curiosity and interest in mechanical things. He loved tools. A hammer and saw were his delight, which was just too bad for the interior of the White House. A friend (evidently a shortsighted individual) gave Tad a box of tools with the result, according to Noah Brooks, that very soon there was nothing in his reach that was not sawed, bored, chiseled, or hacked. Mrs. Pomroy, the nurse, told how "the new saw was tested by cutting away the plank leading from the dining-room to the conservatory," which gives an interesting glimpse of the way people entered it from the White House. Knobs and locks were taken off the doors and nails were driven into the floor through costly carpets. Having taken this course in experimentation, Tad with patriotic zeal decided to open up a cabinet shop to make furniture for the hospitals. He also turned his attention to the repair of an unfortunate wagon. When he commenced the demolition of the stately mahogany chairs in the East Room, the box of tools, like poor Nanny Goat, mysteriously disappeared.

An article in the *Youth's Companion* in 1869, speaking of this mechanical interest, stated: "Young Tad Lincoln was quite a genius in his way. . . ." One day his current project required a board and of course he went to his father about it. The result was that for years a carpenter working at the White House at the time cherished a special order from the President. On a scrap of paper was written over the signature of A. Lincoln: "If you have a piece of board to spare, please let Tad have it."

Tad delighted to visit the patent office (where he was a distinct menace). He constantly went with his father to the telegraph office and one of the cipher operators, Charles A. Tinker, remembered an incident of one of these visits. With Tad holding his hand Mr. Lincoln entered the office, evidently deeply amused about something, for he was chuckling. At a look of inquiry the President explained to Mr. Tinker that he had just read a story in one of Tad's books. It told of a mother hen who was trying to raise her brood and was much disturbed by a sly old fox. While professing to be a very honest fox, the hypocritical Reynard had managed to devour several of her chicks. The mother hen lectured the fox severely about his wickedness. Here Mr. Lincoln stopped, his eyes twinkling. One of the listeners wanted to know what happened after that. "The fox reformed," said Mr. Lincoln, "and became a highly respected paymaster in the army, and now I am wondering which one he is." What made it so funny was that at that time there were rumors of fraud in the Paymaster's Department.

Tad undoubtedly heard much of ciphers and codes in the telegraph office in wartime. It is said that he and his father agreed upon a signal which he could give when he wanted to enter the Cabinet room, evidently an attempt on the part of Mr. Lincoln to put a stop to Tad's explosive entrances. The signal involved a series of short raps and long thumps, a code which had originated in the telegraph office.

People became accustomed to seeing Mr. Lincoln and Tad together on the streets of Washington. Walt Whitman noticed that when President and Mrs. Lincoln rode in an open barouche, Tad would often ride along beside it on his pony. With a small cavalry escort, it was quite a pleasing procession. The destinations of the father and son had infinite variety. Tad went with Mr. Lincoln to see the wounded General Sickles after the Battle of Gettysburg; he accompanied him to sittings for a bust which was being done by a Treasury clerk, W. Marshall Swayne. The bust, which Mr. Lincoln referred to as "a mud head of me," was to be sold to raise money for the soldiers in the hospitals.

In the year 1864 the activities of the family again can be traced in telegrams. Tad and his mother went to New York in April and Mrs. Lincoln, wiring her husband that they had arrived safely and that she needed some more money, added: "Tad says are the goats well?" An answer was sent immediately: "The draft will go to you. Tell Tad the goats and father are very well—especially the goats." Perhaps the boy worried about his pets after the stable disaster.

When his mother went north in June she took Tad with her. He attended a Sanitary Fair in Philadelphia and then returned to Washington from New York while she went to Boston to join Robert. Tad was evidently coming back to keep a cherished engagement with his father. Of course the boy would not be allowed to travel alone. It has been seen that when Mrs. Lincoln went to Long Branch, she took a "servant man" along to look after the boys. Doubtless she continued this custom when she traveled with Tad, and such a companion could bring the boy home. On June 19 Mr. Lincoln telegraphed his wife in New York: "Tad arrived safely, and all well." Tad and his father were going to visit the army again. On June 24 a report went to her in Boston: "All well, and very warm. Tad and I have been to Gen. Grant's army. Returned yesterday safe and sound."

Washington continued "very warm" that summer of 1864. Fleeing from the heat, Tad and his mother went to Manchester, Vermont, late in August. The faithful family man in the White House kept them informed of events at home and of the well-being of the goats, the pony, and "father." On August 31 his message read: "All reasonably well. Bob not here yet. How is dear Tad?" On September 8: "All well, including Tad's pony and the goats. . . . Bob left Sunday afternoon. Said he did not know whether he should see you."

Mr. Lincoln had said, "All reasonably well," but the truth was he was thin and worn and had little appetite. The war was now in its fourth year; its problems, difficulties of government, and doubts of his re-election in November of 1864 were taking their toll. Once, sitting at his piled-up desk, he remarked whimsically but wearily, "I wish George Washington or some of those old patriots were here in my place so that I could have a little rest."

Mrs. Lincoln was worried about his not eating. It must have been about this time that she and Tad and a pleasant member of the domestic staff named Alice Johnstone formed a little conspiracy. Tad had reached the point where he could share his mother's anxiety about his father. In Springfield Mr. Lincoln had delighted in good old-fashioned stewed chicken with cream gravy and hot biscuits. So a special luncheon of this dish was prepared to be served in a quiet room with only the family present. There was only one person, of course, who could be counted on to make Mr. Lincoln come to his meals; Tad fetched him when the stage was all set. When Mr. Lincoln entered and saw what was before him, he exclaimed, "Oh, Mary, this is good. It seems like old times come back." After the meal was over, Tad joyfully announced to the girl who had prepared the chicken, "Oh, Alice, he ate three helps and more gravy than you and me and mother could [together]!"

The election which would decide whether Mr. Lincoln would remain in office took place in November of 1864, and oddly enough Jack, the reprieved turkey of the year before, thereby comes again into the story. Soldiers from Pennsylvania, familiarly called the "Bucktails," were quartered on the grounds of the White House.

Their tents were at the bottom of the south lawn toward the Potomac. A commission from their state was sent to them to take their votes. Tad burst into his father's office one day and dragged him to the window to see the soldiers voting. Stalking around among the men with great gobbler dignity was Jack the turkey, regarding the proceedings with much interest. The turkey was a favorite with the Bucktails. Mr. Lincoln with a twinkle asked Tad what the turkey was doing at the polls: "Does he vote?" Tad was a bit nonplused at the unexpected question but answered quickly, "No, he is not of age." The President, like any fatuous parent relating the bright sayings of his children, told the story for days afterwards.

No one was more enthusiastic than Tad in the celebration which followed Mr. Lincoln's re-election. On the night of November 10 a great crowd of people carrying lanterns and transparencies came surging around the White House. The martial music and the cheers were deafening. To add to the effect they placed a cannon in the driveway and kept firing it off, with the result that occasionally a large pane of glass in the White House would be shattered by the concussion. Tad, who was busily arranging a small illumination of his own in the windows, was utterly delighted each time a pane crashed. The celebration was one after his own heart.

Christmas 1864 was probably the happiest for the family since Willie's death. In spite of the doubts and discouragement of the summer Mr. Lincoln had been re-elected. The military outlook had brightened; after the long heartbreaking struggle, victory for the Union Army was in sight. As if to emphasize this, a telegram from General Sherman had come, saying: "I beg to present you as a Christmas gift the city of Savannah. . . ."

But it was Tad who gave Mr. Lincoln what was perhaps his best gleam of Christmas happiness on December 25. Some dignified officials came to call and as they entered the front door of the White House they witnessed a strange scene: a little band of ragged street urchins following the President's youngest son through the hall. "I'm fetching them in for dinner," Tad called back over his shoulder as they vanished.

Mr. Lincoln was standing ready to receive his visitors. It was said that his face lighted up with a rare smile. There was, of course, the characteristic twinkle in the deep-set eyes, but also something more, perhaps a special tenderness and pride in this son who had his own compassion and good will toward men. Tad knew how to keep Christmas.

CHAPTER 14

Tad's Little Theater and Other Enterprises

BOTH of Tad's parents were devoted to the theater. Attending plays was one of their best recreations in Washington. Mr. Lincoln's superb storytelling and gift of mimicry showed his dramatic instinct; Mrs. Lincoln had delighted to take part in plays when a girl and she too was an engaging mimic. Tad had the love of things theatrical in his very blood. With several theaters within easy reach of the White House, the National, Ford's, and the Canterbury, Tad had ample opportunities to attend plays of all kinds. Sometimes he went with his father and mother, sometimes with just his father or his so-called tutor, and by and by he was quite capable of going over to the National by himself.

Leonard Grover, manager of the National Theater, became a good friend of Mr. Lincoln's and would sometimes visit him in his box at a play. He stated that the President probably attended more than one hundred performances at the National. Mr. Grover long treasured a note Mr. Lincoln sent him. It was written on a piece of the margin of a newspaper and it read: "Dear Mr. Grover, Tad and I will occupy the box to-night." Once Mr. Grover did a real service for the Lincolns. One evening after a play the White House coachman proved so drunk he could not keep his seat in the carriage to drive the President and his wife home. He kept falling off and the gathered crowd was getting much too excited for comfort. Mr. Grover leaped to the driver's seat and drove the Lincolns out of the embarrassing situation, an act for which both of them expressed deep gratitude.

This Lincoln-Grover friendship extended to the younger generation. The Grovers had a little son, Bobby, who was about five years younger than Tad, and the two boys played together and became very chummy. Bobby's father remembered how they used to fish for

Four Pranksters and Restraining Influence

Above, Tad and Willie Lincoln. *Lower right*, Holly and Bud Taft, their playmates. *Lower left*, Julia Taft, who was instructed to see that "those young rascals don't tear down the White House."

From Julia Taft Bayne's *Tad Lincoln's Father*
(Little, Brown & Co.)

Courtesy of F. H. Meserve

Courtesy of the National Archives

Courtesy of the Illinois State Historical Library

Tad Liked Uniforms

Upper left, Tad in what was evidently the bright-colored uniform of " Mrs.
Lincoln's Zouaves," a soldier company of boys. *Upper right,* Elmer Ephraim
Ellsworth, who was so intimate with the Lincoln family he caught measles from
the little boys. *Lower left,* Tad after Secretary Stanton gave him an officer's
commission. *Lower right,* Robert, who was a " good dresser," at about eighteen.

Executive man. Washington D.C. May 3, 1861.

Dear Henry,

I am sorry have not wrote to you at all, since I left youall.

I told my brother bob in my last letter that there was at least ten thousand soldiers stationed at the capitol building. I suppose that you did not learn that Colonel, E. E. Elsworth had gone to New-york and organized a regiment, divided into companys, and brought them here, & to be sworn in— I dont know when. Some people call them the B, hoy's, & others call them, the firemen.

Yours respectfully,
Willie
Lincoln.

Willie Was a Good Correspondent

Willie, going on eleven, writes his friend Henry Remann at Springfield the news from the National Capitol. Note the Southern "you all."

Courtesy of F. H. Meserve

Courtesy of the Library of Congress

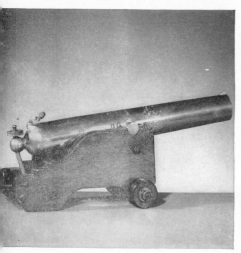

Courtesy of the Illinois State Historical Library

Courtesy of F. H. Meserve

Tad, Cannon, Midgets, and Toyshop

Upper left, Mr. Lincoln showing Tad a photograph album in Brady's studio, February 9, 1864. Robert called this "one of the most characteristic and excellent portraits" of his father. *Upper right*, Stuntz's Toyshop, where Tad and his father bought toy soldiers. *Lower left*, the miniature brass cannon, a model of Dahlgren's Boat Howitzer, which was the result of Lincoln's note: "Capt. Dahlgren may let 'Tad' have a little gun that he can not hurt himself with." *Lower right*, the bride and groom who were entertained at the White House, General and Mrs. Tom Thumb the goldfish in the fountains around the White House, and once they engaged in an escapade which proved what congenial spirits they were. They helped themselves to two "demon" costumes from the wardrobe at the theater, put them on, and started out to make things interesting for people passing by on Pennsylvania Avenue. Unfortunately for them and for the story, a theater official caught them promptly and put a stop to their fun.

With this background Tad soon became a very familiar and privileged figure backstage at the National. He would come to rehearsals, perhaps in company with Bobby Grover, and watch them with rapt attention. Tad always made friends and soon won over the stage workmen. He would frequently aid the property men in placing the stage settings and with his authoritative manner, he probably bossed the job. He had complete liberty backstage and on two known occasions went on stage during a performance as a "super."

One incident was told by the comedian John T. Raymond, who took part in the play involved, a burlesque called *Pocahontas*. In those days, when the soldiers caught a pickpocket, they would placard him—"This is a pickpocket"—and make him walk along the streets of Washington to the tune of the "Rogue's March." The play burlesqued such a scene. Tad had come with his father to see *Pocahontas* and went backstage as usual. The actor said he was "a jolly little fellow; everybody liked him," and someone had the bright idea of dressing him in a very ragged outfit and sending him on the stage with a mob in one of the scenes. Mr. Lincoln, sitting unnoticed in his box, suddenly saw Tad and broke into a hearty laugh. He threw up his hands in a mock gesture of dismay and then let one hand drop over the side of the box. The audience, hitherto unaware of the President's presence, recognized that long, bony hand, for "there was no hand in the world like Mr. Lincoln's." They set up a shout for him and he had to come to the front of the box and make a bow. When Tad returned, his father threw his arms around him in delight. "The pleasure, the affection of the father was so intense, so spontaneous . . . it was glorious to see him."

Another occasion in which Tad appeared on stage was much more dramatic. It was related by Leonard Grover himself. The play was a popular extravaganza called *The Seven Sisters*. It happened that Mr. Lincoln knew the celebrated actor John McDonough, who had a leading part in it. Before the play started its run, Mr. McDonough with several other gentlemen had called on the President, and Mr. Lincoln had seized the opportunity to talk with the actor on a favorite topic, the plays of Shakespeare. It proved to be an in-

volved discussion between experts on the subject. Mr. Lincoln
wanted to know why certain lines were omitted from the stage version of a certain play, and, incidentally, he repeated many lines of
Shakespeare from memory. Perhaps Mr. McDonough's knowing the
President personally made it easier for him to take the step he did
in this incident.

In *The Seven Sisters* Mr. McDonough had interpolated an army
tableau in which he sang a patriotic song that was very popular. The
stage soldiers joined him in the chorus. Tad was delighted with the
play, attended several performances, and finally brought his father
to see it. While his father was intent on what was happening behind
the footlights, Tad quietly tiptoed out of the box and went backstage. There he went to the wardrobe and took out an army blouse
and cap (much too large for him) and put them on. When the soldier
chorus went on stage Tad went right along at the end of the line,
looking a bit grotesque in his oversize uniform but singing loudly
with the best of them. Mr. McDonough, seeing the dramatic possibilities of the situation, stepped over and placed the American flag
he had been waving in Tad's hands. Tad promptly rose to the occasion, stepped a little in front of the line, and, waving his flag to the
music, began the chorus with all the power of his childish treble:

We are coming, Father Abraham, three hundred thousand more—
Shouting the battle-cry of Freedom.

Mr. Lincoln was somewhat taken aback for an instant, then he
shook with laughter. The audience, recognizing the President's
youngest son, was completely captivated. One cannot avoid the suspicion that Mr. McDonough and Tad might have done a bit of planning, perhaps at a rehearsal.

Early in 1864 Tad became the manager of his own little theater.
With his resources it was no problem to get stage paraphernalia;
Mr. Grover mentioned that he "lent him costumes, and stage prop-
erties." It was equally easy to get someone to erect the stage. The
White House carpenter, James Haliday, was a great friend of his,
as the members of the domestic staff generally were. Haliday had
been a member of that military company which Tad organized when
Secretary Stanton gave him his officer's commission. The carpenter
liked to tell how on that evening when Tad dismissed the regular
guard and substituted his own company to protect the White House,
he, James Haliday, escaped duty. He had been appointed sergeant
and that evening he went to Tad (perhaps in the young lieutenant's
headquarters which were opposite the laundry in the basement),

saluted, and said, "Mr. Lieutenant, I would like to have a pass this evening." The lieutenant gravely acknowledged the salute and replied, "All right; I will give the sergeant a pass," and scribbled something on a piece of paper. But when Haliday asked for a pass again the next evening, he received a reprimand and then the softhearted lieutenant gave him the pass after all.

James Haliday and Tad had co-operated in another undertaking. Tad had appeared on the scene when the carpenter and gardener were about to take up the carpet in the state dining room and were having some difficulty with the long table. Tad's executive inclinations at once came to the front; he asked as a special favor if he could assist. Naturally the answer was yes and then he took command. "Now, Jim," he said, "you work with the other man. I will boss the job." Haliday said afterwards, "He told us just how to go about it. And there was no one could engineer it better than he did."

So it was a foregone conclusion that when Tad wanted a stage erected "in the little room just over the entrance," the President would direct James Haliday to do it. It is equally certain that Tad bossed the job. An obscure article in a theater magazine described the scene when the work was all done. The stage was complete with gas footlights, curtain, and appropriate scenery. On either side of it were handsome vases filled with artificial flowers; in the center stood a bust of Edward D. Baker, the one for whom little Eddie had been named so long ago and for whom Willie had written a poem when he died in battle. In front of the stage was a space set off by a wicket fence. This was for the audience and was filled with cushioned chairs, settees, and sofas.

For actors Tad could draw on his beloved "Bucktails" who were camped in his own back yard. One of Tad's friends about his own age, Perry Kelly, whose father was a tinner, sometimes played a part. The audience consisted of any employees of the White House or any Bucktails who could be inveigled into attending, and Tad was a master at inveigling.

One can imagine how interested Tad's theater-loving father and mother were in this project of his and what handsome co-operation he received from them. They, of course, sometimes attended the performances. This little theater was naturally the apple of Tad's eye.

One day he discovered the sanctity of his domain had been rudely invaded. Some photographers from Mr. Brady's studio had come to the White House to take a few views "of the President's office." They were for the use of the artist F. B. Carpenter, who was staying at the White House to paint a picture of the President and his Cabinet, a painting commemorating the Emancipation Proclamation. The photographers requested the use of a dark closet in which to develop their pictures and, knowing that theaters must be made dark and that the men would do no harm, Mr. Carpenter took them to Tad's little theater. Tad discovered that jars of chemicals and alien apparatus had been put into his sanctum and flew into a rage. It was his room and he had the key; he would show them. He locked the door with apparatus inside and photographers outside and refused them permission to enter; "they had no business in his room!"

Both Mr. Carpenter and Tad promptly went to the President and each presented his side of the case. Mr. Lincoln, who was patiently posing for more photographs, said very mildly, "Tad, go and unlock the door." Tad, without obeying, went off to his mother's room, muttering some strong remarks to himself. Mr. Carpenter followed him and tried coaxing, but without result, so he returned to the President. Mr. Lincoln asked, "Has not the boy opened that door?" Mr. Carpenter said no, that Tad was very angry.

Tad's father suddenly arose with his lips set in the determined way that was characteristic of him when he had made up his mind. He went toward the family side of the second floor to which Tad had retreated and one suspects that Mr. Carpenter, like others before him, was hopeful that at last Tad was going to receive a little discipline. Presently Mr. Lincoln returned holding the key to the theater room and unlocked the door himself. "There," he said to the photographers, "go ahead, it is all right now." Then he returned to his office followed by Mr. Carpenter. "Tad," he said to the artist in a tone of apology, "is a peculiar child. He was violently excited when I went to him. I said, 'Tad, do you know you are making your father a great deal of trouble?' He burst into tears, instantly giving me up the key." Mr. Lincoln had long known that Tad, like his mother, must be ruled by affection.

It is not stated whether admission to Tad's theater was free or not, but judging from that young financier's eye for good business, it is a safe guess that there was some charge. The boy's mind was full of schemes for raising funds. Some of these enterprises had patriotic motives. The Sanitary Commission (a national organization which cared for the sick and wounded very much as the Red Cross does today) was constantly trying to raise money, and Tad thought he would help out. He well knew the scores of people who went up the public stairway at the White House to see his father, so he mounted guard at the foot of the stairs and collected tolls from each one. "Five cents for the benefit of the Sanitary Fund," he explained to the visitors.

Sanitary Fairs where articles were sold to raise money for the work of the commission were very common. Tad organized two such sales of his own. It is not clear whether these were private business enterprises to raise money for himself or whether the proceeds went to the Sanitary Commission. In his first venture he commandeered a small table and placed it in the grand corridor of the White House, wheedled fruit and odds and ends of food from the servants in the kitchen, and sold these wares to the various passing visitors. This succeeded so well that like any good businessman Tad expanded his undertaking.

He knew an old woman who sold apples, gingerbread, and candy at a little stand on Pennsylvania Avenue. The avenue itself, with these little stands, had somewhat the look of a fair. There were organ-grinders playing familiar and patriotic tunes, vendors of soap calling their wares, umbrella men with their loonlike cry of "um-ber-ellas to mend," men with a telescope and a sign saying, "Five cents to look at the stars, ten cents to look at the moon," sellers of artificial bugs attached to elastic strings swinging their spidery offerings up and down, little tables on which were displayed huge rocks of candy from which pieces were chipped off according to the buyer's demand. There was the passing parade: soldiers and officers in various uniforms, elegant hoop-skirted ladies, army vehicles of all kinds, and gorgeous private carriages (some of them lined with red satin) driven by liveried coachmen. Pennsylvania Avenue was a panorama of Civil War Washington. It was all a familiar scene to Tad and one of those pictures in his memory which one wishes could be reproduced. Certainly some of his currency went to the various vendors, and from the old gingerbread woman (doubtless to her joy) he bought the entire stock of her little stand near the Treasury Building. He intended to set up shop in the stately and historic portico of the White House itself.

He required equipment of two trestles and a wide plank to display his merchandise, and it is possible this was the occasion, already mentioned, on which Mr. Lincoln wrote an order to a White House carpenter to give Tad a board. Business was brisk: practically every office seeker who entered the White House found it the part of diplomacy to buy his luncheon from Tad. The young shopkeeper received so much money that his pockets overflowed and he had to use his hat for storage purposes, just as his father used to do back in Illinois. Stuffy people of the day (and there were a lot of them) were horrified that the dignified columns of the Executive Mansion should look down on so undignified a scene as the President's son presiding at a gingerbread stand. Tad made money, but Noah Brooks, who told the story, added that he was too generous to keep it very long.

One project of Tad's was of a very different sort. It sometimes happens that a child, hearing of some adult problem and only partially understanding it, suffers a silent but very real anxiety. In 1864 the President issued a proclamation for a day of fasting and prayer. Tad heard of this approaching Fast Day and the main idea that got into his head was that on a certain day he was not going to have anything to eat, a dreadful prospect for a growing boy. He quietly made his preparations. All would have gone well if fate had not been so unkind as to prompt the coachman to clean up the family carriage. In his overhauling the man was astonished to find a queer-looking bundle in one of the boxes under the seat. By this time Tad was standing by, nervously watching the coachman, who opened the bundle and pulled out part of a loaf of bread, some cold meat, and other bits of food. Tad could stand it no longer. "Oh! Oh!" he cried, "give that up, I say! That's my Fast Day picnic." He ran in distress to his mother, who soon comforted him and promised he should not go hungry on Fast Day. Mr. Lincoln was much amused and delighted to tell the story, ending with the remark: "If he grows to be a man, Tad will be what the women all dote on—a good provider."

Tad, like his mother, was much given to making purchases. He conducted some of his business, just as his presidential father did, by military telegraph. A series of these telegrams, sent through the War Department, gives glimpses of his transactions and agencies. Several of them are to the same Thomas W. Sweney (sometimes spelled Sweeney) at Philadelphia to whom Mr. Lincoln had once wired for a pistol for Tad; the gentleman was involved in some way in Tad's shopping. One message to Mr. Sweney read: "I have found a pony to suit me. Please therefore, come on this evening so that you may be able to see him tomorrow." This one is in a good handwriting and bears the notation "By D.H." (perhaps David Homer Bates of the War Department Telegraph Office). Another requests Mr. Sweney to send the money for a "double Sett of harness" bought "at the Same place that you purchased my wagon at." This telegram was to be sent on to Gus Gumpert, another agent in Tad's transactions.

There are telegrams addressed directly to Gus Gumpert (whose name also varies in spelling) and the name of Thomas Cross appears in one of them. A telegram that Mrs. Lincoln once sent suggests that Tom may have served on occasion as the "servant man" whom she took on trips to look after Tad; this message addressed to "Augustus" Gumpert and signed "Mrs. Lincoln" read: "Please bring Tad home immediately. He can come on Tom Cross's car."

Gustav Edward Gumpert, like Thomas Sweney, was a great friend of Tad's who lived at Philadelphia. He and his brothers had a store which Tad delighted to visit, sometimes opening the cash drawer and scattering its contents, and once riding a pony into the store itself, to the great consternation of the customers. On October 4, presumably in 1864, Tad wired Gumpert: "Gus, I want to know about that box you was to send me. Please let me know right away if you Please And Oblige Col Thomas Lincoln." The "Col" of course referred to the officer's commission which Tad had received from Secretary Stanton. (The rank is usually given as lieutenant, however.) A telegram signed by a colonel has a certain air of authority, which Tad doubtless liked, and, of course, such an officer has a perfect right to send his communications by military telegraph.

On October 6, 1864, on the official stationery of the Executive Mansion was written in a far from well-trained handwriting the following telegram: "Dear Gumpert: I send Thomas Cross to see you about the Carriage Bill. It was Sent. to me Aand I ant got any money to pay the man with And Oblidge Thomas Lincoln Yur Friend Tad [.]" This document has been much argued over because Mrs. Lincoln, subsequent to the writing of it, made several statements indicating that Tad could not write when he was in the White House and Mrs. Keckley's testimony gives the impression he could neither read nor write at that time. On June 15, 1865, Mrs. Lincoln wrote from Chicago to Alexander Williamson, a young Scotsman who had been a tutor to Willie and Tad, that her youngest was ". . . at length seized with the desire to *read* & *write*. . . . I hope he will be able to write by fall so that he may be able to write you a letter inviting you *out here* to see him."

Perhaps the strongest statement Mrs. Lincoln made on the subject of Tad's backwardness in learning was that in her letter to Alexander Williamson on December 16, 1867. It was also written in Chicago. "Taddie is well. Can now read, quite well—as he did not know his letters when he came, here, you will agree he learned rapidly." Were Mrs. Lincoln's statements literal or relative? Certainly the telegram of October 6, 1864, was not competent writing. Noah Brooks spoke of the time in the White House when Tad "could scarcely read." If he wrote that telegram, it could be stated truthfully that he could scarcely write. It has been suggested that when Mrs. Lincoln wrote of his not knowing his letters she meant he could not repeat the alphabet. It also sometimes happens that a child learns to sign his name before he knows all his letters or can be said to write.

There is another bit of evidence that pertains to this historical puzzle. Tad's unquestioned signature to a legal document in 1867 is thought by some to bear a marked resemblance to the signature of the telegram in question. The two documents are presented side by side in an illustration, and the reader can judge for himself.

A telegram, of course, can be dictated and written down by anyone. A study of four of the original telegrams at the Illinois State Historical Library shows at least two different handwritings. In most of them the language seems to be Tad's. It has been suggested that Tad got some semiliterate adult, perhaps a servant like Thomas Cross, to write out some of the telegrams, some grown-up person who knew so little he would write "ant" for "ain't." The telegram of October 4 to Gumpert, concerning "that box," is plainly in the same handwriting as the one of October 6, 1864. It is a fascinating point, especially important to collectors as it affects the market value of the documents in question.

In justice to Tad it should be emphasized that while his education undoubtedly was retarded, his mind was not. The boy was not bookishly inclined, as Willie had been, but when he finally decided to apply himself to his lessons he learned rapidly. Dr. W. A. Evans justly stated that "Tad's backwardness in his earlier years was the result of lack of training." And, as has been seen, it was his indulgent father who had said, "Let him run, there's time enough yet for him to learn his letters and get poky."

At all events, it is safe to say that in 1864 achieving competence in reading and writing was not among Tad's major enterprises.

CHAPTER 15

Catastrophe for the Family and the Nation

EARLY in 1865 the long conflict between father and son about Robert's going into the army came to an end. Details leading up to this decision are lacking. Certainly after Robert graduated from Harvard and then entered law school instead of enlisting, he was more subject to criticism than ever. Perhaps Mr. Lincoln had finally brought his wife around to the point where she would face Robert's joining the army, if he could do so in a privileged way. Mrs. Lincoln was now in such a state of instability that he dare not put additional strain upon her. More than a year before, Emilie Todd Helm, speaking of her sister's psychopathic condition, had said to him, "I believe if anything should happen to you or Robert or Tad it would kill her."

That asking special privilege for his son was a matter of embarrassment to Mr. Lincoln is very evident in the letter he wrote General Grant on January 19, 1865. He first asked the general to read and answer this letter as though it were not written by the President but only by a friend. Mr. Lincoln continued: "My son, now in his twenty second year, having graduated at Harvard, wishes to see something of the war before it ends. I do not wish to put him in the ranks, nor yet to give him a commission, to which those who have already served long, are better entitled, and better qualified to hold. Could he, without embarrassment to you, or detriment to the service, go into your Military family with some nominal rank, I, and not the public, furnishing his necessary means?" The close of the letter emphasizes Mr. Lincoln's realization that he was doing something that not only made him vulnerable to criticism but also might bring embarrassment to General Grant. If the answer was no, continued the President, "say so without the least hesitation, because

I am as anxious, and as deeply interested, that you shall not be encumbered as you can be yourself."

General Grant, having no paper, wrote his answer in regard to Robert on the blank half of Mr. Lincoln's own letter: "I will be most happy to have him in my Military family in the manner you propose. The nominal rank given him is immaterial but I would suggest that of Capt. as I have three staff officers now, of conciderable service, in no higher grade." Robert was appointed captain and assistant adjutant general of Volunteers, February 11, 1865. It was undoubtedly a relief to Lincoln to have the matter settled, and now there would be less conflict between him and his eldest son.

His eyes could rest on this son with paternal satisfaction. Robert made a handsome captain. A uniform does much for any young man and Robert's looks had greatly improved. The slight thickness of his features in his earliest pictures had disappeared, his face was more finely cut now and more mature, and his figure was straight, slim, and vigorous.

The recollection of one who later became a friend of Robert's, Mr. F. W. Rice, mentions the proud look on Mr. Lincoln's face as he gazed at his young captain. When Mr. Rice was a boy, his father had taken him to the White House to see President Lincoln. While they were talking and Mr. Lincoln's hand was resting kindly on the lad's head, a slender young man in a captain's uniform entered the room. Mr. Lincoln said to him, "Robert, this is Congressman Rice and his son. . . ." Then placing his arm around Robert's shoulders, he said to the visitors, "You know, my boy here has just been made a captain on Gen. Grant's staff." Young Rice said he could never forget "the look of fatherly pride Mr. Lincoln gave his son."

Apparently Captain Lincoln's courtship of Miss Mary Harlan was progressing satisfactorily. An officer's blue uniform with shining brass buttons has never been a drawback to any gentleman in his wooing. In addition Robert's mother was being most co-operative in the matter. It was not by accident that in the great event of March 4, 1865, the second inauguration of Abraham Lincoln, Mrs. Lincoln's escort was Senator James Harlan, and his lovely daughter Mary was escorted by Captain Robert Lincoln. There were to be knowing looks and wisely nodding heads when the word went around that he was also her escort at the Inaugural Ball.

For many days Washington had been grooming itself for its great pageant. Once more the platform had been erected on the east front of the Capitol and great crowds assembled before it. But where four years before an unfinished truncated dome rose back of the platform, now there loomed the majestic curves of the completed structure holding aloft the great bronze statue of Freedom. It was symbolic of what was happening; the effort to divide the nation was doomed and victory for the Union was now at hand. There was further symbolism. Rain had fallen on the crowd as it assembled, but as the President stepped forward to deliver the immortal Second Inaugural with its "malice toward none," its "charity for all," the darkness of the day vanished and his face was illumined with sudden brilliant sunlight.

Robert and Tad both were destined to look upon great, momentous events in their country's history in March and April of 1865. Again certain telegrams carry the narrative. On March 20 General Grant, no doubt partly inspired by the fact that he had the President's son with him at his headquarters at City Point, Virginia, wired Mr. Lincoln: "Can you not visit City Point for a day or two? I would like very much to see you and I think the rest would do you good." The President replied, accepting the invitation without setting the exact date, and mentioned he would bring Mrs. Lincoln and a few others with him. With their eldest son at the end of the journey, one suspects he would have encountered difficulties if he had tried to leave "Mother" at home. The next day, March 21, Robert sent his own inquiry: "Will you visit the army this week?" The President answered in cipher: "We now think of starting to you about One P.M. Thursday. Dont make public."

Thursday was March 23 and on that day, according to schedule, father, mother, and Tad boarded the *River Queen.* Once more Tad experienced the adventure of steamboat travel down the Potomac cluttered up with gunboats, transports, and other paraphernalia of fighting, and up the James River into the very theater of the war that was coming to its climax.

Among those on board was a bodyguard of the President, William H. Crook. He had been sent to the White House early in 1865, for fears as to Lincoln's safety had increased. A sympathetic young man with a wife and baby, he was well liked by the Lincolns and by Tad, who called him "Took." Crook had not known Tad before and his description of the boy in 1865 shows how much Tad had developed from the lawless little prankster of four years before. "The boy was like his father," said this guard; "he looked like him." He spoke of Tad's tenderheartedness and of how he often borrowed money when some pitiful person asked him for help and how, with that integrity which all the Lincoln sons had, he never forgot to pay it back. Crook described the unique attachment between father and son: Tad, he said, for all his baby tongue "had a man's heart, and in some things a man's mind. I believe he was the best companion Mr. Lincoln ever had—one who always understood him, and whom he always understood." Crook told of Mr. Lincoln's romping up and down the White House corridors with Tad, "playing horse, turn and turn about, or blind-man's buff," and added, "he was happy when he was playing with the boy."

Tad and Crook shared a stateroom on the *River Queen*. As soon as they came on board, Tad's investigating mind took him all over the boat, and by the time he went to bed he had studied "every screw of the engine" and made friends with every man of the crew. Crook added, "They all liked him, too."

Toward morning, as Tad slept in his berth, the alert senses of the guard heard someone enter the stateroom, then Mrs. Lincoln's voice: "It is I, Crook. It is growing colder, and I came in to see if my little boy has covers enough on him." It was Friday evening and dark again when the boat reached City Point. Tad, looking up to the high bluff above the river where the *River Queen* tied up, could see the lights in the buildings of Grant's headquarters on top, where brother Bob was. The boy was eager to get ashore, even though it was so dark, and Crook went with him. They were promptly halted by a sentinel. Crook explained who they were, "but Taddie thought he would go back. He said he did not like the looks of things."

During their stay the presidential party slept on the boat. The first light of Saturday morning revealed the harbor around them crowded with craft of all kinds—fishing boats, sailboats, transports —and the wharf to which the *River Queen* was tied piled high with military supplies. From the higher ground above the river could be seen the tents of General Lee's army. No grand review was scheduled on this visit; the enemy lay too close. They were near the last bitter struggle of the Civil War and the dying of the Confederacy.

Captain Robert Lincoln came early in the morning to see his family. Imagination can fill in the picture of the affectionate greeting of the father and mother to their soldier son and Tad's delight in seeing brother Bob in the glory of his uniform among the other army men. After talking with his eldest son, the President telegraphed Secretary Stanton at eight-thirty that same morning: "Robert just now tells me there was a little rumpus up the line this morning, ending about where it began." Robert was getting what his father had said he wanted: a chance "to see something of the war before it ends."

Robert had his part in the operations that led to the fall of Petersburg. On the rainy night of March 29 the President at City Point could hear cannonading in the direction of that city and see "the flashes of the guns upon the clouds." On April 2 he wired Mrs. Lincoln (who had gone back to Washington for a brief time with plans to return): "At 4:30 p.m. to-day General Grant telegraphs that he has Petersburg completely enveloped from river below to river above. . . . He suggests that I shall go out and see him in the morning, which I think I will do. Tad and I are both well, and will be glad to see you and your party here at the time you name."

Tad was having a glorious time. In spite of evidences of death and destruction on all sides, the morale of the army was uplifted at this time with the certainty of victory. The boy, with his quick interest and enthusiasm, became a great pet among the officers and men. During their stay the headquarters band would march up to an open space near the President's special tent and play popular airs for an hour or so. The music of a brass band was exactly to Tad's taste; he learned to watch for the band at the usual hour in the afternoon, and as soon as he heard the strains of music in the distance, he would jump up and down shouting, "There comes our band! There comes our band!" Of course the men, happy in their knowledge that soon they would be returning to their own young families, enjoyed this buoyant lad.

One day during the visit Tad with his father, mother, Crook, and others went up the Appomattox to Point of Rocks, and Tad looked across to the tents of General Lee's army. And once a sinister incident occurred which would be remembered later. A man came on board and asked Captain Bradford of the *River Queen* if he could see the President. He said he was a personal friend of Mr. Lincoln's and had spent large sums in his behalf in the presidential campaign in Illinois. When asked his name the man at first refused it, then said it was Smith. The man looked like a tramp and those responsible for the President's safety were naturally suspicious. Crook went to the President and told him about the incident and Mr. Lincoln said he knew no such person and that he was an impostor. "Smith" was furious at being refused and said defiantly to Captain Bradford, "If Mr. Lincoln does not know me now, he will know me damned soon after he does see me." Tad saw the man and knew of the suspicions; he would remember.

Apparently Tad did not go with his father when the President visited Grant's quarters at Petersburg on April 3. But Captain Robert Lincoln met him with a mounted escort as he neared the end of the journey and took him to General Grant. In this visit to the war front there was a new relationship between father and eldest son and doubtless a closer one. For the first time they were working together as two men with a common purpose, the winning of the war. One does not know all that they shared during those days packed with action, but there is record that when General Sheridan reached City Point, Robert was the one who went on board the *River Queen* to tell his father "Little Phil" had arrived. The six-feet-four-inch President went ashore to greet the five-feet-four-and-a-half-inch general.

Richmond, Virginia, the capital of the Confederacy, was taken by the Union forces the morning of April 3. When Mr. Lincoln returned from Petersburg on that day, he telegraphed the great news to the Secretary of War, adding, "and I think I will go there to-morrow. I will take care of myself." There was danger in his going into that proud city in its bitterness and ruin of defeat. This time Tad was the son who went with him; it was Tad's twelfth birthday, so how could his father refuse him, even if there was some danger. On April 4 President and son with Crook in attendance went up the James River on the *River Queen* to meet Admiral David D. Porter's fleet. When they got near Richmond, because of obstruction in the river, the party had to go ashore in the captain's gig manned by ten or twelve sailors. The bank was crowded with Negroes crying out at the sight of "Massa Linkum," who had freed them from slavery. As the party which included Captain Charles B. Penrose climbed up from the wharf and with the inadequate escort of those few sailors walked toward the center of the city, Tad's young eyes saw an ever increasing crowd of Negroes, shouting, leaping with joy, kneeling, calling, stretching out their hands toward his father. The party finally reached a stately columned mansion on a hill, the White House of the Confederacy, from which President Jefferson Davis had fled two days before. To a twelve-year-old boy with a martial spirit such a birthday celebration as entering the Executive Mansion of the Rebellion (for Tad indubitably considered the Confederates rebels) must have been a supreme thrill.

After refreshments at this mansion, the presidential party drove through the conquered city. Everywhere were signs of war. The retreating Confederates had fired bridges and warehouses as they left, and the fire, driven by high wind, had spread to the business section. Tad saw houses still burning. The party entered the Capitol on the hill, finding confusion and destruction within. Papers were scattered, desks broken open, furniture wrecked.

The President and Tad spent the night on Admiral Porter's flagship the *Malvern*, which took them back to City Point on April 5. It was on the *Malvern* that Crook, sharing a stateroom with Tad, was again awakened from slumber at night by an anxious parent; Mr. Lincoln, a tall ghost clad in a long white nightgown, came in "to see if Taddie was all right."

Mrs. Lincoln, back in Washington, had sent her husband a telegram on hearing that Richmond had been taken: "Glorious news! Please say to Captain Bradford, that a party of seven persons, leave here tomorrow & will reach City Point, on Thursday morning for breakfast." The party arrived on April 6, as scheduled, and among those seven persons were Senator and Mrs. Harlan with their daughter Mary. Mrs. Lincoln had given her whole heart to this fine girl with whom Robert had fallen in love and it might even be conjectured that one purpose of her return to Washington was to bring Mary to her young captain. One cannot recover the meetings of the lovers at City Point nor Robert's conversations with his parents there, but it is certain that these visits took place and meant much to all concerned.

Robert was able to bring news to the Lincolns of "little sister," Emilie Todd Helm. Late in March he had been sent to escort two unnamed ladies from Fortress Monroe "as far as the flag of truce boat could proceed, which was near Petersburg." The fine-looking young Union captain went on board to fulfill this duty, took one look at the ladies put in his charge, and ejaculated, "Well, if it isn't my Aunt Emilie!" At the same time she exclaimed in great relief and pleasure, "Robert! Oh, how glad I am to see you!" There was strong affection between them. Emilie wanted news of her sister Mary and was distressed at Robert's account of his mother's ailing condition. Robert put his aunt on a pass which would enable her to go south. Again their lives had touched.

Mrs. Lincoln was extremely disappointed that she had not been with the President and Tad when they went to Richmond. To make up for this, the party returned to Richmond, visiting the Davis mansion again. They also went to Petersburg, where the President visited the hospitals filled with wounded soldiers. On the return from Petersburg to City Point the President noticed a terrapin sunning itself outside and had the train stopped so that one of the brakemen could fetch the little creature. Then he and Tad had a fine time playing with it and laughing at its awkward movements. The President had looked very sad and weary after going through the hospitals, but now his face relaxed. As Crook had noticed, he was happy when he made himself a child to play with Tad.

For Robert and Tad the long visit of their father to City Point had meant unparalleled experiences. There was a military review after victory had come. There were lovely evenings when the *River Queen*, with its decks brilliantly illuminated with many-colored lights which had rippling reflections in the water, and with a military band playing patriotic airs, seemed a place of enchantment. Doubtless it was especially so to the boy Tad and to Robert and Mary Harlan, who were in their own iridescent world of two young people in love. But the President must return to Washington, good-by must be said to the eldest son, and on Sunday, April 9, the *River Queen* was steaming on its way back to Washington.

Robert on that Sunday was close to one of the great and memorable scenes in the nation's history. He had ridden with General Grant to Appomattox Court House, Virginia, to the home of Wilmer McLean, where that afternoon, in a small, sparsely furnished parlor, General Robert E. Lee signed the terms of surrender. But modest young Captain Lincoln did not witness that signing; in later years he told how he stood on the porch outside and did not even hear General Lee's voice.

The presidential carriage met the *River Queen* at the wharf, and as the Lincolns drove back to the White House, the lighted bonfires and happy crowds on the streets told them the great news of Lee's surrender had come. "Tad," said Mr. Crook, "was so excited he couldn't keep still." The great dividing Civil War was over and the Union was saved.

The day after the return Tad again went with his father to a photographer's studio, that of Alexander Gardner. Mr. Lincoln posed for several photographs and Mr. Gardner took one of father and son together, with Tad leaning his left arm on a table. The picture shows how much the boy was growing and maturing. Tad lacks in it the little-boy look of the one taken with his father by Mr. Brady in February the year before.

The next evening, Tuesday, April 11, Washington had an elaborate celebration of victory. All public buildings were decorated and illuminated. Pennsylvania Avenue was a gala thoroughfare of banners and bonfires and at the end of it the recently completed dome of the Capitol was bathed in light, even as one sees it today. All feet were hurrying toward the brilliantly lighted White House, for the President was to make a speech that night. A vast, shouting, cheering crowd assembled before it. A small battery from the Navy Yard rent the air with an occasional salute, brass bands were playing, there was the hiss of fireworks. The President and a few friends lingered at the dinner table before going upstairs for him to speak.

As they mounted the stairs, the tumult outside changed; along with the music and cheers there was suddenly a great roar of laughter. Noah Brooks, who was with Mr. Lincoln, saw the cause of the merriment: at one of the front windows to the right of the staircase old Edward the doorkeeper was struggling with Tad and trying to drag him back from the window from which he was waving a Confederate flag. The people, of course, recognized Tad (who frantically waved the flag as Edward pulled him away) and they roared with delight.

Mr. Lincoln spoke from the center window overlooking the portico. There was a tremendous cheer at the sight of his face, then a great silence as he began: "We meet this evening, not in sorrow, but in gladness of heart." It was not a speech of exulting over victory and vindictiveness toward the enemy but one showing kindliness toward the Southerners and the wish to bring them back into the Union. As he finished with each page of his manuscript, he dropped it on the floor and Tad began to collect the loose sheets, chasing them as they fluttered from his father's hand. Having rounded them up and placed them on the table, he whispered, "Come, give me another!" Mr. Lincoln made a restraining gesture with his foot but otherwise showed no sign of being disturbed.

Senator Harlan followed with a speech in different vein. "What shall we do with the rebels?" he asked the crowd, "what shall we do with them?" There was a mighty roar of "Hang them!" Tad looked up into his father's face and said quickly, "No . . . not hang them, but hang on to them." Mr. Lincoln answered, "Tad has got it. We must hang on to them." As Crook had said, these two understood each other.

On the morning of April 14, Good Friday, Robert came home to the White House. He had had an arduous journey with General Grant because of the destruction of railroads and the difficulties of getting through war-torn country. He found his father at breakfast and they had much to talk about. Robert had brought a photograph of General Lee to show his father. Mr. Lincoln studied the picture thoughtfully and said, "It is a good face; it is the face of a noble, noble, brave man. I am glad that the war is over at last."

A great peace and inner happiness had come to the worn President with the ending of battles. Now he could think in terms of normal living once more; now he could give some time to this son whom he had seen bearing himself so well at City Point. The visit there had brought them so much closer together; perhaps each had taken a new and larger measurement of the other. The father's thoughts turned to Robert's future. Looking up at him from the table where he sat, he said, "Well, my son, you have returned safely from the front. The war is now closed, and we soon will live in peace with the brave men that have been fighting against us." Robert must now lay aside his uniform and return to his study of law. The President's face was lighted as he spoke.

He was in the same uplifted happy mood when he went driving with his wife that afternoon. "Mary," he said, ". . . We must *both,* be more cheerful in the future—between the war & the loss of our darling Willie—we have both, been very miserable."

The Lincolns had been invited to attend two theaters, Ford's Theatre, which had a comedy, *Our American Cousin,* and the National, where *Aladdin or The Wonderful Lamp* was playing. It was finally decided that the President and Mrs. Lincoln would go to Ford's while Tad and his tutor would go to the National. The President asked Robert to go with his mother and himself to Ford's, but the son was understandably weary from his journey and said he would like to be excused.

It was in the neighborhood of eight-thirty when Mr. and Mrs. Lincoln drove off from the White House in the presidential carriage. Tad and his tutor could easily walk over to the National. Robert and John Hay went upstairs where they could relax and engage in young men's gossip. John Hay's brilliant and spicy conversation was undoubtedly as entertaining as either play.

More than an hour passed. At the National Theater Tad sat in a front seat gazing into a world of make-believe, his hand perhaps clutching the patriotic red, white, and blue playbill which told of the wonders of "The Great Oriental Spectacle of Aladdin." At its top was a picture of the American eagle above the red, white, and blue shield, for Washington was delirious with patriotic pride in the sweet hour of victory. Between the second and third acts a poem called "The Flag of Sumter" was read; Fort Sumter was where the four years' struggle had begun.

At a few minutes after ten Mr. and Mrs. Lincoln, his hand affectionately holding hers, sat in the box at Ford's Theatre gazing down upon a brightly lighted stage. An assassin crept noiselessly into the shadows behind them. There was the sound of a pistol shot and a woman's scream. The President slumped in his chair.

Back at the White House Robert Lincoln and John Hay heard a commotion downstairs, rushing feet, people bursting through the doors, confused cries. A white-faced messenger rushed up the stairs with the dreadful news that the President had been shot. Over at the National another messenger walked rapidly down the aisle, whispered something into the tutor's ear, and he, with ashen face, led Tad out of the theater and started toward the White House. Robert and John Hay ran downstairs and out the front door, where they found a carriage to take them to Tenth Street. As they started to drive off, a friend breathlessly told them Mr. Seward and most of the Cabinet had been murdered. It all seemed so improbable, so like something in a nightmare that Robert frantically hoped it was untrue. When they reached Tenth Street where Ford's was located, every thoroughfare was blocked by excited, tragic-faced people. The two young men finally got themselves through the crowd and dashed up the curving outside stairs of the house across the street from the theater to which Mr. Lincoln had been carried. On the doorstep as they stepped over it was a large spot of blood. At the door they were met by Dr. Robert K. Stone, the Lincolns' family physician in Washington, who with grave tenderness told Robert there was no hope. For a moment the son was racked with sobs in his shock and grief, then he got hold of himself. Going down the narrow hall whose carpet was covered with oilcloth stained with drops of blood, Robert could hear the labored breathing of the stricken President and the pitiful cries of his frantic mother. In the little back room at the end of the hall he saw the long figure of his father stretched diagonally across the bed, unconscious and dying.

In the endless night that followed, Robert tried tenderly to soothe and comfort his mother. She was so beside herself with shock and anguish she was perhaps only half aware of his presence. He spent part of the time with her in the front room where there was a sofa upon which she could lie exhausted between her paroxysms of grief. At intervals they would go to the back room, where he saw her kiss her dying husband, calling him by every endearing name, imploring him to speak to her, and finally, when realization that there was no hope penetrated her dazed mind, begging him to take her with him. She wanted Taddie sent for, because, as she said in her unreasoning anguish, "she knew he would speak to him because he loved him so well." (Did that unconscious admission of the father's greater love for Tad give an extra stab to Robert's agonized heart?)

Mercifully Tad was left at the White House. He had returned there with his tutor, sobbing and crying out that his father had been shot. One of the staff, Thomas Pendel, whom he called "Tom Pen," told how he gathered Tad into his arms and tried to comfort him. In a half-stunned way the boy kept repeating the dreadful news he had heard. About midnight Pendel said he took Tad into his father's room, undressed him, put him in bed, and lay down beside him with his arm around him. Then he talked soothingly until Tad fell asleep. Perhaps Tom Pen, since Mr. Lincoln was still alive and reports were confused, thought, or made Tad think, his father would recover. In pity one is grateful that Tad could sleep on that awful night.

To Robert it seemed, as he said later, that the interminable agony of that night would never end. It left its mark on him. At about six in the morning it began to rain heavily. The end was very near now. Mrs. Lincoln visited her husband for the last time. She fainted when she saw that his eye, behind which lodged the fatal bullet, had become swollen and discolored. The doctors present gave her restoratives. She was supported to the bedside again and cried out, "Love, live for but one moment to speak to me once—to speak to our children." She was led from the room.

As the President's moans grew fainter, Robert stood at the end of the bed almost directly behind his father's head; he could look down on the dark hair clotted with blood. The room was crowded with doctors, members of the Cabinet and other officials, and close friends. Among them was the loved tutor of Willie and Tad, Alexander Williamson; he was, in all probability, the one who had gone with Tad to the National Theater the evening before.

The death struggle had begun. Secretary Welles, who had great affection for Robert, stood directly behind him at the head of the bed and noted with pitying eyes how "he bore himself well, but on two occasions gave way to overpowering grief and sobbed aloud, turning his head and leaning on the shoulder of Senator Sumner," who stood to his right. At seven-twenty-two his father breathed his last.

Robert put his arms around his stricken mother and supported her to a carriage for that desolate return, through dark and rainy streets, to the White House. Bells were beginning to toll throughout the grieving city, sad and ominous tolling that would soon extend through all the nation.

Robert had to take charge and attend to the things that must be done. His mother was prostrated and alternated between wild outbursts of grief and periods of dazed exhaustion. That very morning of April 15, in a handwriting whose nervous jerking showed the toll that the awful hours had taken of him, Robert wrote out a telegram to his father's old friend David Davis, who was then in Chicago, Illinois: "Please come at once to Washington & take charge of my fa-

ther's affairs—" It was a levelheaded choice and decision. Judge
Davis had been a devoted friend of his father's, who had appointed
him a member of the Supreme Court of the United States, and he
had Robert's own confidence and affection. In addition to being a
most able lawyer, he was a shrewd businessman. He and Robert
would see eye to eye. Judge Davis telegraphed that he would come.

There were many arrangements to make, relatives to consider.
That same day Robert wired his uncle, C. M. Smith of Springfield,
who happened to be in New York, the single word "Come."

Yet while he was meeting the situation clearheadedly and efficiently, he was at the same time doing everything he could to comfort and help his mother. On the morning of the President's death,
perhaps just after his body had been brought back to the White
House, Mrs. Keckley entered Mrs. Lincoln's bedroom to find Robert
"bending over his mother with tender affection. . . ." Tad was
crouched at the foot of her bed "with a world of agony in his young
face." Mrs. Lincoln was an ill and shattered woman and her paroxysms of grief verged on the abnormal; she almost went into convulsions. Tad was the only one who could help her in these outbursts;
he would put his arms around her neck and sob, "Don't cry so,
Mamma! don't cry, or you will make me cry, too! You will break my
heart." It was the one appeal that could reach her; she must not
make Tad cry. Holding this loved child close, she would try to calm
herself for his sake. As always, it was understanding affection only
which could influence Mary Lincoln.

One pitiful glimpse of Tad on that dark Saturday of April 15 was
recorded by Secretary Welles in his diary. The assassination of the
President and the attempt to murder others of the Cabinet had resulted in a state of confusion and wild rumors. John Wilkes Booth
had escaped after shooting Lincoln and some did not know who
the murderer was. Secretary Welles and Attorney General Speed
came to the darkened, silent white mansion that afternoon. They saw
Tad on the first floor looking out at the cold rain and the colored
people in front of the White House who were weeping and bewailing
their loss. They seemed not to know what their fate would be now
that their liberator from slavery was dead. Tad turned his tear-swol-
len face to the two men as they descended the stairs and cried out,
"Oh, Mr. Welles, who killed my father?" Themselves in tears, neither
Mr. Welles nor Mr. Speed could find words to comfort the boy.

Funeral services were held in the great East Room on Wednesday,
April 19. Mrs. Lincoln was far too ill to attend and Tad also was
spared the pain of being present. It was Robert, his young face hag-

gard and drawn, who sat through that affecting service with sorrowing friends. Then, after a lying-in-state in the Capitol, the President's body, on the morning of Friday, April 21, was placed in the blackdraped car of the funeral train for the long circuitous journey back to Illinois. Robert did not go on that trip; he had to remain in Washington to attend to many things and to look after his mother and Tad.

But Mr. Lincoln did not return alone. Some men had gone to the quiet Oak Hill Cemetery in Georgetown, removed a little casket from the Carroll vault, and placed it in the car. Once Willie had written in his little-boy words of a trip which "me and father" had taken. Now Willie and his father, in a new mysterious companionship, were starting another train ride together, home to Springfield.

CHAPTER 16

"I Am Not a President's Son Now"

I T WAS May 22, 1865, before Mrs. Lincoln had recovered sufficiently to leave the White House. The delay was doubtless embarrassing to Robert, who knew that they were being criticized for
staying so long and that the proper thing was to get out as soon as
possible, so that President Johnson could move in. But his mother's
condition was such that he could not do anything about it. The
assassination of her husband had completed Mrs. Lincoln's devastation; she was now a woman physically and, in some respects, mentally ill. In addition to her wild outbursts of hysteria she had reached
a fixed irrationality on matters that pertained to money. This took the
form of a senseless and extravagant buying, while at the same time
she was convinced she was in extreme poverty. Robert had dark
months and years ahead because of this abnormality of his mother's.
Supersensitive to publicity and criticism, he was to be pilloried again
and again by the misunderstood affliction, and these experiences
would leave deep scars on his personality.

He met that humiliating delay in leaving with fine consideration
and levelheaded efficiency. Robert had come a long way from the
bumptious boy described in Springfield. He had had all that Harvard
could give in social and intellectual training, and—very important—
he had fallen in love with a very fine girl. Mr. Crook, who joined the
White House staff early in 1865, found him "a manly, genial young
fellow," and added significantly, "We all liked him." If his father
could have seen him in those remaining weeks in Washington, the
kind gray eyes might well have had that look of shining pride which
Mr. Lincoln had once turned upon his young captain. At that time
and from then on it could be said of Robert Lincoln that he always
did his duty as he saw it.

Mrs. Keckley, who remained with Mrs. Lincoln as nurse during this trying period, noticed that "Robert was very tender to his mother in the days of her sorrow." "He suffered deeply," said Mrs. Keckley, "as his haggard face indicated, but he was ever manly and collected when in the presence of his mother."

Robert, in addition to grieving over his father, was torturing himself with regret. If only he had accepted his father's invitation to go to Ford's Theatre that night, he might have saved him. He understood that the one vacant chair was in front of the door by which Booth entered the box. That would have been the logical chair for him to occupy, with his parents and their two guests in front of him. He could have grappled with Booth when he entered and the whole dreadful tragedy might have been averted. It is said that Robert frequently visited the box at Ford's and sat there trying to figure out how it would have been if he had said yes instead of no when his father asked him to go. Robert was one to brood unhappily over things, and that regret would go with him and haunt him all his days.

He was suffering the agony of losing a father whom he had so lately begun to appreciate. His boyhood relationship evidently had been unsatisfactory; perhaps now Robert began his yearslong realization of what he had missed. It is possible that his refusal to talk of Mr. Lincoln in Springfield days, taking refuge in a brief statement that he had not seen very much of him then, was a dodging of this painful realization. It is possible also that his antagonistic attitude in early days had stemmed from resentment because he did not have from his father the approval he secretly craved.

In a letter written to Professor Francis J. Child of Harvard twelve days after his father's death Robert, for once, gave a glimpse into his own heart. "Our loss is indeed terrible," he said, and then came the sentence of self-revelation: "In all my plans for the future, the chief object I had in view was the approbation of my Father, and now that he is gone and in such a way, I feel utterly without spirit or courage. I know that such a feeling is wrong," he continued, "and that it is my duty to overcome it. I trust that for the sake of my Mother and little brother that I will be able to do so."

Robert was not overlooking anything that needed to be done. On April 21 he telegraphed his resignation of his commission "as Captain and Assistant Adjutant General of Volunteers." (His name, however, was carried on the army rolls until June 20.) Here and there are scattered bits of evidence that show how he was attending to all details for Mrs. Lincoln. In the Stanton Papers one finds his note of

April 28 asking the Secretary of War: "Would you, if convenient, be kind enough to call this evening and see Mother?" He wrote for her the letters of appreciation she was too ill to write. Such a letter is one to a group who had sent her a cross of wax japonicas. Robert thanked them gracefully in his mother's behalf for the "beautiful cross" and "for the kind and sympathetic terms with which the cross is presented. . . ."

Robert supported his mother in an unpleasant controversy that arose even before his father was buried. Without consulting Mrs. Lincoln, a group in Springfield had bought six acres of what were called the Mather grounds in the heart of the town and were preparing to have the President buried there. When she found out about it, Mrs. Lincoln refused her consent for two good reasons: Lincoln had asked that he be buried in a quiet country cemetery, and she also feared she could not be buried beside him in the public location in Springfield. Local interests (which were perhaps financially involved) were furious at her refusal and denounced her in violent terms. This explains the vigor of the telegram which Robert sent Governor R. J. Oglesby on May 1: "There seems to be a disposition at Springfield to disregard my mother's wishes in regard to the interment—Both the temporary and final interment must take place in the Oak Ridge Cemetery—We have reasons for not wishing to use the Mather place for either purpose and we expect and demand that our wishes should be consulted." There was good reason for Mrs. Lincoln to write as she did two months after her husband's death: "Robert, in our day of sorrow and adversity, manifests himself as he really is, a youth of great nobleness."

On May 1 the eldest son telegraphed Cousin Elizabeth Grimsley (Cousin Lizzie, who had been in the White House with the Lincolns for the first six months of their stay there): "I leave this P.M. for Springfield and will be your guest while in town." Robert was the one who had the hard duty of representing the family at his father's funeral on May 4; his mother and Tad remained in Washington. One gets a glimpse of him as he looked on that day in the letter of a lady who went to Springfield for the occasion. After the funeral she said she called at the home of Mrs. Lincoln's cousin John Todd Stuart "& there met Robt. Lincoln, he is fine looking. My heart ached for him, he seemed to feel so sadly. From there we called on Mrs. Grimsley. She went in the carriage with young Lincoln."

Robert, like both his parents, had a capacity for suffering too great for his own good. It was a visit of infinite sadness. His old home on Eighth Street was heavily draped in mourning, its windows, in the fashion of the age, festooned outside with black. In the back yard where he had played as a boy were apple trees incongruously in blossom. Meeting all the relatives stirred old associations and Robert felt family ties keenly. He had to be a part of Springfield's great pageant of mourning. He had to face that moment of leaving a loved body behind in the cemetery which seems to emphasize so painfully the closing of a life.

He returned to his duties in Washington. On May 8 he wrote back to Springfield that his mother was much better and was able to be up for a short time. He must work out the details of their departure. Robert thought his mother should return to Springfield to live, where they still owned the home on Eighth Street, and it did seem the most sensible thing to do. But on the very day of her husband's death she had told him that was not her wish. Bitternesses had arisen between her and some of her relatives there, and she could not bear to face that town and home whose happy memories now brought only pain. So it was decided they would live in Chicago.

Shortly before they left, Mrs. Lincoln had to answer a most important letter. In the veritable avalanche of communications she had received was a four-page letter of sympathy from Queen Victoria of England. In connection with this letter from Her Royal Highness a question arose in which Robert's attitude as his mother's adviser was significant of certain things that he would do later in his life. Mrs. Lincoln, skilled penwoman that she was, composed a beautiful and fitting answer to Her Majesty. That was easy; she and Queen Victoria were very much alike in their great single love and devotion to one man and in their complete and unremitting grieving after his death.

But a letter from the sovereign of Great Britain to the former First Lady of the United States had larger aspects, and pressure arose for the publication of the queen's letter. Years later Robert, speaking of this urging to publish the letter, said they decided not to do so "as it was evidently written with no idea of publicity," and "was so evidently the unrestrained outpouring of sympathy from a full heart, that we felt it would be a violation of propriety to publish it, at least during the life of the writer."

And all the while the letter had been intended for publication! When the President had been assassinated the queen's titled advisers had pointed out to her "that a very good effect would be produced in conciliating the feelings of the United States, if your Majesty would deign to write to Mrs. Lincoln privately, condoling with her on her bereavement by so cruel a crime." Shortly afterwards the queen recorded in her journal that she had written Mrs. Lincoln, "which was much wished."

Robert and his mother, in not publishing the letter, had out-Victoriaed Queen Victoria herself! This attitude of Robert's, that private and personal matters and letters are not for the public, would have far-reaching effects.

Mrs. Lincoln and her eldest son were in agreement about the royal letter, but there were many things in which they did not see eye to eye in their preparations for leaving. She was one of those women who save everything, old hats and dresses and miscellaneous leftovers, and she was finding the packing of her accumulation quite a burden. Robert urged her to burn the stuff. Mrs. Keckley gave some of these conversations: "What are you going to do with that old dress, Mother?" the son would ask.

"Never mind, Robert, I will find use for it. You do not understand this business." Robert replied he hoped he never would understand it, and he wished to heaven the car in which her "old plunder" would be shipped would burn up on the way to Chicago. Then "with an impatient gesture" he would turn on his heel and leave the room. It did not come easily to one of Robert's temperament to give in to his mother, especially as he was usually giving her sound advice. And she was making the mistake of considering him still a child, saying to Mrs. Keckley: "Robert is so impetuous. . . . Well, I hope he will get over his boyish notions in time." That attitude on her part was not easy for him to take either.

How was it with Tad in those remaining weeks in Washington? Ten days after his father's death he sent what may have been his last telegram to Thomas Sweeny. It was pathetically symbolic of the change in his existence; it was not concerned with the purchase of a new pony or wagon or any other source of pleasure but read simply: "Thomas Sweeney . . . please send me that new suit of Black to fit me, one size larger than that Gus. given me." It was signed not "Thomas Lincoln" nor "Tad" but "T. Lincoln." His father's usual signature had been "A. Lincoln"; Tad was now trying in many ways to be like his father.

He was showing his father's own tenderness and understanding toward his anguished mother. When he heard her sobbing in the night, he would come to her bedside, put his young arms around her, and whisper, "Don't cry, Mamma; I cannot sleep if you cry! Papa was good, and he has gone to heaven. He is happy there. He is with God and my brother Willie. Don't cry, Mamma, or I will cry, too." With unerring instinct he had selected the thoughts that would help her. Her one consolation was the belief that her dead husband and children were together and were fondly watching and waiting for her in the beyond. And she would try to stop crying so that he would not cry too but would go back to sleep.

With his strangely mature wisdom, Tad faced up to his changed situation bravely and clear-sightedly. One morning, according to Mrs. Keckley, he looked up at the servant who was helping him and said, "Pa is dead. I can hardly believe that I shall never see him again. I must learn to take care of myself now." He was silent a moment, thinking it out, and then he added, "Yes, Pa is dead, and I am only Tad Lincoln now, little Tad, like other little boys. I am not a President's son now. I won't have many presents any more. Well, I will try and be a good boy, and will hope to go some day to Pa and brother Willie, in heaven."

Tad had been babied and waited on to an extent almost beyond belief. His clothes had been laid out for him in the mornings and a servant had stood by to help him dress. Now he began to make himself independent and was soon getting out his own clothes and disdaining help in putting them on.

There is some reason to think that Robert was an excellent influence on Tad at this time. A deep affection was growing between the brothers now and Mrs. Keckley noticed how Tad took great pride in pleasing his brother Bob. After they reached Chicago the two roomed together.

One unusual item about Tad appeared in a newspaper shortly before the Lincolns left Washington. Lincoln's assassin, John Wilkes Booth, had been shot in the final stages of pursuit, but Washington was agog over the trial of those who had conspired with him. On May 18 a newspaperman noted that "Master Tad. Lincoln was among the spectators at the conspiracy trial this afternoon." It is painful to think of the turmoil in his passionate young heart as he looked at those who had plotted with the murderer of his father.

At long last the family was ready to depart. Robert with due propriety had called on President Johnson to inform him that the White House would be turned over to him in a few days. The new President made no inquiry as to the welfare of Lincoln's widow, who had remained overlong at the Executive Mansion. Fifty or sixty boxes in addition to scores of trunks were carted away to be sent to Chicago. Mrs. Lincoln had been a constant target for abuse as First Lady during the war-torn years. Now tongues began wagging with accusations that she was carrying off the furnishings of the White House. This must have been almost unbearable to Robert, who had advised her to dispose of her useless belongings.

The day finally came when Robert, Tad, and their mother quietly left the great white mansion which had been home to them for four brilliant and tragic years. Robert's feet would again cross that historic threshold when he became a member of the President's Cabinet, but it was a final leave-taking for Mrs. Lincoln and Tad. The most significant and exalted period of their lives was at an end. As they drove off, did Tad, with his instinctive feeling for human values, look back at the house where he and his father had shared so much?

Workmen would come in now to prepare the house for President Johnson. They would tear down the stage of Tad's little theater. In an upstairs room they would find a great accumulation of toys, especially toy soldiers from Stuntz's toyshop, whole regiments of them. Tad had left his playthings behind; the playtime of his life was over.

At the railway station a special green car was waiting for them. Mrs. Keckley as nurse accompanied Mrs. Lincoln, who was still very frail, and Crook, Mr. Lincoln's former bodyguard, was one of the party. Mrs. Lincoln was ill with one of her migraine headaches on the dismal fifty-four-hour journey, and Crook seems to have been the one who looked after Tad. He said there was an observation car on the train and he and the boy spent much time there looking at the passing scenes with Tad asking questions. Tad was interested in travel, fortunately for him, for much traveling lay ahead in his life.

But this journey ended in a way he was not used to. During the past four years when he and his mother or father had gone on trips, everyone knew who they were, and there had been deference and much ado. But now they arrived at Chicago as ordinary citizens. A passer-by might have noticed a little family group, a pale, sad little woman in a widow's deep mourning, a young man whose still immature face looked strained and worn, and a lad of twelve with a friendly air. They took a cab through the noisy, busy streets of a growing city that somehow seemed raw and new in comparison with Washington. Their destination was the Tremont House, where Mr. Lincoln had once stayed with Willie in "a nice little room" where everything was arranged especially for "me and father." There was no glamour to the hotel rooms now. Mr. Crook, who remained in Chicago a week, said he came several times to take Tad for a walk, trying to interest him in what they saw, "but he was a sad little fellow, and mourned for his father."

Mrs. Lincoln soon decided that the Tremont House was too expensive. She was suffering that panic which overwhelms any widow when she realizes the regular income of her husband's salary has stopped and she is dependent upon the interest of the money they had saved. Lincoln left no will and when his estate would be settled three years later it would total over a hundred and ten thousand dollars, of which she, Robert, and Tad would each receive a third. At this time her available funds were limited, but in her irrational conviction that she was very poor, her thinking on the subject was distorted.

She wanted to move from the Tremont House for another reason; she wished to isolate herself from all her friends and relatives. Old faces, she said, would bring back memories that she wished to forget. The mourning customs of the day called for a ritual of grieving, the wearing of heavy black, the use of black-bordered stationery, demonstrations of grief, seclusion, and the avoidance of anything that suggested enjoyment. These things fitted all too well into Mrs. Lincoln's agony of spirit and impaired judgment and cast a heavy shadow on her two sons.

After a week the family moved to a resort hotel, the Hyde Park, in the suburb of that name. Mrs. Keckley, who was still with them though she would shortly return to Washington, gave the details of their arrival at this rather unprepossessing place. The accommodations were second class, the rooms small and plain, the atmosphere cheap and depressing. Mrs. Lincoln wept over the poverty that compelled her to live in such circumstances. Tad tried to be cheerful and furnished the only buoyancy in the party.

Robert, on the afternoon of their arrival, occupied himself with unpacking his books and arranging them on shelves in his room. They were probably his Harvard law books, but there was no possibility of his returning to the Harvard Law School now; he was going to study law in the offices of Scammon, McCagg and Fuller on Lake Street. Mr. Jonathan Young Scammon, the senior member, had been a friend of his father's.

Mrs. Keckley said she helped Robert unpack his books and that he talked pleasantly as they worked. But when they had finished, he stood for a while with a thoughtful and unhappy face, and then, turning to Mrs. Keckley, he asked her what she thought of the new quarters. She answered brightly that they seemed delightful to her. He looked at her "with a quizzical smile" and then said, "You call it a delightful place! Well, perhaps it is. Since you do not have to stay here, you can safely say as much about the charming situation as you please. I presume that I must put up with it, as mother's pleasure must be consulted before my own. But candidly, I would almost as soon be dead as be compelled to remain three months in this dreary house."

If Robert felt his mother's shutting herself off from friends and relatives was unwise and unfair to him and Tad, it is easy to understand. His was not a happy temperament like Tad's and the stay at Hyde Park made bitterly evident how they had fallen from the prominence and luxury of being in the White House. Only one element of their former high estate would remain: the public criticism, misrepresentation, and mudslinging which beat always upon those in the Executive Mansion would continue to assail his unfortunate mother.

CHAPTER 17

"Us Editors of the Budget"

M RS. LINCOLN had been and was deeply concerned over Tad's lack of schooling. When the family settled at the Hyde Park Hotel, one of her first endeavors was to teach him herself. It was there that their argument as to whether "a-p-e" spelled "ape" or "monkey" took place. The various ups and downs of trying to get Tad to study can be traced in the many letters she was writing at this time.

On June 15, 1865, she wrote his former tutor, Alexander Williamson, that Tad "says two or three lessons a day" and that now at last he really wanted to learn to read and write. She added one of her frequent comments on the boy's sweet disposition: "Taddie has a lovely nature & I have not the least trouble in managing him, he is all love & gentleness."

Early in July Tad received a letter from Mr. Crook, but he was still very far from being able to handle his own correspondence. Chicago evidently had impressed Crook favorably and he was thinking of moving there, so he wrote Tad asking about opportunities. To answer such a letter involved adult competence; Mrs. Lincoln, therefore, wrote a helpful reply (signing it "Taddie") telling of conditions, making suggestions, and saying how glad they would be to have him live there. She expressed Tad's homesickness (and her own) for the White House and its people; there are inquiries about "Charlie" [Forbes] and Pendel and the regretful remark: "None of them ever write." One letter shows hunger for information from Washington: "Tell us about the new people in the house. All news, will interest us."

By late summer Tad's new-found enthusiasm for learning was wearing a bit thin. In August his mother again reported to Mr. Williamson: "Taddie is well & . . . is growing very fast & I am sorry to say, he does not apply himself to his studies, with as much interest as he should." She added firmly: "We intend that he shall attend school, regularly after the 1st of Sep." "We" meant herself and eldest son; Robert was also very anxious for Tad to overcome his backwardness in education.

In November, when the family had left Hyde Park and were boarding in the city, Mrs. Lincoln wrote the artist Francis B. Carpenter: "Taddie is learning to be as diligent in his studies, as he used to be *at play*, in the W[hite] H[ouse]. He appears to be rapidly making up, for the great amount of time, he lost in W. As you are aware, *he* was always a *marked character*."

In this same letter to the artist Mrs. Lincoln told of an incident which showed Robert's affection and sympathy for Tad. She had borrowed a copy of Henry J. Raymond's life of President Lincoln. "After reading it," she wrote, "I remarked to Robert, in Taddie's presence, that it was *the most* correct history, of his Father, that had been written. Taddie immediately spoke up & said 'Mother, I am going to save all the little money, you give me, and get one of them.'" The child's sensitive face doubtless grew wistful at the mention of his father, and Robert very quickly told him it would not be necessary for him to save his pennies, that he would buy him a copy.

By January of 1866 the battle over Tad's schooling seems to have been won. Mrs. Lincoln reported again to Mr. Williamson: "Dear little Taddie goes to school, and does not miss an hour. He is already very much beloved in C., his teacher speaks of him in the highest & most affectionate terms." She added: "One of the Bucktails resides here, and T takes great comfort in visiting him." Tad made friends everywhere, and this gift of friendship, coupled with his adaptability, made him the most cheerful member of the family in Chicago.

Since Tad was a minor and had to have a guardian, any money spent for him had to be accounted for in writing. These itemized accounts in the guardianship records at the Illinois State Historical Library come to life with interesting information. Robert acted as Tad's guardian for a while, but he wrote to Judge David Davis in February of 1866: ". . . I would prefer that when he needed advice or restraint, some older person should have authority to give it to him." It was inevitable that Robert would find it difficult at times to deal with his mother in questions involving Tad. In spite of the fact that the eldest son was managing affairs with marked ability and levelheadedness, she still considered him a child. She was also overemotional, and her irrationality in financial matters impaired her judgment. Robert went on in his letter to say that both he and his mother wished Judge Davis to be appointed Tad's guardian. This appointment was made in November 1867.

In Mrs. Lincoln's accounts to Robert for Tad's expenses are found such items as "shoeing pony," "Pd. for wintering pony," and "stabling pony," which show that Tad in Chicago had the pet he loved best. Robert also had brought his horse with him; it was the last gift his father had given him. While the family was still at Hyde Park Mrs. Lincoln had written: "Robert is so worried, that I am sick so much, that he has purchased a neat covered buggy, in which he can drive his horse, otherwise, he says he would sell the horse." Situated as they were out at Hyde Park a horse and buggy was almost a necessity for getting around, and there is a glimpse here of Robert's consideration for his ailing mother. But both of them feared public criticism even in a minor matter like this. "Anything *we do* is seized on—" wrote Mrs. Lincoln truly. ". . . I expect we will hear remarks, about our purchasing a buggy."

Among the rumors that annoyed mother and son that fall of 1865 was one that Robert was traveling in Europe. This hurt the more because he had wanted so to take a certain trip at that time and could not. His particular friend, Edgar Welles, was going to Havana and invited him to go along. Mrs. Lincoln wrote Mrs. Welles with what regret Robert had declined: ". . . the temptation offered by *such a trip* was great & I almost marvelled that R. could withstand it." The letter explained that they were very much restricted financially and that Robert must "attend to his studies." As his mother said later, "He was conscientious, in what he considered his duty, to remain at home. . . ."

Mrs. Lincoln's letters around this time speak constantly of their poverty, and Robert's letters to Judge Davis (much more to be trusted in the matter) show that they were very short of money. But his mother's seeking of inexpensive and inconvenient lodgings was not to Robert's taste. He wrote Judge Davis late in December, 1865: "As I do not see any prospect of keeping house, I propose on the first of next month to rent a room and begin to live with some degree of comfort—a thing not known to my present quarters." On January 3, 1866, he reported to the judge he had taken two rooms to himself.

Perhaps this was one of the factors which caused Mrs. Lincoln on May 22 to purchase a house at 375 West Washington Street, a stately stone front of New York and Boston style. It was a sad mistake financially and one that Robert would not have countenanced; he was having his mother's impulsive and ill-balanced actions to contend with. Such a house with Mrs. Lincoln's standards was beyond their means; they could not afford its upkeep. She, Robert, and Tad were each receiving around seventeen or eighteen hundred a year, and in the postwar inflation everything was, as she said, *"so fabulously high."* But she longed for a home where she could have her sons together, and for Tad, at least, the sojourn in that house was marked by a period of happy normal living.

The new location was a pleasant one on the West Side. Nearby was Union Park, which was plotted out with a lagoon, little rustic bridges, flower beds, and trees. Close by was a colony of Kentuckians of fine families similar to those with whom Mrs. Lincoln had grown up. The Third Presbyterian Church, which Mrs. Lincoln attended, was within reach, and Tad went to Sunday School, sometimes there and sometimes at the First Congregational. He is said to have attended later the Young People's Bible Class at the First Baptist Church on Wabash Avenue.

Best of all in the Washington Street home Tad could attend the Brown School on Warren Avenue between Page and Wood Streets (now 1758 Warren Boulevard). He could loiter and perhaps join in games in that pleasant little Union Park on his way home after school. He was in a class of thirty boys and girls. At last conditions were right and normal for Tad's education; here were associations on equal terms with other children of both sexes and here was wholesome competition in learning. By this time he seems to have given up his ambition to play tricks (he no longer had his father to laugh at them) and his mother mentioned that he was "greatly mortified" when Mr. Carpenter made public some of "his little waywardness" in the White House.

He had abandoned pranks but not projects. The close of 1866 found Tad joining wholeheartedly in plans for a little school newspaper. The former theater manager had turned editor. The Chicago Historical Society has a copy of the *Brown School Holiday Budget,* a quaint little four-page, nine-by-twelve sheet printed in three columns and well illustrated. At the top of the first page, just below the name, is its motto, "Excelsior," and the information that it is "Published occasionally" "By S.P. and Tad." S.P. was Sterling P. Rounds, Jr., and he evidently had the right adult connections for this enterprise, as there is a card of thanks to "Messrs. Rounds & James, Printers . . . who provided us the Type and material for our little sheet" as well as advice. This card is signed "S. P. Rounds, Jr., and Thomas Lincoln, Editors and Proprietors." The date is "West Chicago, Christmas, A.D., 1866"; it is Volume I, Number 1, and as far as is known no succeeding issue ever appeared.

The reader of the *Holiday Budget* is taken delightfully into the juvenile mind of the eighteen sixties. The humor is obvious and teen-age, but here and there is a playful touch rather suggestive of Tad's father. One gets the impression here, too, that Tad inherited his father's humor.

One article is a grave discussion as to whether Santa Claus really exists. This is written by skeptics who admit: "It is not clear, even to *us Editors* of the *Budget,* how he manages to get down the narrow, smoky flue—and how he can *possibly* carry so many traps and notions in his little cutter, and why he don't tip over on some of the steep roofs which will cover our puzzled heads to-night." The writers finally decide that "our Mammas" might have something to do with Santa Claus.

The wit and humor column, headed by the picture of a man riding a pig and entitled "Telegrams per GREASED Lightning," contains a rather unfastidious item: "Weather exceedingly cold, clear and unpleasant—and we miss the balmy and *odorous* breath of Summer. Illinois Canal closed, but Alimentary Canals open and doing a brisk business. Ten thousand lives lost here yesterday—all hogs." There is a sweetly sorrowful poem "Written for the Budget" by somebody's "Auntie," school-day reminiscences by "The Old Boy," and a reprinting of Longfellow's poem from which they took their motto "Excelsior," "because it teaches a lesson which all of us boys and girls would do well to learn."

The *Budget* contains a "School Directory" and "Roll of Honor" for "Pupils distinguished for Punctuality—not Absent or Tardy a single haf day during the year." Tad is not among the seven on this list; he was frail and had frequent colds. But the Brown School period was a happy one for him, and it must have been almost as sad for him as it was for his mother when they had to give up the Washington Street home in the spring of 1867. Mrs. Lincoln rented it and moved to the Clifton House. But evidently both mother and son were homesick for the associations they had left, and in October they moved back to the Union Park neighborhood and boarded at D. Cole's, 460 West Washington Street. Mrs. Lincoln wrote Mrs. Keckley that here they were "very comfortably situated" with parlor and bedroom in a handsome house with "a very kind, good, *quiet* family, and their meals are excellent." The constant flitting around was anything but wholesome for Tad's education and it is difficult to follow all the various moves.

In the early summer of 1867 Robert and Tad saw Washington again. They and their mother were summoned to appear in the trial of John H. Surratt, son of the Mrs. Mary E. Surratt at whose boardinghouse in Washington the conspirators for Lincoln's assassination had met. John H. Surratt had escaped to Canada after Booth shot Lincoln and later went to Europe. When he returned to America, he was arrested and his trial before a civil court took place June 10 to August 10, 1867.

Mrs. Lincoln's health was in such a state she could not go, but Robert and Tad made the trip together and it must have meant much to them in its experiences and companionship. They had seen so little of Washington in peacetime; that itself may have made it seem strange as well as familiar. One imagines that Robert seized the opportunity to see that charming young lady Miss Mary Harlan.

It was July 5 when Tad was called to testify. At City Point he had seen that mysterious man who wanted to gain access to his father and who reluctantly had given his name as "Smith." The question had arisen as to whether "Smith" was really John H. Surratt. One can imagine that scene in the criminal court of the District of Columbia and the tall, thin lad of fourteen, who was beginning to look so much like his father, on the witness stand. He bore himself on that occasion like his father's son. The questions of Mr. Pierrepont and Tad's answers were recorded.

Q. You are a son of the late President Lincoln?
A. Yes, sir.
Q. Were you with your father down at City Point in March, 1865?
A. Yes, sir.
Q. Where were you—in a house or on a steamboat?
A. On a steamboat.
Q. Were you with him during the time he was there?
A. Yes, sir.
Q. Do you remember anybody coming to the steamer and asking to speak to him?
A. Yes, sir.
Q. What did the man say?
A. He said he would like to see the President.
(Question objected to . . . Objection overruled.)
Q. Did he tell you where he came from?
A. Yes; he said from Springfield.
Q. What further did he say?
A. He said he would like to see the President on particular business.
Q. State the mode of his saying it; whether he urged it.
A. Yes, sir; he wanted to see him "real bad."

Q. State whether he tried more than once to pass in where he was.

A. He tried twice, I believe.

Q. State whether they would allow him to see the President.

A. They would not.

Q. Do you see the man here who tried to see the President?
(Prisoner made to stand up.)

A. He looked very much like him.

Q. Like the prisoner?

A. Yes, sir.

Mr. Crook was at the trial also. He said "Smith" had been ragged and sunburned and Surratt looked like a sick man, pale and emaciated, so he could not be sure either whether they were the same. The identification was not established and nothing came of it. Ultimately the indictment against Surratt was dropped and he went free.

Mrs. Lincoln had gone to Racine, Wisconsin, while her sons were East, and they joined her there after the trip to Washington. The guardianship papers show receipts for board for Tad at Racine dated August 4 and August 14, and a letter of Robert's tells of his being there a short while. Mrs. Lincoln was considering placing Tad in an Episcopal institute for boys at Racine. A letter to a friend gives her description of the school and her thoughts on the matter. She liked its location on the lake but the institutional aspect of the place, "an air of *restraint*," as she put it, repelled her. So did the bare dormitories with "the little white cots of the boys, where they are wont, to repose so far away, from the loving Mothers, who would at any moment, give almost their life to see them." Her state of mind and indecision are made very plain in her letter. She realized that Tad was getting to an age when he needed influences that she could not give him, but she could not endure the thought of being separated from him. "I am *now* feeling the necessity for Taddie, being especially cared for and taught obedience by kind & gentle School treatment. . . ," she wrote. The Racine school was in session, but she added: "I had *not* made up my mind to send him to school this summer & I scarcely think I shall."

The conflict in Mrs. Lincoln's mind as to what to do about Tad appears in her letters that fall of 1867. The trouble was that Taddie, her baby, was growing up. He had never had a room to himself, she wrote Judge Davis, and now he must have, but she was worried about the cost of the extra room. Then she added: "It is impossible for me to separate myself from him." She wanted Tad, of course, to have the best of schooling: "His beloved father had he lived would have insisted upon Taddie receiving the advantage of an education," she wrote, "and with the knowledge that my boy has of his backwardness in his studies, he will most readily embrace the opportunities. I shall urge upon him to remain at school & college until he is *twenty one*. . . . I omitted to say, that it is my intention in the future not to be separated from Taddie for a day, going & remaining with him wherever he will be." Robert undoubtedly realized how unfair it was to his younger brother to be so closely tied to a mother who, while all affection, was physically and, to a certain degree, mentally ill and was lacking in balanced judgment.

Tad, after leaving the Brown School, ultimately was enrolled in the Chicago Academy at 218 Wabash Avenue, and receipts for tuition show he was there in the winter of 1867–1868 and through the spring term of 1868. In the guardianship papers there is a printed circular telling of the opening of this school in September 1867. It was coeducational and was divided into Preparatory, Academic, and Collegiate departments. On a blank page of this circular is listed in handwriting the cost of Tad's books: "Geography, 4th Reader, Spell book, Writing book, Book of Nature," and so on, all totaling $4.75. It has been said that the other students laughed at his speech impediment, as children in their teens would be likely to do. But Robert tried to help Tad in improving his speech.

The eldest son wrote Judge Davis early in 1868 that Tad was "learning very fast." He added that his mother had recently taken the boy to a dentist, "a very good one," to have his ill-shaped teeth corrected. The dentist "said that his teeth should be gradually forced into a proper position by means of a spring frame kept in his mouth." Robert found that this was distressing Tad very much: "He could hardly speak so as to be understood & to keep him talking in that way for a year I thought, with his present bad habit of speech, to be asking too much." Robert was looking out for Tad as much as he could and he did something about this intolerable situation: "I got the advice of another dentist, who said such an apparatus was not all necessary. I have stopped his using it & I have put him in charge of a man . . . who teaches Elecution telling him to make him pronounce correctly."

Both the Brown School and the Chicago Academy were coeducational. This made Tad aware that there were such things in the world as girls. Reminiscences of his being attracted to Mary Boone, daughter of Dr. Levi D. Boone, have been given by Mary's sister, Mrs. George B. Carpenter, who remembered Tad. The Boones lived on

Washington Street near State, and Tad came to their house and took Mary skating and to parties. Mrs. Carpenter thought he was in love with Mary. The Boone family regarded Tad as a very nice boy, much devoted to his mother, who was ill a great deal of the time. Mrs. Carpenter thought he looked very much like his father and added that he neither smoked, drank, nor danced. She remembered the imperfection in his speech as slight. Perhaps those elocution lessons Robert had arranged were helping.

Studies, skating, parties, and a girl are all items to show that Tad by 1868 was getting a normal education for a boy in his teens.

CHAPTER 18

For Robert Double Toil
and Trouble

THE PERIOD in Chicago from 1865 to 1868 was tolerable for Tad but not for Robert. For him it was a time of conflict and humiliation. Young as he was, he had to shoulder the responsibilities of the family and deal with his mother's manifestations of irrationality. It is not known how soon after the assassination Mrs. Lincoln frantically told him the secret her husband had never known: that her extravagant buying had left her with piled-up debts. She had bought wildly clothes, furs, jewels, and other things, and now that she was a widow and fallen from her high estate, bills were pouring in on her.

The situation was difficult enough without that dreadful complication. Robert had to finish his law studies before he could be admitted to the bar and become self-supporting; funds were limited at best; and here were thousands of dollars to pay, and pay in secret so as not to disclose his mother's irrational behavior. With complete integrity mother and son began their efforts to pay these debts. This effort shadowed those years in Chicago for both of them. Mrs. Lincoln tried penny-pinching economies, going without dinners, living in cheap quarters, and pawning and selling her belongings. Finally she was to make an unfortunate effort whose consequences seared Robert's soul.

The painful duties all fell to Robert. In December 1865 he took his mother to Springfield for the occasion when his father's body was transferred from the receiving vault into a new one. For Mrs. Lincoln it was a renewing of her three great sorrows. Someone the week before had gone to Hutchinson's Cemetery to get Eddie's little casket. Mary Lincoln looked on the place where her dead husband and two sons were lying and longed passionately, she said, for the time when she would lie beside them. There were niches for Robert and Tad also, but Robert would never lie there with the rest of the family. Mrs. Lincoln wrote Mrs. Welles that she was ill for days after the experience and "too miserable to live." It was also a terrible ordeal for Robert, who was deeply grieved in the year following his father's death. "Poor Robert, has borne his sorrows, manfully," wrote his mother, "yet with a broken heart."

His sorrow and also his loyal friendship and sympathy appear in a letter he wrote to Mrs. Henry when her husband, Dr. Anson G. Henry, beloved friend of the Lincolns, died in 1865. Robert, like his father and mother, would go to great pains to help a friend and he was trying to assist the widow in straightening out a problem. He told her to send "papers to her friends in Congress" and said encouragingly: "I *confidently* hope that we will be successful." He continued: "I can say nothing, my dear Mrs. Henry, of your terrible loss —We can easily feel that our own affliction enables us to sympathize with you most sincerely and deeply. The friendship of the Doctor for us in our distress we shall never forget, and I trust that my efforts to prove it will not be unavailing. My mother sends her love to you." It is a most understanding letter for a young man of twenty-two.

When the year 1866 came in, Robert, to use his mother's words, was still "diligently applying himself, to his law studies" in the office of Scammon, McCagg and Fuller. He did take a brief vacation that fall, going on what he called "the Pacific R. R. Excursion to the plains," but he was working hard and he had his plans. That his mind already had turned to building up a fortune is evident in a letter he wrote Judge Davis in February 1866 in which he spoke of investing in some land ten miles from Chicago. "If the property is what it is said to be," he wrote, "I have no doubt I could realize a handsome profit on it in a short time." He asked Davis for the required amount, three thousand dollars, which perhaps was to be taken from his third of his father's estate, as Robert was frequently mentioning being short of funds at this time. Judge Davis advised against buying the land and Robert accepted his judgment without question.

He was devoted to Judge Davis. He himself said: "Upon my father's death I went to Judge Davis as a second father, and this he was to me. . . ." This fact makes his letters to the judge more valuable in personal information than most. In August he wrote Davis asking if it was all right to let William H. Herndon, his father's former junior law partner, see the box of papers his father had left at C. M. Smith's, papers referring to the senatorial campaign of 1858. Herndon now was collecting material for a biography of Abraham Lincoln and had asked to see them. Robert was willing that he should, if Judge Davis approved; his attitude toward Herndon was friendly and co-operative at this time.

But this attitude soon had reason to change. In the fall of 1866 occurred the first of a number of episodes in which Lincoln's eldest son endeavored to protect his father's memory from untruth. Through life he would try to do this in outstanding cases of injustice but not in minor ones. He wrote about this time, with a touch of the aloofness which was to grow with the years: "Even when I differ with anyone in his views of my father's character &c., unless it were something flagrantly wrong, I would not discuss the subject." In this case the protection was more for his anguished mother. On November 16 Herndon gave in Springfield a public lecture in which he proclaimed that Abraham Lincoln in his youth had loved a girl named Ann Rutledge who died, that his heart had been buried in her grave, and that he had never loved the woman he married, the mother of his four sons. The cruelty of this to Lincoln's grieving and broken widow living in Chicago at the time hardly can be estimated.

Robert's reaction to the lecture is given in his letter to Judge Davis three days later: "Mr Wm H. Herndon is making an ass of himself in his lectures. One he delivered a short time ago is worthy of the 'N.Y. Ledger' and I am getting seriously annoyed at his way of doing things. If you have seen his lecture on 'Abraham Lincoln & Ann Rutledge,' I have no doubt you will feel the impropriety of such a publication even if it were, which I much doubt, all true."

Robert had no way of checking (as historians now have had) by study of the evidence the truth or falsity of the story of the romance. His mother had never heard the name of Ann Rutledge before and he had reason to know the idea that his father had never loved his mother was completely false. He knew too the peculiar characteristics of Herndon. He was a roughhewn, peculiar individual, known in Springfield as a drunkard, who had dabbled a little in the New England transcendentalism of the time. From this he had picked up the idea of the transcendentalists that if one would understand the motives of others, he should look into his own soul, where the same motives prevail. From this idea Herndon progressed to a fixed belief that he himself was clairvoyant, that he could read people's minds, and that he knew what was true by his own power of intuition. The lecture showed his curious method of psychoanalysis, that is, reasoning out "by the lines of human conduct" what should be true. Robert had the right adjective for Herndon's mental processes as he continued his letter to Davis: "His reflections, which make up a large portion, would be very ludicrous if I did not feel strongly that he speaks with a certain amount of Authority from having known my father so long." Robert foresaw what actually did happen; people away from Springfield thought that Lincoln's former law partner (to whom he had never confided personal matters) ought to know the facts. The young man needed Davis's advice. Almost anyone in Springfield would have hesitated to take issue with the garrulous and quickly abusive Herndon, who had such strange mental quirks. "Do you think it would be advisable to write him?" continued the letter. "He is such a singular character that I am afraid of making matters worse, but I think something ought to be done to stop his present course."

Careful study of Herndon's papers in recent years has shown that his starting points in the alleged Lincoln-Rutledge romance were two known facts: Ann was engaged to a friend of the young Lincoln in New Salem, John McNamar—he knew them both very well—and Lincoln grieved when Ann died. There was a posthumous conjecture after her death that if Lincoln grieved, he must have been in love with her. No contemporary evidence of any Lincoln-Rutledge romance exists and historians have shown that it is not authentic history.

Probably Judge Davis advised Robert to go to Springfield and talk to Herndon; at all events, that is what he did, making a personal appeal and being careful not to accuse Herndon of bad motives. After he left, Herndon wrote him what must have been a conciliatory letter and Robert answered in the same tone but driving home his points. Referring to their recent conversation he wrote: "As I said then, I have never had any doubt of your good intentions but inasmuch as the construction put upon your language by everyone who has mentioned the subject to me was so entirely different from your own, I felt justified in asking you to change your expression. Beyond this, I do not wish, nor have I any right, to go. Your opinion may not agree with mine but that is not my affair." Robert's main object, of course, was to protect his ailing mother, to whose overwhelming grief was now added the mortification of the public's saying that her husband had never loved her. He continued: "All I ask is that nothing may be published by you, which after *careful consideration* will seem apt to cause pain to my father's family, which I am sure you do not wish to do."

Robert was controlling his feelings and his language very well under exasperating circumstances. But with Herndon's peculiar slants, his violent antagonism toward Mrs. Lincoln, and his continuing work on the life of Abraham Lincoln, a break between the two was inevitable. A request which Robert made of Herndon the day after sending the above letter unintentionally increased hard feeling on both sides. Robert asked that a certain book that had belonged to his father and had been left in the Lincoln-Herndon law office should be sent to Chicago, as he wished to give it to Dr. James Smith, an old friend of the family. The book did not come, but a letter of explanation from Herndon did, and in this letter he made some inquiries about President Lincoln's religion. Being a freethinker and scoffer at Christianity himself—an infidel, as they called him in Springfield—Herndon was trying to collect material for his later effort to prove that Lincoln had also been an unbeliever. He evidently revealed some of his plans for the biography and Robert had reason to be alarmed. Robert's answer is given at some length because it is the keynote of his attitude later both as to his withholding personal information and as to his abnormal shrinking from publicity.

"I *infer* from your letter," wrote Robert, "but I hope it is not so, that it is your purpose to make some considerable mention of my mother in your work—I say I hope it is not so, because in the first place it would not be pleasant for her or for any woman, to be made public property of in that way—" Here was the old idea that it was "indelicate" to put any personal information about a woman in print; she must remain cloistered in woman's sphere. Robert's letter continued: "With a man it is very different, for he lives out in the world and is used to being talked of—" Then followed what was one of the fundamental reasons Robert later did not wish a political career: "One of the unpleasantest consequences of political success is that however little it may have to do with that success, his whole private life is exposed to the public gaze—that is part of the price he pays. But I see no reason why his wife and children should be included—especially while they are alive—I think no sensible man would live in a glass house, and I think he ought not to be compelled to do so against his will. I feel very keenly on this subject, for the annoyance I am subjected to sometimes is nearly intolerable."

"Intolerable" is exactly what publicity was to Robert's innate shyness and reserve. He was also the burnt child dreading fire: he knew what awful abuse and misrepresentation had poured in upon his father and mother in the White House. His attitude was to deprive the public of personal information he could have given about his parents, himself and his own family, and result in his being thought snobbish and aloof.

In the next sentence of his letter Robert returned to his plea that his mother be left out of Herndon's work. "I hope you will consider this matter carefully, my dear Mr. Herndon, for once done there is no undoing." He signed himself "Sincerely your friend."

The difficulty about the book becomes clear in a letter Robert wrote years later. Herndon, assuming that everything left in the law office was his, had evidently disposed of the book. Robert wrote that after his father's death Judge Davis, in preparing his probate inventory, "enquired of Herndon as to the office property and was told by him, falsely as we both believed, that my father had made him a present of all the contents of the office, as he was starting for Washington." Both Robert and the judge believed Herndon was lying, but in justice to him it should be stated that he was not a deliberate liar, though he said much that was untrue. Herndon doubtless interpreted something Lincoln had said to him as meaning he was to have the office property. The man who believes he knows the truth by his own power of intuition usually ends by believing what he wants to believe. Robert wrote Herndon courteously that it was "all right" about the book and no issue was made as to the office property.

The dispute about the Ann Rutledge lecture was the first incident in a conflict with Herndon that would embitter Robert's existence for a long time. Nearly a quarter of a century later he would be tortured with resentment over Herndon's false statements and misrepresentations about his father and especially about his mother in the Herndon biography of Lincoln.

Early in the year 1867 Robert became a full-fledged lawyer. He was admitted to the bar of Illinois on February 25 and a new law firm was formed. At the top of Robert's letters then appeared this letterhead: "Law Office of Scammon & Lincoln, No. 1 Marine Bank Building, Chicago." Robert's senior partner was Charles T. Scammon, son of Jonathan Young Scammon of the firm in whose office he had studied law. By September of that year Robert was to write Judge Davis: "My business as it is running now, does not fall far short of supporting me. . . ." That meant everything to the young man whose thoughts were concerned with getting married and who had made a trip in July to Washington, where Mary Harlan lived.

In his new situation, however, there was a rather large fly in the ointment. On July 29 he was writing the judge: "My partner has been on a succession of 'sprees' since early in May & is now I believe under treatment in the East." Robert said he felt strongly disposed to "cut loose from him regardless of pecuniary consequences. . . . As I *may* have a good income and dislike personal trouble I am in a quandary." Robert was thoroughly disgusted with his partner and continued: "I cannot tell to what extent his debauches damage me personally. I suppose my experience is that of most men, sometimes smooth and sometimes rough sailing—though I think I have too much of the rough."

By the first of August Robert had made up his mind: "I shall discontinue my connection with the young man, as I find that his course is injuring me. . . . I hope & think that I will work my way out of the trouble with no great damage." However, when his partner returned from treatment some months later, Robert wrote that he was "apparently all right & I hope will remain so." In the end the partnership lasted for several years.

In mid-September a visiting clergyman from England, the Reverend Newman Hall, who was a great admirer of President Lincoln, visited the new lawyer at his office "up a long flight of stairs." Mr. Hall found Robert "modest, quiet, and utterly unassuming." "No one seemed to regard him as possessing any rank, by reason of his father having been President," continued the visitor with his English viewpoint, "nor did he so regard himself. He laughed heartily at a joke of ours about his being called 'His Royal Highness the Prince Robert.' . . . He said he always knew he must get his own living."

The conversation naturally turned to Robert's going into law. The young man told him, said Mr. Hall, "He had been from the first brought up for the law, and he had not allowed his studies to be interrupted a single day by his father being President. The only pause had been when, like other young men, he had served in the army, volunteering as a private." The last phrase is full of interest; if Mr. Hall understood correctly, the procuring of a captain's commission was none of Robert's doing. Whether Mr. Hall was strictly accurate or not, the point that Robert never traded on his father's position is borne out by ample evidence throughout his life. He never had his picture taken in his captain's uniform, which may or may not be significant.

Robert's sense of humor seems to have included appreciation of tall tales. He told the clergyman one about the Far West plains which he had visited the year before. A man out there, he related, was attacked by Indians, shammed dead, and was scalped. Through half-closed eyes the victim watched the Indian go off and saw him accidentally drop the scalp. The scalpee then crept forward to reclaim what was undoubtedly his personal property, put it back on his head, and recovered!

If Robert had known the enterprise his mother was entering upon at the very time he was laughing with Mr. Hall, his laughter would have ceased abruptly. Driven by the necessity of paying her debts and meeting expenses, and even more by her fixed idea that she was destitute, Mrs. Lincoln had decided to sell the costly clothes and jewels she had bought during the Presidency. She would wear black the rest of her life and live in seclusion, so she had no need of them and she desperately wanted funds. Her scores of letters written in this Chicago period are dominated by her efforts to raise money in various ways. She felt that Congress should give her a pension and was embarrassing Robert by writing numerous people about that. It was common at this time to take up subscriptions for or present a handsome home to a national hero, and Mrs. Lincoln, believing that her husband had done more for his country than anyone, was convinced that the public should take care of her and her sons in some such way. Meanwhile, she would sell her clothes.

She went to New York the middle of September, 1867, where Mrs. Keckley joined her to aid in the project. Using the name Mrs. Clarke to conceal her identity, this shortsighted woman arranged with W. H. Brady, commission broker at 609 Broadway, to sell her articles, which were shortly put on exhibition at this address. Of course the brokers soon discovered that Mrs. Clarke was the much-talked-of Mrs. Abraham Lincoln and set out to get all the publicity and advertising they could. Mrs. Lincoln knew many public men in New York and in her distorted thinking she was convinced that those politicians who had received appointments in her husband's administration ought to assist her financially.

She wrote letters to the brokers expressing this idea and expanding on her *"urgent necessity"* for "means of subsistence." She did this at the prompting of the brokers, who said they would show these letters to prominent Republicans to induce them to buy the articles on sale. It was not long before these letters were published in the *New York World* and a terrific furor resulted. The politicians, dismayed at having this unpredictable woman trying to get financial help from them, retaliated by giving out statements discrediting Mrs. Lincoln. The old-clothes scandal, gathering momentum as it went, swept the country.

Mrs. Lincoln, panic-stricken at the antagonistic forces she had set in motion, fled back to Chicago, leaving Mrs. Keckley to continue negotiations. On the train she saw a man reading her letters in a newspaper and heard conversation about herself. At the end of the trip the one bright gleam, as always, was furnished by her youngest son. "At the depot my darling little Taddie was waiting for me," she wrote, "and his voice never sounded so sweet."

Robert was almost frantic. His mother wrote Mrs. Keckley just after her return: "R. came up last evening like a maniac, and almost threatening his life, looking like death, because the letters of the *World* were published in yesterday's paper. I could not refrain from weeping when I saw him so miserable." Her mother feeling responded to Robert's suffering, but she could see only her own point of view that she was justified in what she had done. "Only my darling Taddie prevents my taking my life," she told Mrs. Keckley. "I shall have to endure a round of newspaper abuse from the Republicans because I dared venture to relieve a few of my wants."

To Robert the scandal was unendurable. With his temperament his mother's irrationality was almost a crucifixion in the end. What would it do to the reputation of a rising young lawyer to have his mother the target of such abuse and misrepresentation? If she was in such want as she said she was, it was a reflection on him; it looked as if he was not taking care of her. The affair put him in a false position, for no one could have been more conscientious than he had been in doing his duty to his mother. Some newspapers said she was deranged and Robert himself was quoted as saying his only explanation of his mother's selling her clothes was that she was insane.

He perhaps did imply something to that effect, as by now he fully realized the bitter truth that his mother was mentally ill. Mental illness was not well understood at that time and was often considered a disgrace. What would be the effect of all this scandal on Mary Harlan, the girl he was to marry a year later and to whom he presumably was now engaged?

On October 16 Robert wrote Mary Harlan an admirably straightforward letter telling her the exact nature of his mother's irrationality and warning her that there would be future trouble because of it. "I suppose you have seen some of the papers so there is no need of detailing what I was told they were full of," he said. "I did not read them." Robert here was following the attitude of his father, who avoided reading newspaper abuse of himself. "The simple truth, which I cannot tell to anyone not personally interested, is that my mother is on one subject not mentally responsible." Robert went on to say that he had suspected this for some time and had asked the advice of one or two trusted friends, who told him he could do nothing. (Mrs. Lincoln was normal and highly intelligent on subjects other than money.) He said he found it "terribly irksome" to sit still and say nothing, but it had to be done. His letter continued: "The greatest misery of all is the fear of what may happen in the future. . . . I have no doubt that a great many good and amiable people wonder why I do not take charge of her affairs and keep them straight but it is very hard to deal with one who is sane on all subjects but one." Mrs. Lincoln was willful and probably still had the attitude that Robert was a mere child; he could not take control. Something of his great difficulty appeared in his next statement: "You could hardly believe it possible, but my mother protests to me that she is in actual want and nothing I can do or say will convince her to the contrary." It was a hard letter to write and it is good to know that it went to a young woman whose understanding and affection are reflected in Mrs. Lincoln's own love for Mary Harlan.

Robert was guarded now in dealing with his mother, as one has to be with an abnormal person, but it was impossible for him to agree with her distorted views and efforts to raise money. She, of course, resented this. She had no idea she was irrational in any way and his attitude offended her. By November 9 she was writing Mrs. Keckley complaints about her eldest son: "R. is very spiteful at present, and I think hurries up the division [of his father's estate] to cross my purposes." Robert perhaps hoped that after the estate was settled, she would give up her continual efforts for public subscriptions, a pension from Congress, and other schemes for raising funds. His mother's letter continued: "He mentioned yesterday that he was going to the Rocky Mountains so soon as Edgar Welles joined him." She added that Robert "is very *deep*." She and her eldest son had never understood each other and now her irrationality was pushing them inevitably into a situation that was to be unspeakably tragic for both.

By November 21 Mrs. Lincoln was welcoming the thought that Robert would be "out of the way" for a time. "R. and a party of young men leave for the Rocky Mountains next Monday, to be absent three weeks." Mrs. Lincoln's clothes were still in the hands of the brokers, who now had a scheme for sending out some circulars, and she wanted Robert at a distance when those circulars appeared.

The brokers, who were getting tremendous publicity, kept the affair before the public eye. Early in 1868 Mrs. Keckley wrote Mrs. Lincoln of a proposition to exhibit certain clothes of hers in Europe. By this time Mrs. Lincoln realized she was being used and would not make money from the clothes, and the adverse publicity was wrecking her. The idea of any of her clothes being "paraded in Europe" almost turned her wild, she wrote. "R. would go *raving distracted* if such a thing were done." She implored Mrs. Keckley to head off such a move and to get her clothes back as soon as possible. "R. would blast us all if you were to have this project carried out." The bulk of the clothes was ultimately returned to Mrs. Lincoln, and she had to pay over eight hundred dollars to the commission brokers.

Burdened as he already was, Robert was ready to assume another obligation late in 1867. He was then, and always, generous toward his kin when they were in need. He had made a trip to Springfield and found that his aunt Fannie Wallace and her family were in straitened circumstances following the death of his uncle William Wallace the summer before. Robert wrote Judge Davis: "It occurred to me it would be a good thing if they could have our house there. My mother yesterday suggested the same thing." The difficulty was that part of Tad's income from the estate was fifty dollars a year from that house. Robert told Judge Davis he could not afford to assume taxes and insurance and the fifty dollars, but if Davis could arrange for the taxes and insurance to be paid, he said, "I think I could stand enough to make your report good." Mrs. Wallace thought the house too large, however, and Robert later reported to the judge: ". . . we are going to make different arrangements from those I spoke of to you, so as to benefit her."

If public gossip about the old-clothes episode and Mrs. Lincoln had subsided by the spring of 1868, it was not allowed to remain quiet. That spring a small volume called *Behind the Scenes* was published over the name of Elizabeth Keckley, though she undoubtedly had the help of an interested ghost writer or ghost writers. In this book Mrs. Keckley told of the domestic life of the Lincolns in the White House which she had seen as Mrs. Lincoln's seamstress, maid, and companion. Though it was written in compassionate terms and with good intentions, it laid bare Mrs. Lincoln's weaknesses in full detail. Mrs. Keckley reported conversations between President Lincoln and his wife and gave other intimate details that to Robert's strict sense of propriety must have seemed like disrobing the whole family in public.

The book gave an elaborate account of the clothes-selling scandal and printed Mrs. Lincoln's letters to Mrs. Keckley on the subject, the very letters which have just been quoted, in which Robert's mother in her emotional distress and disordered thinking used such terms about him as "like a maniac," "spiteful," and *"raving distracted."* It repeated his somewhat supercilious remark at the enter-

tainment for General and Mrs. Tom Thumb, calling him "a lofty
soul," which he probably was at that stage of his college-boy development.

Behind the Scenes attracted a great deal of attention. To the thin-
skinned Robert the knowledge that many people were reading all
these private and personal matters about himself and his family must
have been a burning agony. Again he naturally would wonder how
much it would damage his beginning career and what effect it
would have on the girl he was planning to marry.

In the Keckley book there was a full exposé of the debts contracted
by Mrs. Lincoln and of her reasoning that Republicans who had
fared well during the Lincoln administration ought to help her pay
them. Robert and his mother had been trying to pay the debts in
secret, as much as they could. There were so many painful facets
to that problem for the eldest son. The matter of the debts became
known to his future father-in-law, James Harlan, who could not go
along with Mrs. Lincoln's irrational attitudes. She resented this and
was soon writing such comments as: "Mr. Harlan, has acted in the
most contemptible way!"

Ultimately the debts were paid, as Mrs. Lincoln said, "to the utmost farthing." There is some indication that prominent politicians
may have helped out for fear of the affair's injuring the Republican
party, but Mrs. Lincoln wrote in 1870 that she and Robert had paid
most of them themselves so that it could not be said that President
Lincoln had left unpaid debts. Robert had risen to meet this obligation with the integrity that was always to be his.

By the end of 1868 Robert had developed, with reason, a morbid
fear of giving out any personal information; he was permanently
scarred by what he had passed through. He had learned through the
bitter experience of his family that any item, however innocent,
could be twisted into something discreditable and that accusations
could be made up of whole cloth. Even while he was struggling to
complete his law studies and pay his mother's debts, detailed items
had appeared in the papers, as he wrote Judge Davis, crediting him
and Tad with having large private fortunes.

To make Robert's feeling stronger in that same year of 1868 Mary
Harlan's father was the target of vicious political mudslinging. The
girl whom Robert was to marry had been trained, like himself, in
Victorian standards of reticence and propriety, and her family too
was being seared by the fires of public abuse. These two would sus-
pect and fear the seeking of any personal information.

In June of 1868 Tad had a visit to Springfield with his mother. In her behalf he presented to Jesse K. Dubois, Mr. Lincoln's former close friend and an esteemed citizen, a beautiful cane which had belonged to his father. Once more Tad walked the familiar small-town streets, still deep in mud or dust, saw his former playmates, and visited uncles, aunts, and cousins, all doubtless a great pleasure to his responsive and affectionate heart.

A new experience was looming up for Tad; a voyage across the ocean lay ahead for him. His mother had been considering taking him abroad to continue his education in Germany, where she thought they could live more cheaply. The public criticism she had been receiving recently crystallized her intention; she could stand what she called the "persecution from the vampyre press" no longer. She could escape public notice abroad. Also her physician had advised an entire change of air and scene for one in such bad health.

She and Tad were in the East that summer of 1868, spending some time at Cresson and Altoona, Pennsylvania. Robert also journeyed East that spring, to Washington, where Mary Harlan lived. They were planning to be married in September. Mrs. Lincoln was anxious to sail as soon as possible, but in August she wrote a friend: ". . . I am peculiarly situated, being exceedingly anxious to witness the marriage of my son—with a young lady, who is so charming & whom I love so much." Robert's mother had been a recluse now for three years and dreaded any public notice, so she continued: "The terror of having to proceed to *Washington* to witness it, almost overpowers me." But Tad wished it: "My little son is so anxious to remain, until that event takes place & perhaps the regret I may also feel in the future that I had not gratified them all by remaining, has quite determined me." She and Robert could clash, as two high-strung people with strong opinions and tempers are likely to, but usually she humored Tad.

Yet she appreciated the fineness of Robert's attitude, even though she would lash out at him in disparaging terms when she was angry. She wrote Jesse K. Dubois from Cresson in July: "Robert, grows every day, more & more like his father, & is a beautiful character." It was a deserved tribute to his conduct in those three bitter years after his father's death.

At the time she wrote this her eldest son, she said, was in Washington and was planning to meet her and Tad in Baltimore. The two brothers loved each other very much, and it is pleasant to think of all the friends who would be so happy to see Tad again when he arrived in Washington, friends who would exclaim at his tallness and marvel at the change in the mischievous sprite they remembered.

On the evening of September 24, 1868, Robert Todd Lincoln and Mary Eunice Harlan were united in marriage at the Washington home of the bride's father, Senator Harlan. Bishop Matthew Simpson of the Methodist Church, who had been a valued friend of President Lincoln's, performed the ceremony. Only close friends, which included some prominent officials, and relatives were present. The spacious parlors were "elegantly" decorated with flowers formed in pyramids and bouquets. The bride wore a rich white silk trimmed in satin folds and from orange blossoms in her hair fell a flowing veil of "illusion." Her ornaments were pearls. There is no doubt that Mary Harlan was beautiful, and the groom was described as looking the very personification of joy. His mother wore deep mourning unrelieved by jewelry or ornament of any kind. Though the accounts do not mention it, Tad perhaps wore a white vest, as the guardianship records show he bought one in August.

Secretary Welles recorded the event in his diary the next day, mentioning that Robert had made the Welles house his home during the courtship. So that is where he had stayed on those frequent trips from Chicago to Washington. Welles, speaking in his restrained way of his high regard for President Lincoln, wrote in his diary: "I also highly esteem and respect Robert himself and have done so from our first acquaintance in 1861, when he was here with his father at the inauguration. His deportment and character, then and always, impressed me favorably."

Tad remained in Washington for most of the week following the wedding, but Mrs. Lincoln fled from its memories back to Baltimore. Certain comments in letters to her dear friend Mrs. Felician Slatafer at this time indicate that the youngest son was raising some objections to her plans for their departure on October 1 on the *City of Baltimore*. She mentioned him as appearing "a little obstinate and inclined to be argumentative on the subject" and when the sailing date was almost at hand she wrote: "Poor child, he doubtless feels like a victim." Tad apparently did not want to leave Robert and his loved new sister-in-law and one suspects they agreed with him in his opposition to this exile.

Robert's mother leaves no doubt as to the happiness of his marriage and her own great tenderness for her daughter-in-law. A year later she was to write of Mary Harlan Lincoln: "She is so innocent & lovely in character, my son is greatly blessed in so sweet a young wife—and she writes me that she never imagined *such* devotion, as she receives from him." To another friend Mrs. Lincoln said that same year: "My son & his wife write that they are *more* in love, with each other than ever." The daughter-in-law was faithful in writing affectionate letters, calling Mrs. Lincoln "Dear Mother."

Robert's period of great trial was followed by one of tenderness and affection. He was to owe much to this harmonious union and was to be a most devoted husband.

C H A P T E R 19

Tad Goes on a Long Journey

TAD AND his mother sailed from New York for Europe on October 1, 1868. It would be two and a half years before they returned; Tad would have three birthdays, his sixteenth, seventeenth, and eighteenth, on foreign soil. Probably the first thing he did on the voyage was to make a minute investigation of the machinery and workings of the ocean-going *City of Baltimore*, just as he had of that boat of the inland waterways, the *River Queen*. And of course he made friends of everyone on board.

Tad's interest in travel and new things and his gift for friendship were to be doubly valuable to him now that he was removed from his brother and all the people and places he knew and loved. Judge Davis is said to have disapproved of Mrs. Lincoln's taking Tad abroad to educate him, and Robert, loving Tad, must have had grave misgivings and a heavy heart about it. Both men knew Mrs. Lincoln's weaknesses. Whether anyone considered the unwisdom of taking a frail, thin lad like Tad, one so subject to illnesses, to a severe climate and scanty heating is not known.

Mother and son, on arrival abroad, went to Frankfurt am Main, Germany, where Tad was placed in a boarding school, the "Institute" of Dr. Hohagen at Number 17 Kettenhofstrasse. It was a school for German and English boys with an excellent reputation for good teachers. A gentleman whom they had met on the *City of Baltimore*, a former army chaplain named F. W. Bogen, assisted them in the journey to Frankfurt and called to see Tad frequently in the first months and thought he was "very fortunately" situated.

Judge Davis's objection to the sojourn abroad may have been due partly to his realization of how it would complicate his guardianship of Tad. Owing to the necessity of paying bills in a foreign currency, the slowness and unreliability of the mails, the shortness of ready funds, and the legal demands of a guardianship, there were to be many letters, dealing with financial tangles, going back and forth across the ocean. In December Mrs. Lincoln wrote Judge Davis saying that Tad was well settled in the school and asking him to see Robert about forwarding the money to Dr. Hohagen for Taddie's first quarter.

Incidentally, her letter shows that Robert continued to be interested in investments. She told Judge Davis in confidence that Robert wanted to borrow "my 1881 bonds, to be converted into money" and used in a real-estate venture. She said she had at first agreed, then sent a message telling him not to use the bonds. She was quite upset over the incident. "With my great love for my good son, the necessity of refusing his request has made me quite ill." The investment was probably a good one, as Robert was destined to become a shrewd businessman and his taste for business was already showing up.

Mrs. Lincoln's letter was written from the Hotel d'Angleterre in Frankfurt, where she was living in a single room to be near Tad. She had thought living would be cheaper abroad, but she was soon disabused of that idea. People believed the widow of the President of the United States to have a great deal of money and charged accordingly. Before long she would seek cheaper and uncomfortable lodgings.

The receipted bills for Tad's expenses, which she was constantly sending to Judge Davis as guardian, show she was not economizing on Tad. With his mother Tad could always have what he wished, and the guardianship records create some interesting pictures of what he was getting and of his life at Frankfurt.

There are several bills from "Heinrich Best junior, Herren-Kleidermacher," mentioning items like striped brown trousers, suit, and overcoat, and charges for work done on trousers Tad already had, probably lengthening them, as the tall lad seemed to be aiming at his father's lofty height. The bills were paid in florins. After the first year Tad had to have "1 silk hat." Tad seems to have become aware of personal appearance in his middle teens; charges for "warm baths," haircuttings, soaps, oils, and "pomatum" constantly recur. The amount of pomatum bought seems amazing. Possibly his dark hair, like his father's, was unruly and the ointment served to slick it down as well as to give it gloss.

He was rooming and boarding at the school, as many receipted bills show. It is possible to follow his outfitting for Dr. Hohagen's when he entered the school in late October. He had to have German, French, and English grammars. Tad's use of his native tongue in the White House indicates that an English grammar was not beside the mark. He was to learn in Germany not only to speak English correctly but also to overcome his speech impediment. Robert later explained that this was done "by reading aloud as a regular exercise . . . under a German (English speaking) tutor," and while Tad mastered perfect articulation he also acquired the "slight German accent" of his teacher! Before he left Germany, according to Robert, he was "speaking German perfectly." But it was probably difficult and lonely for him at Dr. Hohagen's at first.

It is possible that the one who helped him in his speech difficulty was the special English professor engaged by his mother to give him private lessons, as shown by the receipted bills. One surmises that again Tad had a man to look after him especially and perhaps even take trips with him, when he did not go with his mother. One item, "note of the english professor," arouses the suspicion that Tad on some occasion had to borrow money from him.

The records show that Tad was studying drawing that first winter in Germany and was taking dancing lessons, also that he was attending an English church and contributing to it. After the initial homesickness and strangeness wore off and he began to understand German, there were many things to interest him. And always there was the warmth and affection of his visits with his mother, visits in which they could talk of things at home, of brother Bob and his nice wife and by and by of the baby they were going to have.

To Mrs. Lincoln these visits were the only oases in the desert of her lonely existence. Though she was at home in the French language, she knew no German and this fact made her isolation even more complete. As she wrote a friend: ". . . the young life of my Taddie, is all that makes life endurable to me—" She was exchanging letters of deep affection with Robert and his wife, but it was the giving and receiving of affection with Tad that she lived upon. With infinite tact and understanding the boy rose to her need of him. She called him in those years at Frankfurt, "My bright little comforter, Taddie."

For reasons of economy she left the Hotel d'Angleterre and took a room in a cheap boardinghouse. A friend who visited her the second year in Frankfurt described the quarters in which she found her: "a small cheerless desolate looking room with but one window—two chairs and a wooden table with a solitary candle," at the back of the fourth floor. Mrs. Lincoln told her friend that she could not afford anyone to nurse her when she was ill, as she frequently was, and that Tad left his school at these times and came to take care of her.

Writing this same friend about her various illnesses, Tad's mother drew an unforgettable picture of the gentle lad in the role of nurse.

"My very affectionate young son, is almost continually by my bed-side," ran one letter. He gave her "loving & tender treatment" at all times, she continued, and very especially when she was indisposed. She was seriously ill during the second Christmas in Frankfurt and wrote when she had not yet recovered. The doctor, she said, "has directed me to wear flannel next my skin—and dear careful Taddie has just brought me in, some soft *woollen* ones—Taddie, is like some *old woman,* with regard to his care of me—and two or three days since—when I was *so very* sick—his dark loving eyes—watching over me, reminded me so much of his dearly beloved father's—so filled with *his* deep love."

Mrs. Lincoln had come to Germany in the hope of improving her ill health, but harsh weather and lack of adequate heating resulted in many respiratory infections. The same was true with Tad. The guardianship records show bills for doctors, medicines, and prescriptions for him and very frequently an item which tells of shivering in a frigid room, "extra fuel." But along with discomforts there were many pleasures normal to a boy in his teens.

A bill for "1 pair skates" suggests the thrill of young legs gliding over the ice. Doubtless too Tad had the snow that he had loved in Illinois and missed in Washington. Awakening interests are suggested in the fact that he bought "1 Irving, life of Columbus (bound)." Knowing his love of animals, one can guess the pleasure afforded by "1 ticket for the Zool. garden." He also went to at least "2 cycloramas" and he was well provided with "Pocket money" and "candy." There were many "excursions" and wonderful trips during the various holidays.

All the excitement and thrills that come with foreign travel were Tad's. The records show that he bought an "atlas," that delightful prelude to travel, and he and his mother visited many famous places in Europe. There are bills that show the names Baden, Heidelberg, the Black Forest, the Tyrol, and the Palatinate. Mother and son walked together through quaint foreign streets looking at buildings and sculpture bearing the dates of long-past centuries; they saw, as Mrs. Lincoln put it, all the things that "appear very strange to *fresh American* eyes." She gave excellent descriptions of some of their travels in her letters.

During Tad's summer vacation in 1869 they spent seven weeks in Scotland, traveling incognito. With Mrs. Lincoln, as with Robert, any public notice had become a thing of fear, and the name "Lincoln" was not used on this trip. They went so far north, she said, that "daylight does not entirely cease until 11 P.M. and morning light breaks in upon us at 3 a.m." They visited Edinburgh, "a beautiful city," and went through the Rob Roy country and delighted in the lovely "lochs" and great mountains. Tad's father had loved especially the poetry of Robert Burns, so they made a reverent pilgrimage to Burns's birthplace "& sighed over poor 'Highland Mary's' grave." Their greatest thrill, continued Mrs. Lincoln, was when they "went down into the deep & entered 'Fingal's Cave,' not equal to our Niagara—yet it is *wonderful*." There in that "vaulted region" she and Tad heard the "old hundred" sung by a great crowd of people, Tad's young voice perhaps joining in. The glowing letter continued: "At Oban, we visited the ruined castle where the *first* . . . kings of Scotland lived— a most interesting spot." Tad was learning geography and history in a very pleasant way. There was the added pleasure of seeing a loved old friend in Scotland, Dr. James Smith, who had been the pastor of the Lincolns when Tad was born and was doubtless the one who baptized him. Dr. Smith probably marveled at the tallness of the lad he had known as a baby and noticed how he now resembled his father.

Mrs. Lincoln's enthusiastic accounts show that in travel her natural buoyancy and responsiveness revived and the two had fun together. It is possible to get quite a picture of this pair of enthusiastic travelers from her letter to Robert's wife in May 1870. Mother and son had just returned from a glorious holiday which she described: "At Heidelburg we ascended the mountain one morning about nine o'clock roamed through the ruins of the magnificent old castle and took our breakfast in the grounds where there is a very fine restaurant." A German breakfast on a storied mountain with the appetizer of bracing air and vigorous climb is something to be envied. Mrs. Lincoln loved mountains, a taste Robert and Tad seem to have shared. Her letter continued: "At noon we proceeded to Baden and ascended another mountain height, in the evening to visit the ruins of another grand old castle—centuries back. The next day we went out to 'La Favorita' the abode of the 'White Lady.'" Then followed a statement to Robert's wife that introduces a new topic in the family and gives one a bit of news: "Taddie and I were continually wishing that you and Bob and that precious baby were with us."

Mr. and Mrs. Robert Todd Lincoln of Chicago had a daughter, born October 15, 1869. She was named Mary, to her grandmother Lincoln's great delight, and was soon, according to the family custom, nicknamed, being called "Little Mamie." Robert's reserve usually prevented self-revelation in his letters, but in one or two he gave brief, unguarded expressions of the deep joy and pride he felt in the birth of his first child. On November 4 he wrote Judge Davis of "the new arrival in my family," adding proudly: "The young lady will be of the mature age of three weeks tomorrow and is as fat and hearty as one could wish. My wife has progressed towards her complete recovery very rapidly and is today in all appearances as well as ever but of course has to be careful." Many husbands are a bit taken aback at the changes a baby makes in household arrangements, and Robert's next remark suggests he was one of them: "We have set up a female establishment of our own on Wabash Avenue. . . ."

Like most men, he had wanted a son, a fact he playfully imparted to John G. Nicolay in a letter written a little later: "You may or may not know that I am a happy Father (or rather mother, for my boy is a daughter) of four months standing." His letters frequently show his concern for his wife and he here further reported: "The wife is as well as can be & the baby is better still."

Robert evidently delighted to inform his friends about the new member of his family. He had kept up a close friendship and correspondence with John Hay since the White House days. Hay by now was secretary of legation at Madrid, still unmarried and able to note with a young man's approving eye that "the Spanish women are the most cordial, frank and winning creatures in the world," and "prettier than is necessary." Hay's answer to Robert's announcement was: "Give my best love to Miss Lincoln & tell me next time what her name is. . . ."

Two more children were to be born to Robert to round out the continuing process of his development. But already he had reached what his mother called one of "the happiest stages of life," whose component parts, as she told Robert's wife, are "a nice home—loving husband and precious child." He was settling into his mature role as influential, prosperous good citizen and model, devoted family man. To one who disliked contacts with the public, the refuge of a happy home circle meant everything.

To the new-made grandmother and Uncle Tad in Germany Robert's baby was of supreme importance. Love of children and family affection were outstanding characteristics of the Lincolns. "That blessed baby, how dearly I would love to look upon her sweet young face," wrote Mrs. Lincoln to her adored daughter-in-law, and Tad felt exactly the same way. The desire to see the new baby stimulated their latent homesickness. The travelers wanted the Robert Lincoln family to come abroad and see them; Mrs. Lincoln wrote Robert's wife: "I do so trust that Bob will come over with you if only for three months, it would do him such a world of good." The plan seemed to have been for the young mother and baby to stay longer, but the drawback was, wrote Bob's mother, that Bob "loves you so *very dearly* and misses you very greatly." Mrs. Lincoln's letters to her son's wife could well be entitled, "Love Letters of a Mother-in-law." "I often tell Tad," she wrote, "I can scarcely flatter myself he will ever marry to suit me quite as well as dear Bob has done."

While Tad was at Dr. Hohagen's school in Frankfurt, his mother occasionally took a trip without him. When she came back from such a journey in March 1870, she wrote her daughter-in-law: "I return to find my dear boy much grown in even so short a time and I am pained to see his face thinner, although he retains his usual bright complexion. He is doubtless greatly improving in his studies, yet I am very sure the food he gets at his school does not agree with him." It is the first hint in the records of the heartbreak that lay ahead. Loss of weight and flushed cheeks in a growing boy of seventeen are ominous symptoms. His mother was intensely worried but hoped she could help about the food: "When I am here, I can always give him his dinner as he has their permission to be absent." She added a remark that showed the cold fear that gripped her at any threat to Tad: "His presence has become so necessary even to my life."

Mother and son took a holiday the summer of 1870 that turned into a most distressing experience; they went to the Tyrol, where their pleasant plans were broken up by the Franco-Prussian War. An item in the guardianship papers shows that Tad was prepared for the trip in one respect; he already had bought "1 hat (Tyrolienne)." From Innsbruck, Tyrol, Austria, on July 16 Mrs. Lincoln wrote a friend: "I had come down here with my young son, to give him a little holiday, but shortly after our arrival was notified from Frankfurt that the *French* were on the Rhine and if we wanted to *secure* our baggage which had been deposited at the house of a friend, we must return & see after our effects." To make matters worse they ran out of money. Tad's knowledge of German doubtless stood them in good stead in the complicated days that followed, when they had to get themselves out of a country at war and go to England. Details are lacking except that Mrs. Lincoln said that her heart had been "made sick" by the experience.

Leaving Germany made a complete change in Tad's existence. He and his mother had evidently found life there fairly pleasant; at least, she referred affectionately to "dear old Frankfurt." At Dr. Hohagen's Tad had had friends his own age and a normal schoolboy life; now it was a question what to do about the continuation of his education. He had adjusted himself so well that he was speaking with a German accent, which did not become a native-born young American. Shortly after the flight from the Tyrol Mrs. Lincoln wrote a friend: "I must speak of my young boy. He has become so homesick and at the same time his English education has become so neglected that I have consented with many a heartache to permit him to go home."

If only that plan had been carried out! It seems evident that Robert and his wife were urging Tad's return, justifiably feeling it was time for the loved younger brother to come back and go to an American school. But by September 1870 Mrs. Lincoln had found in England a desirable private teacher for Tad, who was soon "closeted with his tutor seven and a half hours each day, and from Saturday to Saturday." No companionship of other young people his own age, limited time for recreation, only long hours of bending over books for a youth who in all probability was tubercular and needed rest. From Leamington, England, where they located, Mrs. Lincoln wrote even more specifically about this intensive study: "From eight until one o'clock each day Tad is seated at his table—with his tutor studying and from five to seven each evening. . . ."

The family in Chicago apparently did not drop the matter of Tad's coming home. Around December 1 Mrs. Lincoln was writing her daughter-in-law: "Driving down to the bank at noon to-day for letters I proposed to Tad with a trembling voice and aching heart you may be sure, that he would embark on the *Russia* which sails next Saturday week for the U.S. Dec. 10th and go home pass his Christmas with you and Bob and immediately afterwards be placed in school."

But to give Tad up was more than she could face. "To trust my beautiful, darling *good* boy to the elements, at this season of the year, makes my heart faint within me. Each breath I drew would be a prayer for his safety, which only those who have been as deeply bereaved as myself could fully understand." She was still unwilling to return to America herself because of her dread of newspaper misrepresentation. Tad was not one to leave her alone, he had become her protector now, and his quick sympathy would not have missed that tremble in her voice when she spoke of his going.

But he grew more and more homesick. In January 1871 his mother wrote Bob's wife: "Tad is almost wild to see Bob, you and the baby; he thinks the latter must be a rare young lady, I am also of his opinion." Shortly after this was written, his mother had to leave him alone in England. She was ill with what may have been bronchitis, had a very bad cough, and her physician ordered her to go to Italy till spring. She placed Tad in an English school while she was gone and he dutifully reported to her. Writing a friend from Florence, she mentioned receiving a letter "from dear Tad."

Her plan was to return to England in April. At long last she then decided to yield to Tad's wishes and those of Robert and his wife and go home. By this time she had been voted a pension and the publicity attendant upon the matter had died down; she wanted passionately to see her grandbaby and Tad wanted to see his niece. Mother and son together trusted themselves to the elements, which gave them a very rough voyage. The heavy seas evidently delayed their arrival, as on May 10, 1871, Robert wrote Judge Davis: "I am expecting Tad to be here any day as the ship on which he left England is now overdue at New York." The elder brother continued: "I have not thought much as to what I shall advise Tad to do. He is now past eighteen & entitled to be consulted. I have no fears about him if he is as good a boy as I am told."

By May 11 Mrs. Lincoln and Tad had arrived in port and they left for Chicago on May 15. Apparently they saw John Hay in the meantime, as he wrote of the startling contrast between the "modest and cordial young fellow who passed through New York" and "the tricky little sprite" he had known in the White House. Hay thought Tad "greatly improved by his residence abroad" and especially noted the "thoughtful devotion and tenderness beyond his years" which he displayed toward his mother.

The joyous welcome given the travelers by the family on Wabash Avenue in Chicago is reflected in a letter Mrs. Lincoln wrote a few days after arrival: "We are received with so much affection here and notwithstanding the confined limits of this charming little home my son Robert, who is all that is noble and good and his lovely little wife will not hear to our removal." Yet Robert's mother felt that the considerate thing would be for Tad and herself to go to a hotel, as her daughter-in-law "is compelled to go instantly to her mother, who is in a most critical state." However, they could not move "until Saturday," as "my young son is confined to his bed with a severe cold. . . ." Mrs. Lincoln did not seem apprehensive at this time; she spoke happily of the future in Chicago when she and Tad and Robert's family would "be almost always together."

The boy grew somewhat better and he and his mother went to the Clifton House. Years later the man who was keeping the hotel, W. A. Jenkins, remembered how everyone there was drawn to Tad: "He was a very lovable boy, quiet, gentle mannered and good-natured. . . ." Mr. Jenkins remembered also that Tad still had the cold

Puzzle in Evidence

Tad's telegram, *left*, has been the subject of controversy. Since Mrs. Lincoln made several statements indicating he did not know how to write when he was in the White House, it has been suggested he enlisted the aid of a semiliterate person, perhaps a servant, to write the telegram for him. *Right* is Tad's unquestioned signature to a legal document in 1867. Do the two signatures look as if they had been written by the same boy?

Lincoln, Tad, and Robert's Bride

Upper left, photograph of Tad taken in Frankfurt am Main, Germany, when he was between fifteen and seventeen. *Upper right*, a rare photograph of Mary Harlan taken in 1868, the year she married Robert Lincoln. Robert's mother thus described her shortly before the wedding: "a young lady, who is so charming & whom I love so much." *Below*, photograph of Tad and his father taken by Alexander Gardner on April 10, 1865, the day after they returned from City Point and five days before Lincoln's death.

Harper's Weekly, October 26, 1867

Robert Lincoln and His Mother

Above, Robert and Mother. He felt he had to have her tried for insanity for her own protection, but he wept at the trial. *Below*, scene at 609 Broadway, New York, where Mrs. Lincoln's old clothes were put on sale, an episode that humiliated Robert so cruelly that his mother said he almost threatened his own life.

Robert Lincoln and His Father

Ida Tarbell, who interviewed Robert Lincoln when he was president of the Pullman Company, wrote: "I searched his face and manners for resemblances. There was nothing. He was . . . a big plump man . . . perfectly groomed. . . ." Robert was cross-eyed as a child, and here his left eye seems slightly turned inward.

he had caught on the ocean voyage. It grew worse instead of better and at the last of May he developed difficulty in breathing when lying down and had to sleep sitting up in a chair.

On June 8 Mrs. Lincoln wrote her dear friend Mrs. Albert S. White: "My dear boy, has been *very very* dangerously ill—attended by two excellent physicians, who have just left me, with the assurance, that he is better. May we *ever* be sufficiently grateful, should his precious life be spared." The doctor, she continued, "says, that *thus far*, his lungs, are *not at all* diseased, although water has been formed on part of his left lung, which is gradually decreasing." She mentioned she had been sitting up with Tad constantly "for the last ten nights."

Apparently the improvement lasted a while, but the "dropsy of the chest" still made it impossible for the boy to lie down; he had to sit upright in a chair night and day. With the coming of July he grew worse again. He got out of his chair one night, slightly clad, and fainted, which resulted in a setback. Judge Davis passed through Chicago on Saturday, July 8, and visited mother and son at the Clifton House, coming away with a very sad heart. Tad, he wrote a friend, was so ill: "If he recovers, it will be almost a miracle. . . . His mother is in great affliction."

Robert's wife was still out of town with her sick mother. Through Robert's reports to her one can follow the course of Tad's illness, which has now been called pleurisy, "probably tubercular in origin." He had apparently been ailing for a number of months. On Tuesday, July 11, he seemed to be improved again, and the hearts of Robert and his mother lightened a little. On that day Robert wrote his wife: ". . . Mr. Thomas Lincoln has been picking up for the last two or three days and is to all appearances improving, his face has lost some of its expression of distress. . . ."

To see the thin young face in pain made it so hard for Robert and Mrs. Lincoln. They had that supreme agony of helplessly watching a dearly loved one suffer; Tad had that unselfishness that holds back complaint and moan so that the watchers will be hurt a little less. Robert said he had never seen such suffering and such "marvelous fortitude."

The pitiful advance and recession of the disease continued. Thursday night was very bad and Robert wrote his wife next day that the doctor said there was no hope. Yet Tad brightened that day when a picture of his little niece, Mary Lincoln (who was evidently out of town with her mother), arrived, and he looked on the baby face with loving and delighted eyes.

Robert stayed at the hotel that evening until eleven o'clock; then, since Tad had gone to sleep, he dared leave him with his mother and two nurses and return to his home. He had been in bed but a few hours when a message came at half past four to come at once. It was, perhaps, growing light in the summer dawn as he made his way to the hotel. He found Tad in great distress and fighting for breath and saw that he was failing fast. The heartbreaking struggle lasted two or three hours more, then the young shoulders fell forward in the chair and the labored breathing ceased. It was seven-thirty on Saturday morning, July 15, 1871.

Tad's body was taken to Robert's home on Wabash Avenue. Friends and relatives, as always, came to help and sympathize. Robert's wife could not leave her ill mother, but Senator Harlan, her father, arrived Sunday morning. Simple funeral services were held in the older brother's home Sunday afternoon. The members of the Bible class which Tad had once attended came in a group. They paused beside the young still body to gaze upon the pale features and closed eyes of the classmate they had loved. While they did so, Tad's mother sat on a sofa, dazed and distracted; she looked, as one pitying observer said, "truly the woman of sorrow that she was." Robert sat beside his mother to give her what comfort he could; the minister sat on the other side.

As always, the burden fell on Robert's shoulders. His mother was too ill with her long vigil and too overcome with grief to make the trip to Springfield, where Tad was to be buried. Robert also was used up with his watching and his distress, but he must accompany the body on the journey and see that everything fitting was done. The rosewood casket was placed on the train and Robert made the night journey in a car with friends. Senator Harlan, his father-in-law, and Judge Davis, whom he regarded as his second father, were with him.

The train arrived at three-fifty in the morning. Again Robert went through the slow dawning of another day with a sorrowing heart. The body was taken to the familiar mansion on the hill, the home of his Uncle Ninian and Aunt Elizabeth Edwards, where his father and mother had been married nearly twenty-nine years before. Tad's body perhaps was placed in the very room where his parents once stood, a small-town bride and groom, young and with life before them. The casket rested there in the early morning of Monday, July 17.

The funeral was held at nine o'clock in the First Presbyterian

Church, of which Mrs. Lincoln was still a member. The pallbearers were the young friends who had known Tad. Robert had many relatives present, including his three aunts, Elizabeth Edwards, Frances Wallace, and Ann Smith. The Reverend J. H. Brown, now the second husband of Cousin Elizabeth Grimsley, helped conduct the services. He read the passage from Ecclesiastes beginning: "Remember now thy Creator in the days of thy youth. . . ."

Again for Robert there was that sad ride to Oak Ridge Cemetery, where only six years before he had seen his father laid to rest. Willie was there and little Eddie, whom he could remember faintly; now Tad would join them, and he, Robert, not quite twenty-eight, was the last of the Lincoln sons. The assembled people bowed their heads as Tad's body was placed in its niche, the final solemn words were said, and the crowd dispersed.

In the country cemetery, warm and green with summer, there was quiet and peace. Tad again slept with his father.

CHAPTER 20

Tragedy of Mother and Son

FOR HIS mother Tad's death ended all purpose in living. Robert had his wife and baby and she was not essential to him, but she had felt that Tad needed her. Also, differences in personalities in sons cannot be ignored. She loved Robert, he was her good son, but Tad was the one whose presence had brought her joy and comfort. Robert could always be counted on to do what was right and proper and do it in the most efficient way possible, but she often must have felt his disapproval (and she took criticism as badly as he did), while with Tad she felt wrapped in his warm, unquestioning love. No one could express her dark despair more simply and poignantly than she did herself: "I feel there is no life to me, without my idolized Taddie. One by one I have consigned to their resting place, my idolized ones, & now, in *this* world, there is nothing left me, but the deepest anguish & desolation."

Few have considered what Robert suffered in the death of his loved younger brother. He had a terrible vulnerability to hurt and he not only had loved Tad but had begun to have high proud aspirations for him. Robert was to write sorrowingly of Tad to Noah Brooks: "He was only eighteen when he died but he was so manly and self reliant that I had the greatest hopes for his future."

After the burial Robert was almost in a state of collapse. He had planned to spend part of his vacation that summer going over the presidential papers of his father with Judge Davis. (These were the famous "Lincoln Papers" which were finally opened to the public in the Library of Congress in 1947; they were then in a bank at Bloomington, Illinois, under Judge Davis's care.) But, as Robert wrote a friend in September after Tad's death: "My own strength was then used up & I was compelled to leave my office for as long a period as possible & I only returned in time to commence regular fall work." One is reminded here of Abraham Lincoln as a young man getting into such a state of depression over his broken engagement to Mary

Todd that it resulted in physical weakness and he could not attend to business in his law office. Sorrows and stresses were to take heavy toll of Robert through life and they were to pile up in strange ways in the five years after Tad's death.

Robert of course had to help settle the legal and financial details that follow any death. He had shared with Judge Davis the problems of Tad's finances abroad, and, as he wrote the judge, the accounts had caused him "infinite annoyance" and kept him "in constant hot water" with his mother. Tad's estate was more than thirty-seven thousand dollars and his mother and Robert were the only heirs. Mrs. Lincoln was entitled to two thirds, but her obsession about her own poverty did not prevail in this case. Robert wrote Judge Davis: "My mother says she will not take two thirds of the Estate. This is very generous on her part. . . ." The estate was divided equally between them.

The year 1871 was complicated as well as sad for Robert. He was making a change in his law office; the firm of Scammon and Lincoln was dissolved that year. The problem of dealing satisfactorily with the distracted woman his mother had become was both heartbreaking and impossible. She had resumed her restless traveling, going from place to place, and he did all he could do; he employed a reliable woman, Mrs. Richard Fitzgerald, mother of Eddie Foy, the actor, to go with her and look after her.

Mrs. Lincoln was seeking the solace of new places, and in a sense that is what Robert did too in the following year. On May 17, 1872, he reported to Judge Davis: "I am hoping to get off next month for a few months across the water with my family." His passport was dated May 28 and contained the description of himself mentioned in the first chapter. The height of five feet nine and a half inches, the gray eyes, the nose which he had playfully described as "ordinary," the dimpled chin, and brown hair added up to a handsome and distinquished appearance. But there was a certain keen and stubborn determination in his face which the wise would not treat lightly.

He and his family spent the summer and fall of 1872 traveling abroad. There were doubtless many family letters giving the details of their experiences, but they have not been found. The trip was timely, for in the month of his departure a new and dreadful humiliation for him was being avidly talked of in the United States.

The person responsible for this new trouble was that portly and picturesque friend of his father's, Ward Hill Lamon, who had made the journey East to Washington with the Lincolns when Lincoln was President-elect. Mr. Lamon had remained with President Lincoln in

Washington as marshal of the District of Columbia, and after Lincoln's death he, like Herndon, saw the possibilities of capitalizing on his association with the great man by writing a biography of him. But the long, tedious task of study and writing necessary to produce the manuscript was not to his taste or his talents. He was much better in the role of entertaining companion and brawny, devoted bodyguard of the President than he was in that of his biographer. Mr. Lamon worked out one of the most painless ways of producing a book on record: he bought copies of the material Herndon had collected up to September 1869 and engaged a ghost writer to do the work of writing it up. Lamon's choice for this task was Chauncey F. Black, a man politically and temperamentally unfriendly to Lincoln. Herndon's material plus Black's antagonism made a fearful combination. The resulting volume, Lamon's *Life of Abraham Lincoln*, was being gossiped about furiously in the summer and fall of 1872.

It was Robert's fate through life to fight and suffer over falsehoods and misrepresentations about his father. Lamon's book, made up of Herndon's records, letters, interviews, and "truth by intuition," had, of course, the untrue statements and misconceptions that were to appear later in Herndon's own biography, including the Ann Rutledge romance, the theory that Lincoln had not loved his wife, and the attempt to prove that the President had not been a Christian. Most crushing of all, perhaps, to Robert was the statement that of the marriage of his father's parents Thomas Lincoln and Nancy Hanks "there exists no evidence but that of mutual acknowledgment and cohabitation." In other words, Lamon's book set loose in a gossiping world the impression that Abraham Lincoln had been an illegitimate child. Anything more calculated to torture Robert and his mother (both steeped in the rigid conventionality of the Victorian age) can hardly be imagined. If his grandparents had not been married, that fact took away from Robert the cherished name of Lincoln; he, his mother, his wife, his child were all Hankses. The public shame and humiliation was almost beyond endurance to one of Robert's temperament. Mrs. Lincoln fled from the country into Canada to get away from it.

The insinuation of illegitimacy was utterly false, being based upon a few wisps of ignorant gossip and Herndon's habit of jumping to conclusions. Robert, resourceful lawyer that he was, at his first opportunity sought and found indisputable proof of the marriage of his grandparents over two and a half years before his father was born. Robert put the document (which once more made them all Lincolns "safe & sure," as his mother put it) in his vault in the bank, but to erase the idea from the public mind was as hopeless as trying to gather up a mass of feathers thrown to the wind. He had to burn in silence. But there would be a sequel eleven years later when he had become a Cabinet member in Washington.

In 1883 Ward Hill Lamon very much wanted an appointment as postmaster at Denver. The appointment was not forthcoming as expected and word came to Lamon that Robert had blocked it at Washington. Hurt, angry, and obtusely unaware of the agony he had inflicted, Lamon wrote Robert saying he could not understand such action on his part, adding: ". . . it is so unlike anything your father ever did or was capable of doing. . . ."

Robert wrote Lamon an answer in which he delivered his punches with full force. Yes, he, Robert, had taken "an early opportunity to say to the Postmaster General that your appointment would be personally offensive to me. . . ." He stated the reasons; Lamon's *Life of Lincoln* was so objectionable in its character that not until that day had he opened it. He had been made aware by various newspaper articles that it contained "one insinuation which was especially offensive in itself," and he had looked at Lamon's book that day in order to specify page and paragraph, "first paragraph on Page ten." Robert did not mince words: ". . . the burden of the paragraph has always appeared to me to be an astonishing exhibition of malicious ingratitude on your part to your dead benefactor." Robert ended his letter devastatingly. His father, he wrote, "was charitable and forgiving to the last degree; but I think that no man attempted while he was living to give him such a wound as you tried to deal when his friendship was no longer of practical use to you except to be advertised to increase the sale of your merchandise."

Lamon answered Robert's letter with a veritable avalanche of language, a long, lofty, offended letter belittling Robert. He defended what his book had said as true, which did not help matters as Robert knew it was not true. But Lamon did write the truth when he said in this letter that he had loved Lincoln with a sincere affection. And one of his statements must have hurt Lincoln's son deeply: "You seem to form a melancholy contrast between yourself and your noble sire. If you possess one single characteristic that you could possibly have inherited from the male side of your house, you have not as yet developed it to the satisfaction of the people." It was a comparison and contrast from which Robert would never be able to escape.

The year 1873 held several important events for Robert. After he returned from abroad he formed a new law connection with a senior partner of excellent standing, Edward S. Isham. The firm of Isham and Lincoln prospered, and much later (in 1887) William G. Beale was to be added to it.

During the first half of 1873 Robert and his wife were looking forward to the birth of another child. He had wanted his first-born, Mamie, now an engaging little individual going on four, to be a son; undoubtedly he desired a boy even more now. There was a very special name waiting for a Lincoln son. Robert must have felt a deep joy when a boy was born on August 14, a fine child on whom was bestowed the illustrious name of his grandfather, Abraham Lincoln. The baby, of course, promptly received a nickname, a rather unexpected one, "Jack." There is a legend that Robert later told this son not to use his given name until he had proved himself worthy of it. At all events, the name Jack headed off the less appealing nickname "Abe." Jack was to develop into a gifted and lovable boy whom his father loved as Abraham Lincoln had loved Willie and Tad.

Robert needed a refuge from humiliation and indignation late that year when William H. Herndon on December 12 delivered in Springfield another lecture on his father. Lamon's book had set in motion a controversy over Lincoln's religion.

Actually no one ever lived a more Christian life than Lincoln, and his deep faith in God was expressed over and over again in his speeches and writings, so Robert had good reason to feel outraged at Herndon's misrepresentation of his father. In addition, Herndon in this lecture took occasion to repeat the insinuation of Lamon's book that Lincoln had been illegitimate. Herndon mentioned in this connection that Robert claimed to have a record proving his father's legitimacy, but, said Herndon, "I aver there is no such record," thus practically calling Robert a liar in a public lecture in his home town.

Robert read about the lecture in the papers in Chicago, the city in which he was building up his reputation. On December 16 he wrote Mr. Nicolay, enclosing a clipping from the *Tribune* and a penciled draft of a reply to Herndon. "My idea is this—" he said, "I have hastily written what is enclosed—& if Judge Davis coincides, do you write it out in your own name, for I do not wish personally to enter the controversy—change and rewrite just as you choose . . . & get Mr. Harlan to print your letter in the Chronicle. . . ." (Mr. Harlan, Robert's father-in-law, had become editor of the *Washington Chronicle*.) Mr. Nicolay, as President Lincoln's former secretary, could speak on Lincoln's religion as one closely associated with him. However, two days later Robert telegraphed Nicolay that his friends opposed the answering of Herndon, and in a letter written January 10, 1874, he asked for the return of his "screed written in pencil."

While Robert thus avoided a public quarrel with the vituperative and unpredictable Herndon, his mother did not. In his lecture Herndon had quoted something Mrs. Lincoln had said to him in an interview some years before as showing that Lincoln was not a Christian. Mrs. Lincoln had truthfully said that her husband had not joined a church and Herndon had interpreted this as meaning Lincoln was not a technical Christian. But Mrs. Lincoln had also in that interview spoken beautifully and feelingly of her husband's deep faith, and she was outraged that Herndon had omitted this and seized on a phrase to make her a witness against her husband's Christianity. She indignantly denied such perverted meaning of her words, and a newspaper article gave the impression she had denied having the interview with Herndon at all. This impression made people think that Herndon had told a falsehood about having the interview, and stung by this, he let loose his fury and hate of Mrs. Lincoln in an open letter to newspapers over the country. In this letter, which he called "Mrs. Lincoln's Denial and What She Says," he presented Robert's mother as a liar and referred to her "spasmodic madness."

To be branded as a liar and lunatic over the nation was a frightful thing to a woman already so bruised by public abuse that every blow fell upon an oversensitized spirit. Robert's mother had not lied. A letter used for the first time in the author's biography of Mary Lincoln shows that she had not denied the interview at all but had given a full account of it. The publication of the "denial" was equally humiliating to Robert. Both mother and son had the dreadful frustration of not being able to stop Herndon's calumnies. The reference to his mother's madness was especially terrible to Robert because he himself believed she was insane in some respects and could well be fearful of the effect on her of this latest blow. And the effect was terrible. Mrs. Lincoln had become a pitiful, frightened woman who would walk the floor at night with bright lights burning because of imagined dangers and would enter a public dining room to look fearfully around and whisper, "I am afraid; I am afraid."

Mrs. Lincoln had returned from her travels to Chicago in 1873, probably drawn there by the lure of that baby grandson, whose name was Abraham Lincoln. Now she fled again from this new public humiliation. It was a constant worry to Robert to have his mentally ill mother traveling from place to place. As he had said to Mary Harlan before they were married, the greatest misery of all was the fear of what might happen. But the pitiful climax of her irrationality was not reached until the spring of 1875.

In March of that year Mrs. Lincoln was in Florida. In the treacherous world which she now mentally inhabited, Robert was the one person she could turn to with confidence, her one protector. One does not know what touched off her sudden apprehension that something was wrong with him—it could have been a bad dream, a delayed letter, or a bit of twisted information—but on the twelfth she sent the following telegram to Robert's physician: "My belief is my son is ill; telegraph. I start for Chicago to-morrow."

The physician soon got in touch with Robert and found he was in good health. As a matter of fact, he had not been sick in ten years. Robert at once telegraphed his mother saying he was well and suggesting that she remain in Florida. She evidently did not receive this telegram before she sent a second one, this time directly to him: "My dearly beloved son, Robert T. Lincoln—Rouse yourself and live for your mother; you are all I have; from this hour all I have is yours. I pray every night that you may be spared to your mother."

She arrived in Chicago March 15 and went to the Grand Pacific Hotel. She was in a highly disturbed nervous condition and would not go to Robert's home as he begged her to do. He necessarily took a room in the hotel adjoining hers and stayed there to look after her. During the following nights his sleep was frequently broken by her tapping at his door and rousing him to tell him of her fears. She thought people were trying to get at her to injure her and told wild tales of attempts to rob and poison her. It seemed as if she was expressing in physical terms what gossip and publicity had really done to her.

Robert did everything in his power to meet the situation and to help his mother. He employed a woman at the hotel to stay with her as much as possible and to sleep in her room at night. On April 1 she went into the hall not fully dressed and entered the elevator, and when he put his arm around her to lead her back to her room, she screamed, "You are going to murder me." He could not persuade her to go to his home; she had had a misunderstanding with his wife, probably another item which existed only in her feverish, distorted thinking. The evidence all indicates that Mary Harlan Lincoln was most affectionate and considerate toward her mother-in-law.

During the daytime Mrs. Lincoln would go on shopping expeditions, buying extravagantly of watches, perfumery, trunks, lace curtains, jewelry, and other items for which she had no need. Toward the last of April she showed Robert securities for fifty-seven thousand dollars which she was carrying in a pocket on her person. This was a dangerous situation, and Robert, without her knowledge, employed a man to follow and watch over her when she left the hotel. Robert's accounts show that the man was a detective and add details: "Paid A. Pinkerton for services and expenses of special attendant for three weeks" $151. These records also show how he was paying various servants at the Grand Pacific Hotel for special services for his mother.

The impossible situation continued for two months. Robert was apprehensive that his mother might be victimized, robbed, or irresponsibly dissipate the bulk of her estate. Also, she plainly needed rest, protection, and medical care. As he was to testify on the witness stand, she had never heeded his advice and she would not heed it now. The only way he could put her in a sanitarium and get control of her property was by a legal judgment of insanity. He asked the advice of his mother's cousin, John Todd Stuart, and of Judge Davis, and both agreed that calling for a sanity trial was the only course he could take. He sought the opinion of six physicians of high standing, describing her actions, and after a consultation they informed him that by further delay he was making himself "morally responsible for some very probable tragedy, which might occur at any moment."

It was a fearful decision for a son to make. He knew it would be a terrible blow to his mother, who had always been so tender and affectionate to him. (He probably did not foresee that she would attribute his action to a base motive.) He also knew how much of the publicity he so feared and abhorred would attend the holding of the trial. But he had exhausted his resources and himself and saw no other course to take. With great reluctance he did his painful duty as he saw it and called for a sanity hearing.

The date was set for May 19, 1875, and the place was the Cook County Court in Chicago. When the day dawned, Mrs. Lincoln knew nothing of the impending trial. Someone had to break the news to this unsuspecting woman that people thought she was crazy; someone had to get her to appear in court. The one who undertook this painful duty was Leonard Swett, a good friend of Robert's father who had been associated with him on the judicial circuit, a man of strength combined with fine feeling. He was also Mrs. Lincoln's friend; she liked and trusted him, and counted on his sympathetic understanding, as her letters to him show full well. He had been one of those who urged Robert to call for the trial, feeling it was necessary for Mrs. Lincoln's own protection. The trial was set for two o'clock; at one Leonard Swett went to Mrs. Lincoln's hotel.

A new, unpublished document has come to light which brings the scene that followed in Mrs. Lincoln's room into focus as vividly as if it were done in technicolor. It is Leonard Swett's letter to Judge David Davis written five days after the trial describing what was said and done. The letter is written with a lawyer's precision as to details and with great restraint, yet one catches in the lines Mr. Swett's utter agony at what he had to do to the cherished and beloved wife of Abraham Lincoln, his revered friend. He said the matter of taking Mrs. Lincoln into custody "presented more real terrors than anything I have ever undertaken. To have advanced on a battery instead would, it seems to me, have been a real relief."

When he entered her room, he said, Mrs. Lincoln "seemed cheerful and glad to see me." Mr. Swett was a tall man with a figure not unlike that of President Lincoln; she doubtless lifted to him trusting blue eyes warm with welcome. He asked her to sit down and said, "I have got some bad news for you." She seemed startled, as well she might; probably her first thought was that something was wrong with Robert, but she sat down as he had requested. Mr. Swett then told her that her friends had come to the conclusion that the troubles she had been called to pass through had been too much and had produced "mental disease."

"You mean to say I am crazy, then, do you?"

"Yes," said Mr. Swett, "I regret to say that is what your friends all think."

"I am much obliged to you," she answered, "but I am abundantly able to take care of myself, and I don't need any aid from any such friends. Where is my son Robert," she continued. "I want him to come here." It was probably the last time she ever turned to Robert with trust. Mr. Swett told her she would see him in court.

"The Court," she said, "what court do you mean; who says I am insane?"

"Judge Davis said so," replied Mr. Swett, "and your cousin John T. Stewart [Stuart]; Robert says so; and as I do not want to throw the responsibility of this upon others, I say so."

Mr. Swett then pulled from his pocket letters from several physicians giving their opinions that she was insane. She very naturally answered, "I haven't seen those physicians, they do not come to see me, they know nothing about me, what does this mean?"

Mr. Swett explained that Robert had filed an affidavit in the county court that she was believed to be insane, whereupon a writ was issued that gave the sheriff authority to arrest her and take her to court. Two officers, continued Mr. Swett, were downstairs ready to seize her by force, handcuffing her if necessary, and take her to court. To prevent this he was asking her to go quietly with him.

Mrs. Lincoln refused and protested about this monstrous plot against her. She denounced Robert bitterly and reproached Mr. Swett: "And you my husband's friend, you would take me and lock me up in an asylum, would you!" Mr. Swett's account continued: "and then she threw up her hands, and the tears streaming down her cheeks, prayed to the Lord and called upon her husband to release her and drive me away."

Finally the trapped creature asked him to leave while she changed her dress. He refused and she asked him why. He answered, "Because if I do, Mrs. Lincoln, I am afraid you will jump out of the window." At last she stepped into a closet and made the change. As they started he said, "Will you take my arm, Mrs. Lincoln," and she answered with a flash of spirit, "No; I thank you I can walk yet."

When he opened the door of the courtroom and she saw the forbidding interior and only men about, she shrank back. Mr. Swett coaxed her to enter by saying Robert was inside. When her son came to her, she received him kindly and he sat down beside her. Her counsel, Isaac N. Arnold, who had been a good friend of her husband's, sat on her other side. A reporter noted how modest and "gentle looking" she was as she sat silently through the three-hour ordeal. She heard various doctors give their opinions that she was insane, various individuals recount her eccentric sayings and actions.

What the ordeal was doing to Robert was apparent when he was called to the witness stand. An observer noted that his face was pale, his eyes red with weeping, "and his whole manner was such as to affect all present." His mother looked upon him with sympathetic eyes. She was probably numb with shock, and he had been her beloved son and was so evidently suffering deeply. Robert gave a full account of what had happened since she had telegraphed in March thinking he was ill. When he told of those nights at the hotel when she would tap at his door to wake him and tell him her pitiful fears, he broke down and wept. To shed tears in public is an ordeal for any man, but to Robert, supersensitive to the public gaze, that being on the witness stand was pure torture. The courtroom had become crowded, but the scene was so touching that some in the audience were wiping their eyes in sympathy.

He was asked if he regarded it as safe to allow his mother to remain unrestrained. He answered, "She has long been a source of much anxiety to me," and again he was affected to tears. He said she had always been "exceedingly kind" to him. In his opinion she had been of "unsound mind" since the death of his father, had been "irresponsible" for the past ten years. She was "unmanageable" and would never heed his advice. He told of her purchases which had no reason, "for her trunks are filled with dresses and valuables of which she makes no use. She wears no jewelry and dresses in deep black."

The jury returned a verdict of insanity. Robert then went up to his mother and took her hand tenderly. She looked at him sadly and reproachfully and exclaimed, "O Robert, to think that my son would ever have done this." He turned his face away that she might not see the pain in it.

Before she left the courtroom Mr. Swett asked her for the securities she was carrying on her person. He told her he could get an order of court or have the sheriff take them forcibly but he hoped she would not impose that necessity upon him. He asked her if she would not give the bonds properly to Robert, and she said no, Robert never could have anything that belonged to her. Swett then asked if she would give them to Mr. Arnold, who was standing by. She said she could not, as they were in her underclothing and "you would not be indelicate to me in the presence of those people." She implored Mr. Swett to take her to her room. Accompanied by Mr. Arnold, they left the courtroom through the tunnel. As soon as they arrived at her room Mr. Swett urged her to give him the bonds, until she was forced to yield. She rose and with tears streaming down her face said, "And you are not satisfied with locking me up in an insane asylum, but now you are going to rob me of all I have on earth; my husband is dead, and my children are dead and these bonds I have saved for my necessities in my old age; now you are going to rob me of them." Completely defeated and physically exhausted, "she yielded as to force," and gave Mr. Arnold $56,000 in government bonds. She evidently had cashed one bond since she had shown them to Robert.

Mr. Swett summed up the pathetic situation in the last paragraph of his letter to Judge Davis: "From the beginning to the end of this ordeal, which was painful beyond parallel, she conducted herself like a lady in every regard. She believed she was sane. She believed that I, who ought to be her friend, was conspiring with Robert and you, to lock her up and rob her of her money."

Mr. Swett had indeed looked into her tortured mind. Mrs. Lincoln sincerely believed that Robert, her only remaining son, was an unscrupulous and callous man who had deliberately trumped up the terrible charge of insanity in order to get rid of her and obtain her money. As the numbness of shock wore off and full conviction of this untrue and unjust theory took possession of her, she felt death was the only way out. She managed to elude those who were watching over her at the hotel and went to several drugstores asking for camphor and laudanum, ostensibly as an application to an aching shoulder. The clerks were cautious and finally one of them, being forewarned, gave her the prescription without the laudanum in it, and she drank it, believing it would end her life. This woman, in whom affection was predominant, had had the greatest of sorrows before but never treachery from one she loved; it was her first attempt at self-destruction. Robert was sent for immediately and stayed with her during her few remaining hours in Chicago. He did not know the terrible motive she attributed to him, for with the belief that he had become her enemy she began to conceal her thoughts from him. The day following the trial she was taken to Bellevue Place, a private sanitarium at Batavia, Illinois, and put under the care of Dr. R. J. Patterson. Robert was appointed conservator of her estate.

Detailed accounts of the proceedings at the trial, including mention of Mrs. Lincoln's gentle behavior and her wounded remark: "O Robert, to think that my son would ever have done this," were telegraphed to newspapers over the nation. People began to ask questions: what had this hardhearted man done to this gentle, harmless, and bereaved mother? Robert was sharply criticized. A devoted friend of Mrs. Lincoln's, Mrs. J. H. Orne, wrote him in distress, asking about his mother, whom she greatly loved. Robert's letter in reply showed such full consideration and conscientiousness that Mrs. Orne was completely satisfied that he had done the best that could be done.

The son explained that the regrettable "public proceedings in court" had been necessary, because such procedure was the only legal method by which he could commit his mother to a sanitarium. He thought she was "as happily situated as is possible under the circumstances." He gave details: "She is in the private part of the house of Dr. Patterson and her associates are the members of his family only. With them she walks and drives whenever she likes and takes her meals with them or in her own room as she chooses, and she tells me she likes them all very much." His only consolation "in this sad affair," he continued, was "in thinking that she herself is happier in every way, in her freedom from care and excitement, than she has been in ten years." He said: ". . . we are on the best of terms," and, "So far as I can see she does not realize her situation at all." (He was wrong there: Mrs. Lincoln was nursing her resentment against him and was setting to work to obtain her release.) The son went on to say with truth: "It is of course my care that she should have everything for her comfort and pleasure that can be obtained." He ended that his responsibility was one he would gladly share if he could, "but being alone as I am, I can only do my duty as it is given me to see it."

That he dutifully visited his mother once a week at Batavia is attested by a newspaper correspondent who called upon Mrs. Lincoln at the sanitarium. Frequently he would bring "her favorite grandchild" with him, doubtless Mrs. Lincoln's own little namesake. The correspondent noted on the visit that the patient had two "very expensive doll-babies" which she said were for her little granddaughter. Robert and his mother had at least one unspoiled meeting ground, their great love for his two children, who were named Abraham and Mary Lincoln. Perhaps he told her that summer that he and his wife were expecting a third child. (Jessie Harlan Lincoln was born on Nobember 6, 1875.)

But mother and son on these visits talked for the most part almost as strangers, neither knowing what was in the other's mind. She thought of him now as one who had basely betrayed her for the sake of money; he thought her far more mentally ill and uncomprehending than she was. For Mrs. Lincoln was quietly using her effective and fluent pen to enlist the aid of friends to get her from behind her barred windows. Her many letters denouncing Robert for locking her up from mercenary motives were constantly going out from the sanitarium. Among those who received them were Judge and Mrs. James B. Bradwell, two influential people with legal training, Mrs. Bradwell being the first woman lawyer of Illinois. The Bradwells came to see Mrs. Lincoln in Batavia and were convinced that she was in her right mind and that her detention in an asylum was an outrage. Questions being raised had results; in September she was removed to the home of her sister Elizabeth Edwards at Springfield, though she was still under judgment of insanity and was in the custody of the Edwardses. Robert was undoubtedly glad and relieved to have his mother in the home of his uncle and aunt.

An item in his scrupulous accounts as conservator indicates that he himself took his mother to Springfield; he lists the expenses of the trip for the two of them and his return. He arranged for "Amanda from Batavia" to be "an attendant on Mrs. Lincoln" in Springfield. Between September 13, 1875, and June 7, 1876, he sent checks totaling $4599.28 to his uncle, Ninian W. Edwards, for his mother, "to be expended by her for her comfort and support." Robert met her constant demands; she wanted her box of jewels and he got it out of the bank and sent it to her; she seemed to have an endless supply of trunks containing possessions she never used; he arranged for nine trunks of wearing apparel to be sent to her at the Edwards home. He was a busy man with his lawyer's practice, his wife and three children, and his obligations as an increasingly important citizen, but every detail as to his mother's care was well attended to.

Mrs. Lincoln remained quietly at the Edwards home in Springfield for nine months. Then Ninian W. Edwards petitioned for another sanity trial for her, saying, "She has not spent all she was allowed to spend during the past year, and we all think she is in a condition to take care of her own affairs." This trial took place on June 15, 1876, in Chicago and occupied only a few minutes. Robert did not appear, but he was represented as not offering any objection. The relatives had probably agreed this was the best course to take. Mrs. Lincoln was declared "restored to reason" and capable of managing her own estate. Leonard Swett was her attorney in her petition to have Robert Lincoln removed as her conservator. It doubtless meant much to him that he could act in this move to restore her to legal sanity, when what he had had to do to her the year before had hurt him so terribly.

Robert's mother returned to Springfield with Mr. Edwards. Four days after the trial she sat down and wrote her son a letter in which she let loose all the anger and resentment that had seethed within her for those thirteen bitter months when she had been branded and treated as a lunatic. The agitated handwriting itself indicates the fury with which she wrote. The letter began: "Robert T. Lincoln Do not fail to send me without *the least* delay, *all* my paintings . . . my silver set . . . [and] other articles your wife appropriated. . . ." (Evidence of the injustice of this accusation to Robert's wife is in a letter Mrs. Lincoln had written her from abroad six years before. Speaking of household articles left in Chicago, she had said to her daughter-in-law: "*Anything* and *everything* is yours—if you will consider them worth an acceptance. . . . It will be such a relief to me to know that articles can be used and enjoyed by you.") Mrs. Lincoln enumerated the articles at length and continued her letter to her son: "Two lawyers and myself, have just been together and their list, coincides with my own & will be published in a few days." (What would a published list of articles he and his wife were supposed to have stolen do to his standing?) The next sentence indicated that his Aunt Elizabeth Edwards shared his mother's opinion of him, "Aunt Lizzie," to whom he had so often turned for help and understanding: "Trust not to the belief, that Mrs. Edward's tongue, has not been *rancorous* against you all winter & she has maintained to the very last, that you dared not venture into her house & our presence."

His mother's excoriation went on: "I am now in constant receipt of letters, from my friends denouncing you in the bitterest terms, six letters from prominent, *respectable* Chicago people such as you do not associate with. . . . Two prominent clergymen, have written me, since I saw you—and mention in their letters, that they think it advisable to offer up prayers for you in Church, on account of your wickedness against me and High Heaven. In reference to Chicago you have the enemies, & I chance to have the friends there." The letter concluded: "Send me all that I have written for, you have tried your game of robbery long enough. On yesterday, I received two telegrams from prominent Eastern lawyers. You have injured yourself, not me, by your wicked conduct. Mrs. A. Lincoln."

The cruelty of this letter to a blameless and supersensitive man makes one cringe. He had turned his tear-stained face away from her after the verdict of insanity in order that she might not be hurt by the grief in it. Now she wanted to hurt him and destroy his reputation because that very mental illness made her believe he had done a terrible thing to her. He had tried conscientiously to do what was right and best for her; not once had he failed in his filial duty as he saw it. He would some day try to collect and destroy those letters of denunciation she had written, as evidence of her irrationality, but he would find it a hopeless task. The bitterness of this whole experience would hurt him all his life. Here were two well-meaning human beings, mother and son, caught, through no fault of their own, in fateful circumstances from which neither could escape and which brought each intolerable pain.

CHAPTER 21

"A Man Ought Not to *Shirk* Public Duties but—"

ROBERT'S mother, feeling herself branded as insane, again fled
from the country. "I cannot endure to meet my former friends,
Lizzie," she said to Elizabeth Edwards; "they will never cease to regard me as a lunatic, I feel it in their soothing manner. If I should
say the moon is made of green cheese they would heartily and smil-
ingly agree with me. I love you, but I cannot stay. I would be much
less unhappy in the midst of strangers." She spent the summer of
1876 in her sister's home in Springfield, but in the fall she went to
Europe to be gone until October 1880.

During these four years she did not care to write to the son who, as
she believed, had so cruelly wronged her. She did send letters continually to the relatives in Springfield, especially to a most lovable
grandnephew, Edward Lewis Baker, Jr., who reminded her, she said,
of Willie and Tad. Lewis, the grandson of Mrs. Edwards, was in his
later teens, and Mary Lincoln had to have an outlet for the maternal
affection which was now blocked in Robert's direction. Her letters
frequently expressed the bitterness and resentment she felt toward
her eldest son.

On his side he could well have been smarting under a sense of
the injustice of her accusations which put him in a false light with
regard to his treatment of her. It was doubtless humiliating to him
to be forced, three years after his mother's departure, to answer an
inquiry from a New York clergyman with the statement: "My mother
is now somewhere in Europe but she has, for unfortunate reasons,
ceased to communicate with me, and I do not know her present
address although, of course, I can by writing to some of her friends
obtain it in case of need."

Yet his mother's habit of maternal love and pride was too basic to

be broken off completely. Writing her grandnephew, "Dear Lewis,"
from Pau, France, in June 1879, Mrs. Lincoln said: "There is a paper
published at Paris called the 'American Register,' which is issued
once a week, & which I sometimes see." In this paper, she went on,
she had recently seen a short article mentioning the name of Robert
T. Lincoln as a prominent lawyer in Chicago "with *quite* the *certainty* of being at no distant day" a candidate for the Presidency. She
continued: "You can imagine how elated I felt, in my quiet way,
over such a prospect— The triumph of the '*just*—' *slightly different*
from the great & good father, however who was kind even to *his
Stepmother*—" Yet in spite of this mention of Robert's fancied un-
kindness to her, she began buoyantly to run over in her mind what
this great honor would mean to him and his family and even to plan
his Cabinet for him! In imagination she pictured the loved little
granddaughter in the stately White House rooms where her own
children had once played: "*Little Mamie* with her charming manners
& presence, in the event of *success*, will grace the place." Her next
words indicate she had been sending gifts indirectly to this little
namesake: "By the way, dear Lewis, should I enclose any thing for
this dear child again, I will not trouble your good Grandmother—
only if you will write R. T. Lincoln—the formal note—remitting what
is sent." The situation between Robert and his mother during these
years abroad was unjust and full of hurt for him.

If Robert had seen that article in the *American Register,* elation
is the last emotion he would have felt. He had no liking nor desire for
politics, but politics was not letting him alone. Republican politicians
were not likely to overlook the possibilities of a candidate with the
magic name of Lincoln. Here was an extremely able and upright
man, a model husband and father, and a staunch Republican, who
would be associated in the minds of the public with the shining qualities of his father, the great Emancipator and Civil War President
who had saved the Union. The fact that Robert was not like his
father and had no taste for either the public or politics was not known
or considered.

Robert's letters show that even in the late eighteen sixties he was
giving much thought to politics in a resisting sort of way. He had
always a strong sense of public duty. And one with his shrewdness
would realize what an advantage he had as his father's son, though
that fact was as distasteful to him as politics itself. He scorned special
privilege and really leaned over backwards so as not to trade on his
relation to President Lincoln. Also, a man of his ability does not enjoy

being spoken of merely as the son of his father, and not in the right of his own achievement. It is in many ways a hampering and fearful thing to be the son of a great man, and Robert, thin-skinned and with the instinct of a recluse, was to get the maximum of suffering from it.

Keeping in touch with those close friends of the war years, John G. Nicolay and John Hay, Robert wrote Hay early in 1868 expressing his contemptuous opinion of politics. Hay sent the letter to Nicolay, who had some revealing comments to make on returning it: ". . . I send you back Bob's letter which is certainly characteristic, and shows that latent power of observation and comparison which is evidently in the blood. He still looks at politics through a refracting medium—perhaps I should say an opaque one—either making him incapable of arriving at a true estimate." Mr. Nicolay continued that politics was a thing to take or to leave "but by no means to be despised, either in its nobler or baser relations to the times we live in. Nobody had a clearer perception on that point than his father." Nicolay thought that a little more age and experience would "probably enable Bob to see it as well."

It is possible that among the many pressures pushing Robert into politics in the eighteen seventies was one within his home circle. At least, a remark he made in a letter early in 1875 awakens the suspicion that Mrs. Robert Todd Lincoln was one of those in favor of a political career for her husband. Robert wrote Nicolay: "I shall tell my wife about Mrs. Nicolay leaving Washington on account of the climate. There's millions in such an item for me." If the conjecture that Mary Harlan Lincoln wanted to return to Washington is correct, it is easy to understand. Her father had been prominent as senator and Secretary of the Interior and she had known the thrills of official life at the nation's capital. It is true that by this time his public career was practically over and that it had involved much public abuse, a fact which Robert, with his phobia about publicity, was not likely to forget.

At all events, politics did claim intermittent periods of service from this reluctant individual whose taste was primarily for the life of a businessman. In April 1876 he was elected supervisor of the town of South Chicago, an office he held for about a year. His election was part of a movement to oust a corrupt gang of petty officeholders and the situation undoubtedly appealed to his sense of public duty. Robert was firm in his convictions and was always a good fighter. He took a zealous interest in the presidential election of 1880 and was a member from Cook County to the state convention at Springfield that nominated delegates to the Republican National Convention which met in Chicago early in June. When he went to Springfield on this occasion, perhaps his uncles, aunts, and cousins there wondered whether they were witnessing the beginnings of another notable Lincoln career in politics. At this time he was an ardent advocate of a third term for President Grant, the general on whose staff he had served in the last few months of the Civil War. He was one of the electors on the Republican ticket for the State of Illinois and thus participated in the actual election of James A. Garfield and Chester A. Arthur in 1880.

That autumn Robert's mother came back from abroad, a pitiful little gray-haired woman weighing only a hundred pounds, ill, painfully crippled by a fall, and beginning to lose her eyesight. It was her grandnephew Lewis Baker, Jr., not her one remaining son, who met her ship in New York and took her back to Springfield to the Edwards home on the hill. She was still bitter about the great wrong which she believed Robert had done to her. It was a sad situation and, now that she was living in the same state as Robert, a difficult one. One Sunday late in May, 1881, he came to visit her at the Edwards home and tried to make peace with her. He brought with him the most effective advocate possible, a pleasing little girl going on twelve, his daughter "Mamie," her favorite grandchild. Mrs. Lincoln was one who could not fail to yield to maternal affection; after all, this was her son, her first-born, with his child named for her. She promised to forgive and forget. One doubts whether things were ever the same between her and Robert as they were before the sanity trial, but at least normal relations were resumed.

Robert had much kindness in his nature and it was without doubt painful to him to see what a pathetic wreck his mother had become. But a comment of his shortly afterwards makes one doubt whether he had that quality which his father and Tad had had to such a marked degree, the quality of actually feeling the pain of another. Robert found a letter of inquiry about his mother from Mrs. Orne when he returned from Springfield and replied to it from Washington on June 2: "The reports you have seen about her are exaggerated very much. She is undoubtedly far from well & had not been out of her room for more than six months and she thinks she is very ill. My own judgment is that some part of her trouble is imaginary." It is true Mrs. Lincoln's mental trouble and her continual grieving made her sufferings much worse, but her fall had inflicted a painful spinal injury.

Perhaps it was easier for Mrs. Lincoln to become reconciled with

Robert because at this time she could again feel an upsurge of pride in his increased political prominence. It has been noted that his letter to Mrs. Orne was written in Washington. In February of 1881 President-elect Garfield had written Judge David Davis a letter marked *"Confidential"* in which he had asked the judge's opinion of Robert Todd Lincoln, as he was considering him "in the make up of the Cabinet." Judge Davis could well recommend Robert's high ability, integrity, patriotic sense of duty, and ardent Republicanism. After President Garfield was inaugurated, he promptly appointed Robert Secretary of War. It is doubtful that he was pleased by the appointment. It is possible that his mother, broken as she was, mustered more enthusiasm over the news than he did. Robert was well established now as a member of one of the foremost law firms in Chicago, one that represented the interests of many New York and other Eastern corporations. He was a charter member of the Chicago Bar Association and was considered one of the brightest and ablest young lawyers in the city. Early in 1880 the governor of Illinois had appointed him one of the trustees of the Illinois Central Railroad. He was showing marked executive ability in the management of large business interests and was turning his thoughts to the business world, which would ultimately woo him away from the practice of law.

He was getting his life into exactly the grooves in which he wanted it to run. He and his charming wife moved in the best social circles. Loving children, as the son of Abraham and Mary Lincoln almost inevitably would, he found his home life made warm and rich by "Mamie," who was approaching twelve, "Jack," nearly eight and a boy any father would be proud of, and little Jessie, going on six. Robert had no enthusiasm about being uprooted and moving to Washington, where he was to remain four years. Perhaps it was a sort of homecoming to Mary Harlan Lincoln to be once more in the swing of Washington official life. Many papers, of course, remarked that Robert had received the appointment because he was the son of his father.

That summer of 1881 Robert had a shattering experience. He was to accompany his chief on a trip starting July 2, and he arrived at the Washington railway station just in time to see President Garfield shot by Charles J. Guiteau. Robert's nature was ill adapted to receive such a shock, yet by a most extraordinary coincidence he was to undergo another of the same kind. Twenty years later he was among the invited guests at the Buffalo Pan-American Exposition and was nearby when the assassin Leon Czolgosz fired the fatal shot at President McKinley. These tragedies, added to the memory of the awful night he had spent at the bedside of his dying father, affected Robert deeply. After the McKinley assassination he would sometimes remark sadly and fatalistically that not many men had been near at hand for the murder of three American Presidents. When he was asked later if he would attend a presidential function, a newspaper quoted him as saying: "No, I'm not going and they'd better not invite me, because there is a certain fatality about presidential functions when I am present."

President Garfield lingered for eleven weeks before he died. During this interval a reporter from the *New York Tribune* interviewed the new Secretary of War and published an account of their conversation which gives some sidelights on Robert. The reporter came away with an irreducible minimum of information. He first wanted to know what was new in the War Department. Mr. Secretary replied there was nothing to tell; the department went on "in the routine way."

"Do you expect new Indian troubles?"

Secretary Lincoln admitted the Indians were causing "a little trouble" but he had not received "any late official information" and he felt sure there would not be "any serious disturbances."

"Are you making any extensive preparations for the Yorktown celebration?" the reporter next inquired.

"No, I am very sorry to say that I am not, simply because I am powerless to do anything that costs much money." Robert grew a bit more expansive on how poor the department was. The reporter finally asked the secretary what he thought of President Garfield's condition. Secretary Lincoln was positive that he would recover.

President Garfield died on September 19, 1881, and Lincoln's son continued as Secretary of War under President Arthur. It is not within the scope of this story to go into the many details of Robert Lincoln's public and business career, but certain other incidents throw light on his views and maturing personality. *Frank Leslie's Illustrated Newspaper* for October 11, 1884, carried an article called, "Secretary Lincoln and The Color Line." Brigadier General William B. Hazen, chief signal officer in the War Department, had objected to the enlistment of a colored man into his corps and appealed to Secretary Lincoln to sustain him. The secretary took the opposite view and threw all his influence into helping the enlistment of the colored man, which was accomplished.

It was not the only conflict between General Hazen and his superior in the War Department; a bitter controversy had developed between them. The Signal Corps had organized an arctic expedition in 1881 and sent a party of men under Lieutenant A. W. Greely to Lady Franklin Bay. Relief ships sent the following year and in 1883 were unable to reach them. Hazen wished a second attempt at relief to be made in 1883, but Secretary Lincoln decided it was too late in the year to send it. This left Greely and his party for a third winter in the Arctic without reinforcement of supplies, and when rescuers finally got through to them in June 1884, only seven of the original twenty-five members were still alive and they were starving. General Hazen bitterly criticized the secretary for his inaction in 1883. Robert Lincoln in his annual report for 1884 censured Hazen for his criticism. Hazen then wrote a letter to Robert (which was returned to him) and published a statement that he had written such a letter in the *Washington Star* March 2, 1885. The result was that he was ordered before a general court-martial and by sentence of this court was reprimanded by the President for "unwarranted and captious criticism" of his superior.

Secretary Lincoln could not avoid the controversies and accusations that are the tax paid for holding high office. And he had become a man whom the discreet neither slapped lightly on the back nor antagonized. Even after he left his post as Secretary of War, certain criticisms followed him. It was in 1888 that a question arose as to some Rebel flags said to have been boxed up by his order when he was in Washington with the intention of returning them to the Southern states from which they were originally taken. One has to get back to the inflamed attitudes of the time to realize that this was a touchy subject; the accusation carried an implication of disloyalty. Robert, who had had so many relatives fighting on the side of the South in the Civil War, was especially sensitive about the subject. The *New York Tribune* quoted the short angry sentences he snapped out when asked about the Rebel flags: "Well, what of it? . . . I don't know anything about the matter. . . . If the flags were boxed and anybody wants to insinuate that they were so boxed for the purpose of returning them to the Southern States, it is all poppycock. The thing was never once spoken of, nor even thought of while I was in the Department. We had more important things to think about when I was there than the disposition that should be made of a few, rotten old rebel flags."

Robert's temper evidently was not adapted to the exasperations of public life. Yet he was said to have been unusually popular among the subordinates in the War Department. He showed consideration and helpfulness to those near to him and *Leslie's Newspaper* mentioned an item revealing his sense of fairness: it stated that Secretary

Lincoln wanted to issue an order that would help do away with favoritism in the army, through which some officers were permitted continuous easy staff duty and others were always sent to do the fighting. To issue that order would inevitably bring up the old accusation that he had been shown favoritism when he had been appointed a captain on General Grant's staff.

David C. Mearns in his introduction to *The Lincoln Papers* thus sums up Robert Lincoln's record as Secretary of War: "Although he made an excellent civil servant, he was not distinguished for fostering public relations." He supported President Arthur for renomination, but when the Democratic President Grover Cleveland was inaugurated in March 1885, he gladly returned to his law practice in Chicago. Of his four years in the War Department he felt there was nothing "worth recording," and he was "satisfied to have got out of it without more grief." Both remarks were characteristic of his way of looking at things.

During his second year in Washington the long sad story of his mother's life came to an end. In the fall of 1881 Mrs. Lincoln, seeking relief from the suffering of her injured back, had come to New York to be under the medical care of Dr. Lewis A. Sayre, the leading orthopedic surgeon of his day. She told a reporter that Robert and his wife Mary came from Washington to see her "at intervals of two or three weeks," and she spoke of the kindness of them both to her. She still had her irrational conviction of poverty, and in January 1882 Congress increased her pension to $5000 a year. This movement stirred up all the old unfavorable publicity about her, which was without doubt very embarrassing to the Secretary of War, whom the public would naturally blame for not taking care of his mother. Mrs. Lincoln herself said Robert and his wife were most willing to take care of her, but he "had his own brood to look after" and she did not wish them to do so.

She died at the Edwards home in Springfield on July 16, 1882. Robert made the trip to Illinois to attend her funeral. On July 17 his mother's body lay in state at the Edwards home, where eleven years before to the very day Tad had lain in his casket. Once more in the hushed atmosphere of death Robert renewed ties with his Todd relatives and saw the old familiar streets and homes. He attended the funeral services at the First Presbyterian Church, where doubtless there were elderly people who stared at this mature, impressive man, now a member of the Cabinet at Washington, who had once been the mischievous little Bobbie Lincoln they remembered. Again Robert rode in procession to the Oak Ridge Cemetery, where his mother was laid in the place she had so longed to be—beside his father. With them now were Eddie, Willie, and Tad, and Robert was the only one left of that lively group that once gathered around the dining table in the house that stood, with the ironic imperishability of inanimate things, at the corner of Eighth and Jackson.

Robert would not come to Springfield often in the future, perhaps because it held so many sad memories for him, perhaps because he had grown away from the little town into a more complicated environment of which its good people knew little. Five years later he and his wife would sign a deed giving the Eighth Street house to the people of Illinois on condition that it would always be kept in good repair and open to the public. They would go back to that old home once more, at the celebration of the hundredth anniversary of President Lincoln's birth in 1909. Robert asked to go upstairs to his old boyhood room, and when he had entered, friends quietly withdrew, leaving him there a while with his memories.

To Robert's three children the Harlan grandparents were, through circumstances, much more a reality than the Lincoln ones. When Senator Harlan retired from public life, he moved to Mount Pleasant, Iowa, where he had formerly been president of Iowa Wesleyan College. During the period when their father was Secretary of War and after the family returned to Chicago, the Lincoln children in summer would visit the Harlan home, a comfortable, two-story frame dwelling just north of the campus. Robert himself made frequent trips to Mount Pleasant when his duties would permit it. A concrete evidence of his children's presence in that house is still treasured. On September 4 and 7, 1883, Senator Harlan backed his three grandchildren up against a closet door and marked their heights with a pencil and wrote down the date.

Mary (Mamie), Jack, and Jessie Lincoln were bright, natural, unpretentious children well liked by the people of the town. Jack especially was remembered as a handsome boy with a charming personality. Robert and his wife looked upon this son of great promise even as Abraham and Mary Lincoln had looked with happy surmise upon their son Willie.

A unique Lincoln relic is preserved at Iowa Wesleyan College, a collection of stones and bits of colored glass in a cardboard box which bears the label, "Collection Illustrating Rounded Pebbles & Sharp Stones Made by A. Lincoln." Little is known about it, but the imagination likes to play upon it. Abraham Lincoln was interested in many branches of knowledge, and geologists are pleased to suggest that this collection shows he was a "rockhound." One knows he used to take his little sons for walks in the country, pointing out and explaining various objects of interest to them. If the collection is genuine, Mrs. Lincoln might well have saved it, and Robert, in addition to inheriting all her money, had also received all the keepsakes treasured by her.

In 1887 the Robert Lincoln family in Chicago moved to 60 Lake Shore Drive. They could indeed afford a fine residence now. Robert wrote to Nicolay in December of that year: "We are now getting really settled after six years vagabondizing—nothing but the sheriff or undertaker shall ever move us. Mrs. Lincoln has recovered her health & we are all very happy." It is clear that happiness for Robert lay in his home life, a chosen circle of friends, and in the challenge of his prospering financial affairs. In the summer of 1888 he enjoyed another trip to Europe. Once more he had got his life into the groove he preferred.

One can therefore imagine his surprise and consternation when one day late in March, 1889, a reporter called at the office of Isham, Lincoln and Beale and asked Mr. Lincoln if he would comment on his appointment as minister to England. Robert stared and said incredulously, "What is that you say?" The reporter told him a dispatch had been received saying that President Benjamin Harrison had sent his name to the Senate as minister to Great Britain.

"It is news to me," said Robert. "I have never heard a word about it." He went on to say he had not been a candidate for that or any other position and, "How the appointment came to me is beyond my knowledge, information or belief. I have not yet been officially informed of it and have no other information than that you bring me."

When the reporter asked whether he would accept, Mr. Lincoln replied he did not care to discuss the matter in any way until he had official notification. It was plain to the reporter and to Robert's friends that the news was most unwelcome. But those who had planned this surprise for him were well aware that he would not dodge his duty.

So once more this man who liked settled habits was uprooted and sent across the ocean in the role of diplomat. He sailed in May 1889 to serve four years as Minister to the Court of St. James's. With him and his family went his secretary Charles Isham (a distant cousin of his senior law partner), who in 1891 was to marry his eldest daughter Mary.

A letter written from London about two months after they arrived shows the Lincoln family well settled in their new life and enjoying certain aspects of it. "We are very well here," wrote Robert, "Mrs. Lincoln especially so, except that the combination of our 4th of July reception & two 'Shah' functions on the same day rather tired her out." He mentioned that he had had to add to her fatigue by making a speech! His letter continued: "Yesterday I took Mary & Jack to a house on the Thames for the afternoon racing."

Jack (Abraham Lincoln II) was sixteen in August of that year 1889 and plans for his education required working out. Of course he must go to Harvard as his father had done. It was decided to send him to school at Versailles, France, to study French in preparation for entering Harvard. Robert had good reason for believing in adequate preparation for those entrance examinations.

By November Jack had developed a carbuncle under his arm. It seemed a slight ailment at first, but on November 6 the French physician decided it was necessary to operate and did so. The Lincolns with Robert's secretary Charles Isham went to France to be with their idolized son. The course of Jack's illness can be traced in his father's letters to the legation secretary at London. No special alarm was felt at first, but the boy's condition fluctuated between improvement and relapse and the wound refused to heal. On November 26 his father wrote a letter in which his intense anxiety and tender concern are very evident. He mentioned "blood poisoning" and described Jack's condition: "He is weak and emaciated but cheerful and his appetite continually increases. This afternoon he is inclined to think us a little hardhearted for denying him a piece of beefsteak, which he would prefer to mere beef juice, but he has the promise of a little substantial diet tomorrow."

The illness dragged on through Christmas and into January 1890, with the worried father and mother keeping vigil. On January 12 Mr. Lincoln's letter brought up the subject of moving his son back to London. He and his wife felt that Jack was not getting the treatment he needed in France, though they dreaded the hardships of taking so ill a boy on railroads and across the channel. A physician from London came to Versailles and made the journey back with the patient and his parents to the Lincoln London residence at 2 Cromwell Houses.

Hope soared again. On February 5 Robert reported: "I am happy to tell you . . . that the attending medical men . . . this morning expressed their united belief that he will get well. . . ." It was the old sad story of fluctuating hopes and fears that moved inexorably to despair which Robert's parents had lived through in the loss of their sons. A physician in the nineteen forties has said that Jack Lincoln had septicemia and could have been saved by modern medical treatment, but many have thought that the "carbuncle" was of a malignant nature. By February 21 the crowding of the patient's lung by "pleuritic effusion" caused difficulty in breathing, and Robert was inevitably reminded of the agonizing days of Tad's final illness. It was on March 5, 1890, that Robert Lincoln's son breathed his last. With him died the possibility of continuation of the Lincoln name.

The loss of his son was the greatest sorrow of Robert's life. He knew now the full agony in Abraham Lincoln's heart as he had looked down upon Willie lying dead. In answer to a letter from John Nicolay, Robert gave a moving expression to the change this sorrow had made: ". . . I must thank you for your note and answer you that your sympathy is gratefully felt. You can imagine that for more than common reasons our boy's life was very precious to us and as his character & ability became year by year more assured, I had good reason for setting no limit in our hopes for him. Now that there is nothing left but a memory, the loss is very hard to bear."

Robert's remaining three years in England were shadowed by the sadness of losing his son. Apparently, he and his wife did not want to face the Christmas following Jack's death so far from home; at all events, they, with at least one of the daughters, returned to this country at the end of the year and went to Mount Pleasant, Iowa, where Mrs. Robert Lincoln's father was still living. It probably helped to renew family ties. Robert wrote a letter on mourning stationery from Mount Pleasant on December 26 in which he mentioned that he would return to his duties in London a few weeks ahead of his wife and daughter.

He discharged his obligations fittingly and efficiently, but he found many factors connected with his position irksome. When Senator George F. Hoar visited England in 1892, Robert described to him a special vexation. When the Minister for Foreign Affairs received the diplomatic representatives of other countries at the Foreign Office, ambassadors ranked above ministers and were received first. (Robert Lincoln was our last envoy to England who was a minister; after his return the rank was raised to ambassador.)

Robert further told Senator Hoar, who relates this story in his autobiography, that the members of each class were received in the order of their seniority and that the ministers from the United States, being changed with different administrations, were likely to be among the juniors. This sometimes meant waiting all day to be received and then like as not having to return the next day to repeat the performance. If an ambassador happened to arrive just when Robert's turn had come, he was given precedence at once. It was a situation no efficient American businessman could view with tolerance.

On October 17, 1892, a New York newspaper announced that the minister to England had just arrived in this country on a two months' leave of absence. Reporters of course came to interview him, but it was a skillful reporter indeed who could extract any interesting news from Robert Lincoln. His comments for the newspapers were: "My personal relations with the British Government have been very pleasant. There is nothing connected with my official duties that I feel I can properly speak about except the forthcoming International Monetary Conference, in arranging for which it has fallen to me to have some share. . . ." He had evidently been criticized for not attending the funeral of the poet Tennyson. He explained that the invitation to be a pallbearer came just as he was entering the train to go to Liverpool to embark.

Theodore Roosevelt is quoted as saying that "all of our envoys to London have been pro-British except Bob Lincoln." But there were pleasant features of those four years and much meeting of notables. One finds an amusing account of an occasion when Robert dined at a home where Gladstone was also a guest. As the dinner started, a topic came up which interested Mr. Gladstone greatly. He seized the conversation and discoursed on that topic until long after the suitable hour for leaving. In the carriage which bore Mr. Gladstone belatedly to his own home, someone asked him what he thought of Mr. Lincoln. The answer was: "Mr. Lincoln is a charming personality, but he does not seem to have much conversation."

Robert Lincoln was to have increasingly an inner circle of congenial friends among the wealthy and prominent people of his country. One finds him writing from 2 Cromwell Houses, S.W., in London warm personal letters to Andrew Carnegie, who had invited him to visit him in Scotland.

Mr. and Mrs. Lincoln dined with Queen Victoria, and she wrote in her journal at Windsor Castle: "Mr. Lincoln is very pleasant and sensible." One cannot help wondering what the conventional little queen would have written if Abraham Lincoln had dined with her.

Robert and his family returned from England in 1893 when Ambassador Bayard succeeded him. That same year Harvard conferred upon him the degree of Doctor of Laws. He had now given eight years of his life to public service. Ever since his mother had seen that little notice in the *American Register*, there had been recurring talk of him as a candidate for President. The drawing power of the name of Lincoln (especially to the colored people) and his undoubted ability and integrity were powerful attractions for a candidate. But he did not have his father's great magnetic personality which included a love of people and politics and the last thing he desired was to be President. "It seems difficult for the average American to understand that it is possible for anyone not to desire the Presidency," he once said, "but I most certainly do not. I have seen enough of the inside of Washington official life to have lost all interest for it. The Presidential office is but a gilded prison. Its cares and worries outweigh the honor which surrounds the position."

Even as late as 1912, when Robert Lincoln was sixty-nine, it was suggested that he be a candidate for President. His letter to his friend George H. Thacher gives his emphatic refusal. By that time he was in such poor health that he could decline with a clear conscience. "A man ought not to *shirk* public duties," he wrote, "but equally he ought not to undertake them if he knows he has become unfit to do them."

CHAPTER 22

Attention of President Lincoln's Son

AFTER the Lincoln family returned from England in 1893, Robert found that law practice had lost its charms for him. He wrote John Nicolay just after the New Year of 1894 had come in: "I am trying to get to work again but the shop has ceased to interest me, I am sorry to say." Robert was cut out for a businessman and business claimed him from that time on. By his own statement later, "the conduct of a business . . . was in every way pleasant to me," its "regularly renewing problems" were "a positive pleasure to tackle."

He succeeded so well that in 1897 he was made president of the Pullman Company. By that time he had become one of the nation's well-known financiers and business leaders. He was spoken of as a "Captain of Industry" and associated with the other men of money and power in the United States. The son of the President who had been born in a log cabin was a millionaire.

During the White House years he and his mother (in the summer of 1863) had fled from the Washington heat which neither of them could well endure to the coolness of Manchester, Vermont. The summer climate and the charm of the scene appealed to Robert, and in 1902 he bought several hundred acres of the beautiful mountain and valley land, upon which he built his country mansion called Hildene. It was like the estate of an English gentleman and included gardens, lawns, and woodland. Here he could be secluded with his family and accessible only to his chosen inner circle of friends. He had other places of retreat and recreation also. On May 7, 1896, he wrote a friend from Chicago: "I am just leaving town for our spring fishing in Lake Erie (The Peter Club, Sandusky, Ohio), where I want to stay until May 20th. . . ." Once more he was getting the pattern of his life as he wished it, and this time he would keep it unbroken by the demands of public life.

But he retained a keen interest in politics. He had even done some campaigning on his leave from London in 1892. In 1894 a group of young men in New York appropriately named their Republican club the Robert T. Lincoln Club. They gave a reception for him and he talked with them for an hour. He was intensely Republican and a conservative Republican. He took a dim view of the opposing party, especially as regards business matters. "If we don't all bust before this Democratic trouble passes on," he wrote Nicolay in that same year of 1894, "I have a scheme for an addition to my house. . . ." But he wanted to be fair and he gave the Democrats credit where he felt he could. The following year a newspaper quoted him as saying: ". . . I think Mr. Cleveland has made a remarkably good President in many respects, and I am glad the country has such a good President, even if he is a Democrat and although I do not agree with him politically."

Robert made a speech at Danville, Illinois, in the campaign for McKinley in 1900. It is said this was his last political speech, and in the accounts of this occasion appears a most appealing story. With his usual aversion to public notice he arrived and registered at his hotel as quietly as possible. Then he disappeared. Several hours later, when the time for his speech was approaching, those in charge, getting into something of a panic, began to search for him. They found him at the home of an aged Negro woman, Mrs. Maria Vance, eating corn pone and bacon! Mrs. Vance had once been cook at the Lincoln home in Springfield and, learning that she was in Danville, Robert had looked her up. They had had a fine time visiting and though he had to leave to make his speech, he returned after it and stayed with her until time to catch his train. The aged servant undoubtedly found him a most sympathetic, approachable, and entertaining visitor and from that time on she received a substantial check from him every month. Robert was quietly generous to many who were in need.

He had acquired a becoming mustache comparatively early. One does not know exactly when the dimple in his chin retreated behind a beard not unlike that of his father. Ida M. Tarbell, biographer of Abraham Lincoln, interviewed Robert when he was president of the Pullman Company and gave a description which brings him into sharp focus. It was almost unbelievable to her, she wrote (in her autobiography, *All in the Day's Work*), to be drinking tea with the son of Abraham Lincoln. She searched his face and manner for resemblances but could not find them: "He was all Todd, a big plump man . . . perfectly groomed with that freshness which makes men of his type look as if they were just out of the barber's chair, the admirable social poise of the man who has seen the world's greatest and has come to be sure of himself; and this in spite of such buffeting as few men have had." She reflected that the Republican party would have been happy to make him their leader, if he had had the "political genius" of his father, but she thought they had tried him out and found he was not "political timber." She, of course, wanted material from him for her writing on his father. He was "very friendly" but said "he was afraid he had little that would help me."

Biographers of his father were always besetting him with questions and requests for material; it was one of the penalties he paid for being Lincoln's son. After 1865 his existence was conditioned in many ways by the fact that Abraham Lincoln had been his father. It was, paradoxically, both a shadow and a glare always upon him. It denied him credit for his own achievements; it threw him in painful contrast with his father, rather unfairly so, as the nation has produced only one statesman like Abraham Lincoln, and it is a devastating thing for anyone to be measured by his greatness.

Robert shrank from the role of President Lincoln's son in general but he was zealous in one phase of it, the protecting of his father's memory from what he considered misrepresentation or error. His quarrel with Ward Hill Lamon over Lamon's biography of Lincoln was an example of the son's resentment of untrue statements about his father. Lamon's book had been written from the material Herndon had collected, and one can well imagine Robert's furious indignation when in 1889, the year he went to England, the Herndon-Weik biography of Lincoln, based on the same material, was published. Robert had written Herndon twenty-three years before that exposing the private life of an individual "to the public gaze" was one of the worst penalties of political success, and he saw no reason why a man's wife and children should also be given to the public. Herndon's book laid stress on Mrs. Lincoln's emotional instability in terms slanted by his hatred of her. It contained the Ann Rutledge legend, a dramatic description of a wedding occasion at which his father as bridegroom failed to appear (the product of Herndon's vivid imagination), the theory that his father had not loved his mother, and other misconceptions at which the son had good reason to be outraged. Robert expressed his opinion of what Herndon had done as follows: "I became convinced that he was actuated by an intense malice, and was possessed of a most ingenious imagination. The malice arose, I am quite sure, from the fact that my father could not see his way, in view of Herndon's personal character, to give him some lucrative employment during the War of the Rebellion."

There can be no doubt that Robert Lincoln loathed Herndon. Herndon in his turn gave vent to his feeling about Robert by describing him in such belittling terms as little, mean, malicious, pig-headed, silly, cold, and a damned fool. These terms were ultimately to find their way into print and probably contributed to the present-day public opinion of Robert Lincoln.

Much as Robert resented the Herndon-Weik life of his father, there was little he could do about it. To make the matter more embarrassing, an English edition was issued while he was in London as minister. A story was circulated that he bought up this English edition and destroyed it, but David Donald, Herndon's biographer, thinks this doubtful. Mr. Donald found no evidence that Robert tried to suppress the book either in England or America. He did find that Robert influenced one publisher not to republish the Herndon-Weik biography, but another company did so in 1892. Robert's justified bitterness about the misrepresentations in the Herndon biography had to go on to the end of his life, with each new generation avidly reading the book and forming from it their impressions about his father and mother.

First and last the biographers of his father took up a great deal of Robert's time and attention. In the early eighteen seventies John G. Nicolay and John Hay were already taking their first steps in the work which would ultimately become their ten-volume life of Lincoln. They were also to edit what they called the *Complete Works of Abraham Lincoln*. Their biography had to be submitted to Robert's eye and to his very definite ideas of what it should contain. Their letters to him show how extremely anxious they were to write nothing that would offend him or interfere with his co-operation. There is some justification for Herndon's opinion that they were "afraid of Bob." In their work Robert let them use his father's presidential papers, that vast and famous collection commonly called "The Lincoln Papers."

David C. Mearns in his introduction to his two-volume work *The Lincoln Papers* has given a detailed and fascinating account of the various happenings pertaining to this collection from the year 1865 up to that memorable night in July 1947 when it was at last opened to the public. J. G. Randall in Volume III of *Lincoln the President: Midstream* has discussed the contents of the papers in general and their value to historians. The concern here is with Robert's actions and attitudes in regard to these papers. From the first the possession of them was a heavy responsibility to him, and by and by he found it hard to decide what was best to do with them. Through the years he was constantly besieged with requests to see them. "I confess to a great disinclination to looking over the papers," he wrote David Davis as early as 1871, "for I will have a host of people after one thing or another." Robert was the last person to want a host of people after him. The present author, having worked daily in this collection for several months, can appreciate Robert's difficulty in trying to sort out any particular item from the vast miscellany of forty-one thousand pieces with millions of handwritten words, some of them very hard to decipher.

After Nicolay and Hay had used the papers, Robert still pondered what he would do with them. "If my son was still alive," he wrote Herbert Putnam, Librarian of Congress, in 1902, "I should probably leave these papers in his hands. . . ." By that time Mr. Putnam had diplomatically suggested that the Library of Congress would be a most appropriate place to deposit them. Mr. Putnam's many letters to Robert on this subject show almost superhuman tact and caution, as is the case with the letters of Nicolay and Hay to "Bob." One gets the impression that the letter writers knew they were dealing with an individual who must be handled with gloves.

Robert was taking good care of his father's papers. In 1911 he resigned as president of the Pullman Company and became chairman of the board of directors. The following year the Lincoln family broke up the home in Chicago and moved to Washington, D.C. Robert gave the address in an invitation to William Lincoln Shearer to visit him: "My residence there is 3014 N Street, in a part of Washington which was formerly Georgetown. I live in a very old house which is interesting in various ways." The three-story colonial brick mansion was indeed interesting; it had been built in the seventeen hundreds, was beautifully furnished, and became a show place.

From this time on, it was the custom of the family to go to Hildene in Vermont in the spring and return to Washington in the fall. Robert loved Hildene. "We are all very well & happy up here in the Mountains & all dread being driven away by the cold winter to come," he wrote Nicolay's daughter Helen in November 1912. The Lincolns made the trips back and forth in their private railroad car, and Robert took the Lincoln Papers (there were eight trunks of them) back and forth with him to Manchester and Washington.

The question is often asked: "Did Robert Lincoln burn his father's presidential papers?" The answer is no. The source of the impression that he burned them is a reminiscence related by Nicholas Murray

Butler, president of Columbia University, both in an article in the *Saturday Evening Post* and in his autobiography. According to the *Saturday Evening Post* account Mr. Butler in 1923 visited Robert at Hildene and noticed in the library "an old-fashioned trunk which was standing near one of the bookshelves." He asked about the trunk and Robert answered: ". . . it contains only some family papers which I am going to burn." Mr. Butler, jumping to the conclusion that the papers were Lincoln's presidential papers, launched into a prolonged and eloquent argument that Robert must not destroy these papers, that they belonged to the nation and he should put them in the Library of Congress. One suspects that Robert, who of all men knew the uses of taciturnity, said little and let the flow of language pass over him without attempt to check it. Mr. Butler's memory may have been faulty after the passage of years, for he believed he had saved the presidential papers of Abraham Lincoln for the nation. But at the time this visit and conversation took place in 1923 Robert had already put the Lincoln Papers in the Library of Congress; they had been there for four years. When Robert said "family papers" he undoubtedly meant private family papers in his own files, which were a very different thing from the papers that had been in his father's files in the presidential office.

The Lincoln Papers (the full title is "The Robert Todd Lincoln Collection of the Papers of Abraham Lincoln") were deposited in the Library of Congress with the condition they were not to be opened to the public until twenty-one years after Robert's death. Another question frequently asked is: "Why did Robert Lincoln put this restriction on them?" He himself said in his deed of gift: "This condition is imposed by me because said papers contain many references of a private nature to the immediate ancestors of persons now living, which, in my judgment, should not be made public. . . ." Robert knew from experience how much pain "references of a private nature" could cause. At one time, speaking of this feature of the papers, he told Ida Tarbell that he was considering burning them. He also felt that Nicolay and Hay had used most of the material of historical importance in the papers, but those who have examined them know how very wrong he was in this. Robert with his circumscribed Victorian ideas of what history and biography should contain was anything but a judge of what is useful historically. Nicolay and Hay had written under his surveillance a useful but lifeless biography with little of the personal life of Lincoln. As J. G. Randall has said: "The papers are highly valuable for the kind of book that Nicolay and Hay did not write."

Many believe that the twenty-one-year delay was also stipulated by Robert's determination to prevent Albert J. Beveridge from using them. Beveridge, while writing his biography of Lincoln, had used every pressure on Robert to get his permission to use the papers. Beveridge had the use of Herndon's papers before they were finally opened to the public in 1942 and rated Herndon very highly. Robert, knowing the distortions and falseness of some of Herndon's conclusions, did not care to assist Beveridge in the circumstances.

One can thank Robert Lincoln that he preserved his father's papers and presented them to the Library of Congress substantially intact. He did give a few of them, a very few, away, but these were not destroyed. The matter of his own papers and family letters, however, is another story. He did destroy some of his mother's letters and one does not know how many more private and personal letters. Robert Lincoln's own papers have not become available and scholars have been unable to determine their whereabouts or what they will contain, if they ever come to light.

He inherited his mother's papers as well as his father's. Robert's attention had to be given to matters that devolved upon him not only because he was President Lincoln's sole surviving son; many perplexing questions were forced upon him because he was also the son of the unfortunate and misunderstood Mary Todd Lincoln. Her mental illness with its resulting complications in his life had scarred him. He sometimes in letters to friends described what he had suffered from it. He wrote Robert Sterling Yard, editor of the *Century*, in 1914 mentioning his mother's derangement and adding bitterly: "I could not hold her back from doing many things that distressed me beyond any power of description; advertising her old clothes for sale and writing begging letters by the hundreds were only a part of what I had to grieve and be mortified about; there was any quantity of newspaper publicity about her actions and writings and much of my time was spent in sadly answering inquiries about her. It all nearly wore my life out."

For a while he tried to gather up and destroy those of her letters which disclosed her irrationality, but he found the task was hopeless. He wrote a friend in 1913: "Of course I regret the existence of these relics of the long years of the distressing mental disorder of my mother but it is idle to think of gathering them up. Hundreds of them have been kindly sent me for destruction and I am quite sure that there exist still other hundreds."

His wish to destroy these letters which were evidence of his mother's irrationality is at least understandable, but there are indications that Mrs. Lincoln's papers contained documents which would have been treasured infinitely by posterity. Mrs. Lincoln, writing to Mrs. Welles about three months after her husband's assassination, spoke of arranging "a large package of *his,* dear, loving letters to me, many of them written to me, in the 'long ago,' and quite yellow with age, others, more recent & *one* written from his office, *only* the *Wednesday, before* [his death]." Fourteen years later she answered one who had asked for Lincoln's autograph from Pau, France: "I regret to inform you, that all his letters to me were enclosed in a small trunk & left in America." The swift, wild conjecture arises: could this have been the trunk that Nicholas Murray Butler saw? These priceless letters almost certainly were among Mrs. Lincoln's papers which Robert inherited and they have not come to light. Robert wrote shortly after his mother's death: "I have not examined any of my mother's papers, and do not believe that anything will be found among them of sufficient importance for preservation." Had he but realized it, the publication of his father's loving letters to his mother would have quickly scotched Herndon's theory that Abraham Lincoln did not love his wife. (Fortunately, a few did not come into Robert's hands and these have been used in this story.) To Robert such documents were like Queen Victoria's letter to his mother, of too private and personal a nature to be given to the public. He acted according to his own ideas of what was proper, but if Robert destroyed those letters from his father to his mother, as seems likely, it is hard for present-day biographers to be reconciled to the loss. Mr. Mearns says in his introduction to *The Lincoln Papers:* ". . . it seems certain that Robert Lincoln did actually destroy some Lincoln letters, for the family tells how his granddaughter, Mary Lincoln Beckwith, once watched him as he threw some on the grate."

One knows that many of Robert's private papers were disposed of when the family moved to Washington. When asked about a certain letter in 1916 Robert replied: "It was probably destroyed with an immense number of old letters and papers when I broke up my residence in Chicago about five years ago. . . ."

In justice to Robert it should be stated that he did help in giving information to people, if he felt they ought to be helped. His letters in mature years show courtesy, consideration, and the desire to do the right thing when people made reasonable requests for information about his father. If he knew and trusted them, he would go to great pains. Incidentally, there is an interesting bit in a letter he wrote Helen Nicolay in answer to some question she had asked. Robert's postscript is intriguing: "In the Chase item," he wrote, "what my father actually said was not 'something' but 'some deviltry of Chase's,' but it is perhaps better to leave it as you have it."

To Robert the destroying of his father's personal letters was doing unto others as he would have them do unto him; it was protecting his father's privacy from an improper and distasteful curiosity. Robert was kept busy protecting his father's memory from a number of things. Every student of Abraham Lincoln knows there are fradulent claims concerning him and writings said to be his which are forgeries. Robert properly resented any such hoax. He objected to the so-called "birth cabin" as not authentic and wrote indignantly in 1919: "The structure now enshrined in a great marble building in Kentucky is a fraud when represented as the actual house." He disapproved of the "Lincoln Family" pictures which are all composite pictures. He felt they were a kind of fraud too, because, "There was never such a group actually assembled." His objection to the cabin as unauthentic was apt to be interpreted in the public mind as shame that his father had been born in a log cabin. One does not find false pride in the mature Robert Lincoln; he was a modest and retiring man, but his natural reserve sometimes gave the impression of snobbishness. It should be noted that he took pains to mark the lowly graves of his grandparents, Thomas and Nancy Hanks Lincoln.

Robert even tried to protect his father from what he considered sculptural slander. A small book could be written about the controversy over George G. Barnard's statue of Lincoln which raged especially in the latter part of the year 1917. (This has sometimes been called "the stomach-ache statue," because the hands are placed over the middle of the torso in a way that suggests hidden woe.) There are those today who consider it a great work of art, but to Robert Lincoln it was a "monstrosity." When he heard that a replica of this statue was to be erected in London, he started a determined fight against the move and enlisted the support of many prominent people. He wrote former President Taft a long letter which seethed with indignation over this "monstrous figure which is grotesque as a likeness of President Lincoln and defamatory as an effigy."

It was an international matter and a delicate one, as the Barnard statue had already been accepted by the public authorities in London. But Robert was a tenacious fighter and had all the resources of wealth and of knowing the right people. It is sufficient here to say that after a long-drawn-out war of words a replica of the superb Saint-Gaudens standing statue of Lincoln was unveiled in London with great ceremony in 1920. The Barnard statue in question was placed in Manchester, England.

Robert had been caused genuine unhappiness by the thought of the Barnard statue in London and felt deep gratification when the battle against it was won. In writing Nicholas Murray Butler to thank him for his support in the matter he made the comment: "I am more than ever proud of a father for whom friends came so nobly to the rescue of his memory from an enduring outrage. . . ."

The words "more than ever proud" are the keynote of what had been happening in Robert's feeling about his father during the long years. What Allan Nevins has called "the great, turbulent, confused experiment of living" is likely to bring to anyone a better comprehension of fundamental values. As Robert met the complications and afflictions of his own life, he could better understand the patient wisdom of his father in meeting the far more difficult problems of his. He came increasingly to appreciate his father's qualities of greatness.

In his later years nothing pleased him more than to hear his father praised. But he wanted no mention of his mother, he would not talk or write of her. Nor did he want others to write of her. He asked Abram Wakeman, Jr. (son of Abram Wakeman of New York, who had been a good friend of his father's and mother's), not to publish any letters written by her because so many of them showed her "derangement" and "were a source of great unhappiness to me." Because he would not give his cousin Elizabeth Grimsley the nod of approval for publishing her long and valuable article, "Six Months in the White House," its publication was delayed until after his death. It was not that this article contained anything to which he could reasonably object. But it was an intimate account of the Lincolns in those first months in Washington and contained much about his mother.

Robert's love and veneration for his father grew until it was a marked characteristic in his later life. Sometimes one gets a glimpse of his regret that he had not had him longer. Writing William Lincoln Shearer upon the death of Dr. Shearer, Robert said: "Let me assure you of my earnest sympathy in this affliction, which should be tempered to you by your having had your father with you for so many years."

The son shunned writing about Abraham Lincoln. "I think that publications respecting my father had better come from others than myself, and I have always acted upon that feeling," he once wrote Abram Wakeman, Jr. But on one occasion he broke his rule and made a speech about Abraham Lincoln. It was at Galesburg, Illinois, on October 7, 1896, the thirty-eighth anniversary of the Lincoln-Douglas debate in that town. It is hard to know how far the son, whose whole make-up tended to give him tastes and views different from his father's, could enter into Abraham Lincoln's basic thinking, but in this speech Robert dealt with American democracy, the rule of the people, in which his father had had a great sustaining faith. To President Lincoln the Civil War was a testing of that democracy; it must be won in order that the American form of government might survive. He had said on the battlefield of Gettysburg, above the new-made graves of the soldiers who had died there: "It is rather for us to be here dedicated to the great task remaining before us . . . that we here highly resolve that these dead shall not have died in vain—that this nation, under God, shall have a new birth of freedom—and that, government of the people, by the people, for the people, shall not perish from the earth."

It is rather fascinating to consider Robert Lincoln's statement on the American democracy for which his father, in effect, had given his life. Robert at Galesburg first spoke of the issues of that year 1858 when Abraham Lincoln debated with Stephen A. Douglas. His father, said Robert, had "called the struggle one between right and wrong. In spite of the great odds against him he battled on, sustained by conscience and supported by the idea that when the fogs cleared away the people would be found on the side of right. . . . Now, as then, there can be but one supreme issue, that between right and wrong."

Robert continued with his own declaration of faith: "In our country there are no ruling classes. The right to direct public affairs according to his might and influence and conscience belongs to the humblest as well as to the greatest. The elections represent the judgments of individual voters. . . . The power of the people, by their judgments expressed through the ballot box, to shape their own destinies, sometimes makes one tremble. But it is times of danger, critical moments, that bring into action the high moral quality of the citizenship of America. The people are always true. They are always right, and I have an abiding faith they will remain so."

To Robert, in his mature appreciation of his father, the building of the Lincoln Memorial in Washington was a supreme joy. He once wrote Charles Moore of the Library of Congress: "I cannot find just the word I would like to express my feeling of admiration for it in every way. . . ." He watched every step in the progress of its construction with intense interest, and to Representative John W. Dwight, who had worked earnestly for the appropriation to build it, he gave a rare gift, the original manuscript of his father's speech to the crowd who gathered outside the White House after the election of 1864.

In his later years when Robert Lincoln would drive out on winter afternoons in Washington, the route was very apt to include a turn around that lovely temple on the Mall. There would be a stop and a pause while the son of Abraham Lincoln gazed with silent emotion through the temple's portals at that beautiful luminous statue of his father. Perhaps the soft radiance that played upon it in the twilight was like the feeling that had come to shine upon the memory of his father in his own heart.

CHAPTER 23

The Enigma of Robert Lincoln

JUDGING from the questions asked about him, the eldest son of Abraham Lincoln is today an enigma in the public mind. Over and over again one is asked: "What was Robert Lincoln like?" Along with these questions there is often an attitude of hostility. And if people come across the various things that have been said about him, their confusion is increased, as the statements are so contradictory.

His father's well-known comments on him ("one of the little rare-ripe sort," "a little rascal," and so on) perhaps have given him a bad start in public opinion. There is little doubt that he was a cantankerous, unadjusted child, but like everybody else, Robert Lincoln had to be a number of individuals before he emerged into his mature self. The difficulty of adjustment, however, lasted through all his life. Dr. W. A. Evans, writing in the nineteen thirties, spoke of his "peculiarities of personality," but realized with a physician's understanding that he had had terrible experiences which had left deep scars and maladjustments. Dr. Evans disagreed with those who thought he had in youth "a phlegmatic temperament" and found him "supersensitive," "over-emotional," and many of his attitudes "defence reactions."

His friend Nicholas Murray Butler thought he had "an inferiority complex." He quoted him as saying that he was not Robert Lincoln but Abraham Lincoln's son. "No one wanted me for Secretary of War," he remarked gloomily; "they wanted Abraham Lincoln's son. No one wanted me for minister to England; they wanted Abraham Lincoln's son. No one wanted me for president of the Pullman Company; they wanted Abraham Lincoln's son." There hardly could be a better expression of the frustration that goes with being the son of a great man; Mr. Butler thought it "darkened" much of Robert's life. It increased his aversion to publicity, as he felt he received attention merely because he was his father's son. He was almost morbidly anxious not to trade upon this fact. This aloofness in turn made people think he was snobbish. Society does not adjust to a maladjusted personality any better than such a personality adjusts to society. The fact that Robert was wealthy, powerful, and lived like an aristocrat increased the resentment at his apparent snobbishness.

Added to these unfavorable impressions in general have been the attitudes of certain groups whose opinions differed from his. Historians and biographers have resented his withholding or destroying historical material. They feel a helpless anger that one who was in an incomparable position to give a close-up, personal view of a great national hero declined, because of a set, outmoded notion, to do so. Perhaps this feeling is that Lincoln belongs to the nation and it is a sort of cheating for one individual to withhold any part of him. One finds historians calling him "narrow-minded," "lofty," "pompous and misanthropic." Carl Sandburg describes him as "a distinguished, troubled, peculiar, and sometimes smug individual."

Politics being what it is, he has, of course, been denounced by those who disagreed with him politically. Robert Lincoln was sincere in his views as a conservative Republican. This drew the fire of liberals, who called him "arch-conservative and orthodox," " 'respectable,' " and as stereotyped in his time as his father was unique. He has received censure because he was George Pullman's attorney at the time of the Pullman strike. As the result of the panic of 1893 the Pullman Company reduced the wages of its employees, and this was followed by the famous Pullman strike of 1894. Robert was accused of refusing a living wage to Pullman porters, who belong to a race his father had set free.

One can see the points of view which selected certain of these descriptive terms. Robert Lincoln's pattern of thinking was set in the Victorian era in which he grew up, and the Victorians seem very "narrow-minded" and "pompous" (perhaps stuffy is a better word) today. He was certainly a "troubled" personality. He was "smug" in the sense that he believed firmly in the rightness of his own opinions. The other side of this is that a sincere man (and Robert was sincere) lives by what he believes. It is the word "misanthropic" which gives one the longest pause. Robert shunned the public, but he was no hater of mankind.

The above were the views of those who did not know Robert personally and were disagreeing with his ideas. They had no impression of the kindly, genial man, devoted husband, father, and friend described by those who visited with him at Hildene and Washington. These friends have set their words of praise and affection against the various terms of blame. Congressman Joseph Cannon of

Illinois, "Uncle Joe Cannon," was one of those who broke through the barrier of Robert Lincoln's reserve to understand him and he told the result. "Uncle Joe" did not warm up to him at first; as he said: "I got the early impression of him that thousands of others had. Later, as I learned him, I loved him." This warm tie doubtless was strengthened by the fact that in many ways the two thought alike.

Those who knew Robert Lincoln intimately did love him. One can assemble an anthology of praise from them. They spoke of him as "intensely patriotic," and "a genial acquaintance, a most delightful companion and the most loyal of friends." Senator George F. Hoar, who had urged his appointment as minister to England, said: "He was a very modest man indeed, never pressing any claim to public consideration or office, either on his own account or as his father's son. . . . But I had noticed that when he had anything to say or anything to do, he always said or did the wisest and best thing to be said or done under the circumstances."

Nicholas Murray Butler found him "shy and reserved, but full of human kindness and generous feeling which he often hesitated to reveal." Looking at him as he sat in the home of the aged Negro woman in Danville, Illinois, talking eagerly with her of old times, eating her corn pone and bacon, and afterwards adding her to the list of those whom he quietly pensioned, one sees a close-up of that kindliness and generosity.

His consideration is revealed in an incident told by Mary Grimsley Donaldson, granddaughter of his cousin Elizabeth Grimsley. Robert came to Springfield once when Mrs. Donaldson's mother was very ill. On hearing this, as Mrs. Donaldson relates the story, "he came to our house right away. He stood at the door when I opened it with a beautiful basket of fruit and a very large armful of big pink roses. He asked me about Mother and when she heard his voice she called 'Come up Bob.' He sat in the rocker by her bed for some time and was most affectionate and sympathetic."

One gets closest perhaps to Robert Lincoln in the memorable letters he wrote his Aunt Emilie Todd Helm and her daughter Katherine. There are more than fifty of these letters to draw a well-rounded portrait of him in later life. Here is a loving and considerate man watching over Emilie and her children, taking pains to help her untangle her problems, telling her the family news, speaking of the pleasure of their visits together, remembering her birthday with "enclosures," and giving warm, understanding sympathy for illness or trouble. They reveal Robert the father anxious about "our girl Jessie," who was approaching her second confinement: "She had such a bad time before. . . ." They show his enjoyment of his grandchildren: "Jessie & her two kids are with us & do their best to make us feel young." He wrote appealingly of his granddaughter Mary with her hair "flying in the sun," calling her by her nickname "Peggy" and adding fondly, "she is a great pet whatever she does."

Pleasure in his relatives is in these letters. After meeting a new one who was "jolly & pretty & fascinating" he remarked: "I have a pretty nice lot of cousins & am proud of them." One can trace the deep devotion between himself and his wife as ill health darkened his days: "Mary . . . takes the best possible care of me." "We are alone here, leading a very quiet life & sliding down the hill as gently as we can."

Many of Robert's friends stress what a charming conversationalist and excellent storyteller he was. Occasionally a passage in one of his letters gives a glimpse of this personal charm which had even won the approval of Her Royal Highness, Queen Victoria. "He had his father's sense of humor," said a friend who had chatted with him in the "Bob Lincoln Corner" of the Metropolitan Club in his later years, "and was a most delightful raconteur." Senses of humor are of many kinds and degrees and while it is not questioned that Robert had one which was a delight to his friends, it might be questioned that it was the same kind as his father's. Abraham Lincoln used his humor, and his storytelling, as an instrument in his great art of dealing with people. His humor went with a marked ability to see the viewpoint of others, and with a broad tolerance and compassion. It was that great type of humor which has as its complement a vast sympathy for the sorrows of mankind.

The comparison of Robert's qualities with those of his father is inevitable. Much of the hostile attitude of the public stems from the fact that he was so unlike Abraham Lincoln. He was miscast in the role of his father's son. Joseph Cannon in speaking of his initial not too friendly feeling toward Robert coupled it with the statement that he was "wholly different in views, actions and physique from his father." People have been positively indignant at Robert because he did not inherit his father's qualities. It was a handicap he could not overcome and Mr. Cannon added with keen perception: "The public, I do not suppose, ever will come to regard the man at his true worth." Robert had said truly that he could never be just himself, Robert Lincoln, that he could only be regarded as Abraham Lincoln's son. A corollary of this was that he was constantly being compared to his father to his own disparagement. In basic integrity of character, in high abilities, and in the determination to do the right as he saw it, Robert was his father's son. Few good and distinguished citizens, however, can stand up under comparison to Abraham Lincoln's self-lessness, his vision as a statesman, and his concern for the welfare of mankind.

In 1894 Robert Lincoln was fifty-one years old. It was a time when he should have felt vigorous and happy in his successful career, but the buffetings and pressures of the years had begun early to take their toll. He wrote Nicolay in December of that year: "I wonder if you are getting to feel so miserably old as I do. My daughter & her baby live a thousand miles away & the whole future seems merely so many days to be passed." The baby was Lincoln Isham, son of his daughter Mary, who had married Charles Isham.

Those who looked enviously on his luxurious manner of living did not know his secret worries. In that same month Nicolay wrote "Bob" that he had been having trouble with his eyes and Robert answered: "I have been pulling along with only one eye for many years in a lopsided way, like a cab-horse in Vienna & have been a little worried at times but now have confidence in its lasting me out." Presumably this weak eye was the one that had been crossed in childhood and had earned him the nickname "Cockeye" from his schoolmates. The good eye, as he had hoped, was destined to last him out and he read much in his later years.

His increasing ill health runs through his letters. Four years later he was writing Nicolay again: "I hope you are very well. I am sorry to say that I am not." In 1906 he wrote Herbert Putnam of the Library of Congress: ". . . I was so foolish as to permit myself to go down very much in the condition of my nerves, so that instead of devoting some time last winter, as I had hoped to do, in the examination of my father's papers, I was compelled to lay up for more than three months, and did absolutely nothing whatever, not even replying to private notes. I am, I believe, a good deal better, and hope for a complete recovery in a few months." His letters to his Aunt Emilie frequently mention his "nervous dyspepsia" and "nervous prostration."

Abraham Lincoln in his youth had considered himself as having "defective nerves" and certainly his wife's nervous system was ill-balanced; perhaps the son had a heritage of "nerves." His father, however, had developed a selfless philosophy that helped him endure; his mother in her youth had had buoyancy and a cheerful interest in people and the details of living. But it had been hard for Robert ever to attain serenity of spirit; there had always been something to spoil it. When a friend had congratulated him on becoming president of the Pullman Company, he had answered: "I am afraid that the work thrown upon me makes me the subject of anything but congratulations." That triumph had come at a time of great distress for him. The *Chicago Tribune,* on the same page where it had a long article on his election to this presidency, carried an account of his daughter Jessie's elopement with an attractive young athlete, Warren Beckwith, a member of the football team at Mount Pleasant, Iowa. It was a marriage which Robert and his wife had bitterly opposed, and they had thought the attachment broken off. On November 10, 1897 (this was the day before his election), word of the elopement had come to them at their home, and dumbfounded they had hurried to Jessie's room, only to find her gone. She had been married several hours before. Robert's comment to the avid press was: "There is no use denying it, my daughter is of age, and she married against my advice." On November 12 the *Chicago Tribune* quoted him as saying: "I have not seen the young man, and I shall not extend my pardon to him." Perhaps it was the familiar case where a parent with a determined will encounters the same determination in his offspring.

The marriage ultimately ended in divorce. Many years later Warren Beckwith was quoted in the *Chicago Tribune* as saying that Robert Lincoln was nice to him, but it was Mrs. Robert Lincoln who "was always interfering in our marriage." Jessie Lincoln had two children by Warren Beckwith: Mary Lincoln Beckwith and Robert Lincoln Beckwith. They with Lincoln Isham are, as of this writing, the only descendants of Abraham Lincoln living today. As they have no children, it is expected that the Lincoln blood will die out with them.

The poor state of Robert's health was demonstrated dramatically in 1909. In May he attended the unveiling of the Lincoln statue by Adolph A. Weinman at Hodgenville, Kentucky, the birthplace of his father. The dedication took place on Memorial Day. It was a great event for the little county seat; visitors from all over Kentucky poured in, among them a number of Civil War veterans, some who had worn the blue, some who had worn the gray. Robert Lincoln came in his private car, which stopped at Louisville, Kentucky, to welcome aboard his Aunt Emilie Todd Helm, now well past seventy but retaining still her spirited charm. Aunt and nephew greeted each other with great affection and talked eagerly together as the train moved on toward Hodgenville.

A carriage met "Bob Lincoln," as they called him, at the station, and he was driven in a parade which marched behind a band to the public square. Here in front of the flag-draped statue was a wooden platform. Robert, as always, took an inconspicuous place upon it.

The day was very warm and there was so much to stir his emotions. An old friend who had gone to school with him in Springfield came up to greet him and to recall memories of his boyhood. Some little girls brought him a nosegay and a wreath. With his characteristic love of children he patted them on the head and caressed them tenderly.

The high moment of the unveiling came. Emilie Todd Helm was the one who pulled the cord, releasing the flags which fell to the base revealing a beautiful seated statue of Abraham Lincoln. It was noticed that Robert was deeply moved and was having difficulty controlling his emotions. Then followed the oration of the day. The speaker was Colonel Watterson, "Marse Henry" Watterson, editor of the *Louisville Courier-Journal* and "an old and very dear friend" of Robert's. He delivered a deeply stirring, old-fashioned, eloquent oration. Robert, who now loved to hear his father praised, heard him extolled in golden phrases which led up to the lofty peroration: " . . . inspired by God was Abraham Lincoln; and a thousand years hence no drama, no tragedy, no epic poem, will be filled with greater wonder, or be followed by mankind with greater feeling than that which tells the story of his life and death."

It was all too much for Robert, the stirring of old memories, the meeting with his Aunt Emilie, the sight of that figure of his father seated in a chair in quiet and thoughtful mood, just as the son had often seen him at the home in Springfield. The combination of emotion and heat exhaustion overcame him. He determinedly had stayed on the platform until the ceremonies were over; then he had to be helped off it, put in a carriage, and rushed to his private car. He was in a state of almost complete collapse and complained of numbness over his left side. This passed in a few hours, but it was thought he narrowly escaped a paralytic stroke.

On the train returning he told how disappointed he was that his illness had prevented him from going out to the farm where his father had been born. He hoped he could return in the fall, he said. "Then I can walk over the farm and drink from the spring." His heart was warm toward those he had met; he felt he had never seen finer people than those at Hodgenville. He repeated how "grieved" he was that he had not seen his father's birthplace.

While Robert's health was becoming increasingly frail and he was much with doctors, it appears that his wife had become interested in Christian Science. Evidence of Robert's own attachment or connection with any particular church appears to be lacking. He seems not to have shared his wife's sentiments toward Christian Science, at least one finds an amusing passage (with sidelights) in a letter he wrote a friend apparently about fifteen years after his marriage. "Mrs. Lincoln is here [said her husband] & has what she calls a 'belief' that she has a little attack of Grippe. I am quite sure of it but she insists on fighting it out by herself, as she has done every thing else for now 15 years!" The exclamation mark showed his amused tolerance of her firmness of character, and his letters mentioning her reveal in general what a fortunate marriage this was for him; she was his "good wife" and he missed her terribly when she was away.

Incidentally, Mrs. Robert Todd Lincoln's attachment to Christian Science was to be revealed in her will. She was to survive her husband by nearly eleven years. She directed that after her death the income from the large estate which she had inherited from him should be distributed annually to the direct heirs. But if and when a time should come when there were no issues by blood descent, then the residuary estate was to be divided equally among the American Red Cross, the Christian Science Church, and Iowa Wesleyan College. Since the present three descendants have no issue, it is expected that this provision ultimately will go into effect. Some have estimated the recent value of this Lincoln fortune as more than three million dollars; if this is correct, the three organizations stand to be much enriched.

Because of his ill health Robert Lincoln resigned as president of the Pullman Company on May 18, 1911. He remained chairman of the board of directors until early in 1922. After his resignation his health improved somewhat, and following the move East, his life settled into a pleasant routine, winters in Washington, long summers at Hildene in Vermont. He had his chosen group of friends whom he met at their homes or his, or at his many clubs. He belonged to the Ekwanok Country Club at Manchester, Vermont (serving as president for many years), to the Union and Century Clubs of New York, the Metropolitan and Chevy Chase Clubs of Washington, and the Chicago and University Clubs of Chicago. He shunned public functions but nevertheless took an active interest in Manchester affairs, was a trustee of the Mark Skinner Library and a generous contributor to local charities and improvements.

He had his own special recreations at Hildene. With his great love of mathematics he delighted in working out its most complicated problems. He would take his surveying instruments and survey the grounds of the Ekwanok Club just for the fun of it. Astronomy fascinated him. He had a private observatory at Hildene with a powerful telescope, and a special wire ran to it to enable him to check his chronometer for accurate work in his astronomical calculations. In a letter to Nicholas Murray Butler on June 16, 1913, he described in imaginative terms what this relaxation meant to him. Mr. Butler was to pass near Hildene and Robert wrote him the exact time to look from his train to the left in the valley, where he would see on a hillside "a bright spot in the trees which is the dome of my observatory. From it I look nightly into a universe wherein there is no Referendum or Recall and only one body which is at once powerful and incalculably erratic, and though still influential upon the Tides, is said to be dead. I refer only to the Moon." Robert invited Mr. Butler to come and have a look and a brief relaxation from "political grief." He added: "Other consolations on call." One of the "consolations," and an important one to Robert, was golf.

Nicholas Murray Butler remembered that Robert would visit Augusta, Georgia, with a group of impressively prominent gentlemen who were facetiously dubbed "The Little Mothers." The name seems to have been bestowed upon them because they were charged with trying to take care of the whole world. This circle, according to Mr. Butler, included from time to time men who had been or were to be President of the United States. Presidents and other dignitaries were almost commonplace to Robert Lincoln. President Taft visited Hildene; President Coolidge was his friend. When visiting princes came to this country, the former "Prince of Rails," son of the great President Lincoln, was the nearest thing to royalty that the nation had. So when Prince Henry of Prussia arrived in Chicago in 1902, it was Robert Lincoln who rode in an open carriage with him through cheering crowds when he went to lay a wreath at the base of President Lincoln's statue.

Lloyd George came to this country in the fall of 1923 and passed by train through Manchester, Vermont. He had great admiration and reverence for Abraham Lincoln and wished to meet his son. Robert had been very ill, but in spite of his physician's advice against it, he went to the station to greet the British statesman. The two talked together a few moments and Lloyd George asked Robert what he remembered of the Civil War. Lincoln's son answered: "It is not much, except that I saw my father grow older and sadder as the struggle went on." He heard the distinguished visitor from England say: "There is no man in all the history of the world that I place higher than Abraham Lincoln."

He was eighty years old when he went to meet Lloyd George on that October day in 1923 and had become very frail. In his early seventies he had had something of a nervous breakdown and from that time on had lived a more retired and restricted life than ever. He retained his lively interest in business affairs, but small pressures which he would have taken in his stride in his prime had become intolerable to his tortured nerves. When he journeyed back and forth between Manchester, Vermont, and Washington in his private car, he now always took a physician with him.

His days settled into the sheltered routine of the semi-invalid. He would have breakfast in bed and remain there for his daily checkup by his physician. In the last few years he suffered from a chronic conjunctivitis, an inflammation of the eyelids, which the doctor treated every morning. After the medical examination he would get up, dress, and go to his library to attend to his correspondence. When the weather permitted he usually took a drive in the afternoon or saw something of his close friends. In the evenings he customarily dined with his family and sat with them in the library afterwards. He had with Mary Harlan Lincoln that fine and understanding companionship which comes only after many years of marriage; he had his interest in his two daughters and the three grandchildren, who were now grown up. At night when he retired he usually read in bed before going to sleep.

In 1922 the suggestion was made that President Lincoln's body be moved from Springfield to Washington. Robert wrote Nicholas Murray Butler that he strongly opposed it. He asked Mr. Butler to read again his father's farewell address to his old friends and neighbors at Springfield. The son then comprehended Abraham Lincoln's affection for the little town where he had lived so many years and his premonitory homesickness at leaving it. As to the Lincoln tomb in Oak Ridge Cemetery Robert wrote: "Within it are entombed the bodies of my father and my mother and my only son, and it is arranged that my wife and myself shall be entombed there." "Jack" Lincoln's body had been brought back from England and placed with that of the grandfather who had never known of him. The tomb contained four dear young lads named Lincoln whose lives had been pitifully brief.

To Robert Lincoln was given a swift passing at the end. On the morning of July 26, 1926, the servant who went to his room preparatory to serving his breakfast found he had died in the night. The physician said the cause was cerebral hemorrhage. Had he lived six days more, until August 1, Robert Lincoln would have been eighty-three.

The funeral held at his beloved Hildene was private and very simple; only the family and a few very close friends were present.

The services were conducted by the minister of Manchester's Congregational Church, D. Cunningham-Graham, who read the Twenty-third Psalm and some other passages from the Bible. No eulogy was spoken—he would not have wished it—but the poignant lines of Tennyson's "Crossing the Bar" were read. The casket was placed in a vault in Dellwood Cemetery near Hildene pending its removal to its final resting place. Manchester mourned; it had lost, as a Vermont newspaper said, "one of its greatest benefactors and its foremost citizen."

Strangely, the body remained in the receiving vault nearly two years, until March 14, 1928, and then it was removed, not to the Lincoln tomb at Springfield, but to Arlington National Cemetery at Washington. One does not know the why of this change of plan or whose decision it was. About two years later, in May 1930, "Jack" Lincoln's body, at the request of his mother, was taken from the tomb at Springfield and placed beside that of his father. They sleep under a large, impressive, pink granite monument in beautiful Arlington. There seems something almost symbolic in this final burial and in Robert Lincoln's birthplace. He was born in the Globe Tavern, but the other Lincoln sons were born in the home itself. They rest with their father and mother in Illinois, while he lies far way in the East. He had been different from them and had seemed a little outside that warm, inner circle of deep love, understanding, and mutual tastes that his parents and his brothers had known.

When the word went out over the wires on July 26, 1926, that Robert Lincoln had died, flags flew at half-mast at all army posts and stations out of respect for the former Secretary of War. Newspapers gave the news front-page headlines, and there was much reviewing of his outstanding career. The *Philadelphia Ledger* commented that few sons of Presidents had achieved such a national reputation. To Mary Harlan Lincoln, who had been his wife for nearly fifty-eight years, came a flood of telegrams and letters of sympathy and praise from all sides. The message of Frank B. Kellogg, Secretary of State, was typical of what his friends were saying on the death of Robert Todd Lincoln: "He had a distinguished public career and the nation will look back with gratitude and affection upon his great services as a statesman and a publicist. His death is the nation's loss. His career covered more than a half century of a notable period in American history. Those who knew him as I did will mourn the passing of a friend, a warm-hearted, charming gentleman."

Bibliography

In the years when I was engaged in research for the writing of *Mary Lincoln: Biography of a Marriage,* I made it a rule, wherever I found material on the Lincoln sons, to take a record of it. The bibliographies for the Lincoln marriage and the children of that marriage obviously overlap. In the research for this book, where the focus was on the sons, Robert Todd Lincoln's later life has been the most difficult task. It was his firm conviction that the personal life of an individual is no concern of the public and he acted on that conviction. His papers are not available and historians cannot get information as to their whereabouts.

The most substantial body of material on Robert Lincoln I have found is that collected by David C. Mearns, Chief of the Manuscripts Division, Library of Congress, when he was preparing his introduction to his two-volume work *The Lincoln Papers.* This extensive collection, which I used through the courtesy of Mr. Mearns, contains photostats and transcripts of many varied and valuable items. Its assortment of Robert Lincoln's letters from many sources has been most important to this study. The collection includes Robert's letters to J. G. Nicolay and John Hay, his extensive correspondence with them concerning the Nicolay and Hay biography of Abraham Lincoln, and their illuminating letters to each other commenting on him. It also contains Robert's correspondence with many people in regard to the Lincoln Papers, especially with the officials of the Library of Congress. There are articles from contemporary newspapers and magazines; there are photostats of legal documents, such as Robert Lincoln's commission as captain in the Civil War and the will of his widow Mary Harlan Lincoln. One legal item proved to be of special interest: American Security and Trust Co. and Mary H. Lincoln, Executors, etc., *vs.* Commissioners (1931), 24 *Board of Tax Appeals,* 334–338. After Robert Lincoln's death in July 1926 question was raised as to whether certain gifts which he had made to his wife that spring were "in anticipation of death" and were actuated by a wish to reduce inheritance tax. It was finally decided that the gifts had not been made in anticipation of death, but the proceeding involved a detailed account of Robert Lincoln's state of health and routine of living in his last few years, very useful material for a biographer. An interview which the author and her husband had in 1947 with Norman B. Frost, formerly secretary and counsel of Robert Lincoln, dovetailed with this record in completing the picture of the man of tortured nerves Robert Lincoln became in later life.

Other sources, taken from the annotations in the original manuscript of *Lincoln's Sons,* are given below.

Manuscript Collections

Abraham Lincoln Association Collection, Ill. State Hist. Lib. Valuable for transcripts, photostats, recollections, and other material. Special files on Robert Todd Lincoln, William Wallace Lincoln, and Thomas Lincoln.

Brown University Collection. Especially letters of Mrs. A. Lincoln.

Chicago Historical Society. Has numerous letters of Robert T. Lincoln and letters of Mr. and Mrs. Abraham Lincoln and their friends with items about the Lincoln sons. Contains the *Brown School Holiday Budget.*

University of Chicago Collection. Includes the William E. Barton Collection. Especially letters of Mrs. Lincoln and Willie Lincoln's letter of June 6, 1859.

Clinton Levering Conkling MSS., Ill. State Hist. Lib.

James Cook Conkling MSS., Ill. State Hist. Lib.

David Davis MSS. Photostats in possession of Willard L. King and used through his courtesy. Originals owned by David Davis IV. Very valuable for letters of Robert Lincoln, Mrs. Lincoln, Leonard Swett's letter concerning the sanity trial of Mrs. Lincoln, and letters of Judge and Mrs. Davis with intimate references to the Lincolns.

Benjamin Brown French MSS., Lib. of Cong.

Helm Collection. Papers of Emilie Todd Helm and her family in the possession of William H. Townsend. This collection contains more than fifty intimate family letters written by Robert Lincoln.

Herndon-Weik MSS., Lib. of Cong.

Henry E. Huntington Library Collections. They include the Ward H. Lamon MSS. and letters of Mrs. Lincoln.

Illinois State Historical Library Collections. Listing by groups of papers cannot give an adequate idea of the richness of this library in Lincoln material. Originals of letters and telegrams of Lincoln, Mrs. Lincoln, and Robert Lincoln and originals of Tad's telegrams have been indispensable to this study.

University of Illinois Library Collection. Includes many photostats and transcripts of manuscripts, especially the Emanuel Hertz collection of photostats.

Lincoln National Life Foundation Collection, Fort Wayne, Ind.

Lincoln Administration Papers. Original records of Robert T. Lincoln as conservator of his mother's property while she was under judgment of insanity. Ill. State Hist. Lib.

Lincoln, original Estate Papers of Abraham, Mary Todd, and Thomas Lincoln. Ill. State Hist. Lib.

Lincoln, Mary Todd, Court Records of Sanity Trial of, photostats. Ill. State Hist. Lib.

Lincoln, Robert Todd. Autobiographical sketch written on his graduation from Harvard in 1864. Harvard Archives.

Robert Todd Lincoln Collections of the Papers of Abraham Lincoln. Lib. of Cong.

Lincoln, Thomas, Guardianship, Papers of. Ill. State Hist. Lib.

Little, Henry G., Recollections of. Manuscript in possession of his grand-daughter, Mrs. W. A. Noyes.

New York Public Library. Letters of Robert T. Lincoln to Andrew Carnegie and others.

J. G. Nicolay MSS., Lib. of Cong. Very valuable to this study because of Robert Lincoln's letters.

Alfred Whital Stern Collection of Lincolniana. Contains letters of Robert Lincoln valuable to this study.

Stuart-Hay MSS., Ill. State Hist. Lib.

Charles Sumner MSS., Harvard University Lib. Letters of Mrs. Lincoln give details valuable to this study.

Joseph Wallace Scrapbooks, Ill. State Hist. Lib.

Gideon Welles MSS., Lib. of Cong. Valuable to this study for letters of Mrs. Lincoln to Mrs. Welles.

Books and Articles

Angle, Paul M. *"Here I Have Lived": A History of Lincoln's Springfield, 1821–1865.* Springfield, Ill., 1935.

—— *Lincoln, 1854–1861: Being the Day-by-Day Activities of Abraham Lincoln from January 1, 1854 to March 4, 1861.* Springfield, Ill., 1933.

—— "Tad Lincoln's School Paper," *Chicago History* (Winter 1948–1949), 41–43.

Ayres, Philip Wheelock. "Lincoln As a Neighbor," *Review of Reviews* (Feb. 1918), 183–185.

Bailhache, Preston H. "Recollections of a Springfield Doctor," *Jour. Ill. State Hist. Soc.* (Spring 1954), 57–63.

Barrett Collection. *The Immortal Autograph Letters . . . and Other Lincolniana, Collected by the Late Oliver R. Barrett of Chicago.* Catalogue of public auction sale, Parke-Bernet Galleries, New York, 1952.

Bates, David Homer. *Lincoln in the Telegraph Office.* New York, 1907.

Bayne, Julia Taft. *Tad Lincoln's Father.* Boston, 1931. One of the most valuable sources on the Lincoln boys.

Beale, Howard K., ed. *The Diary of Edward Bates, 1859–1866* (Ann. Rep. Amer. Hist. Assoc.). Washington, 1933.

Boyden, Anna L. *War Reminiscences or Echoes from Hospital and White House.* Boston, 1887. A rare book which contains the recollections of Mrs. Rebecca R. Pomroy, who nursed Tad Lincoln in his illness after Willie's death.

Brigham, Johnson. *James Harlan.* Iowa Biographical Series, ed. by Benjamin F. Shambaugh, 1913.

Brooks, Noah. "A Boy in the White House," *St. Nicholas* (Nov. 1882), 57–65.

—— "Personal Reminiscences of Lincoln," *Scribner's Monthly* (Feb. 1878), 561–569.

—— *Washington in Lincoln's Time.* New York, 1895.

Brown, Virginia Stuart. *Through Lincoln's Door.* Springfield, Ill., 1952.

Browne, Francis Fisher. *The Every-Day Life of Abraham Lincoln.* Chicago, 1913.

Browning, Orville Hickman. T. C. Pease and J. G. Randall, eds. *The Diary of Orville Hickman Browning* (Ill. State Hist. Lib. *Collections,* XX, XXII). Springfield, Ill., 1925–1933.

Bullard, F. Lauriston. *Lincoln in Marble and Bronze.* New Brunswick, N. J., 1952.

—— *Tad and His Father.* Boston, 1915.

Busey, Samuel Claggett. *Personal Reminiscences . . .* Washington, 1895.

Butler, Nicholas Murray. "Lincoln and Son," *The Saturday Evening Post* (Feb. 11, 1939), 23 ff. Valuable for Butler's recollections and extracts from Robert Lincoln's letters to him.

Carpenter, Francis B. *The Inner Life of Abraham Lincoln: Six Months at the White House.* Boston, 1883.

Clark, Allen C. *Abraham Lincoln in the National Capital.* Washington, 1925.

Colman, Edna M. *Seventy-Five Years of White House Gossip: From Washington to Lincoln.* Garden City, N. Y., 1925.

Crook, William Henry. *Through Five Administrations: Reminiscences of Col. William H. Crook, Bodyguard to President Lincoln.* Ed. by Margarita Spalding Gerry. New York and London, 1910.

Cunningham, Frank H. *Familiar Sketches of the Phillips Exeter Academy and Surroundings.* Boston, 1883.

Darrin, Charles V. "Robert Todd Lincoln and a Family Friendship," *Jour. Ill. State Hist. Soc.* (Autumn 1951), 210–217. Contains letters of Robert T. Lincoln.

—— "Your Truly Attached Friend, Mary Lincoln," *Jour. Ill. State Hist. Soc.* (Spring 1951), 7–25.

Davis, George T. M. *Autobiography of the Late Col. Geo. T. M. Davis.* Pub. by his legal Representatives. New York, 1891.

Dennett, Tyler, ed. *Lincoln and the Civil War in the Diaries and Letters of John Hay.* New York, 1939.

Desmond, Alice Curtis. *Barnum Presents: General Tom Thumb.* New York, 1954.

—— "General Tom Thumb's Widow," *New York Historical Society Quarterly* (July 1954), 311–324.

Donald, David. *Lincoln's Herndon.* New York, 1948.

Evans, W. A., M.D. *Mrs. Abraham Lincoln: A Study of Her Personality and Her Influence on Lincoln.* New York, 1932. This careful study from the medical approach includes the Lincoln sons.

Fuller, Frank. *A Day with the Lincoln Family.* Rare booklet in the Ill. State Hist. Lib.

Gernon, Blaine Brooks. *The Lincolns in Chicago.* Chicago, 1934.

Glyndon, Howard (Mrs. Laura Redden Searing). "The Truth About Mrs. Lincoln," *The Independent* (Aug. 10, 1882).

Goltz, Carlos W. *Incidents in the Life of Mary Todd Lincoln.* Sioux City, Iowa, 1928.

Grimsley, Elizabeth Todd. "Six Months in the White House," *Jour. Ill. State Hist. Soc.* (Oct.–Jan. 1926–1927), 43–73. It was written about thirty years before its publication, but because of Robert Lincoln's objection was not published until after his death.

Grover, Leonard. "Lincoln's Interest in the Theater," *The Century Illustrated Monthly Magazine* (April 1909), 943–950.

Hall, The Reverend Newman. "My Impressions of America" (interview with Robert Lincoln), *The Broadway: A London Magazine* (March–August 1869).

Harvard College: Class of 1864. Secretary's Report No. 6, 1864–1889 (Printed 1889). *Ibid.* Report No. 7, 1864–1904 (Printed 1904). *Ibid.* Report No. 8, 1864–1914 (Printed 1914).

Harvard Graduates' Magazine (Sept. 1926), article on R. T. Lincoln, 162–163.

Hay, John. "Life in the White House in the Time of Lincoln," *Century Magazine* (Nov. 1890), 33–37.

―― For Hay diary, see Dennett, Tyler.

Helm, Katherine. *The True Story of Mary, Wife of Lincoln, Containing the Recollections of Mary Lincoln's Sister Emilie (Mrs. Ben Hardin Helm), Extracts from Her War-Time Diary, Numerous Letters and Other Documents now First Published.* New York, 1928.

Herndon, William H. *Herndon's Life of Lincoln . . . by William H. Herndon and Jesse W. Weik with Introduction and Notes by Paul M. Angle.* Cleveland and New York, 1942. The Herndon-Weik biography was first published in 1889.

―― "Mrs. Lincoln's Denial, and What She Says." Broadside, Jan. 12, 1874. Mass. Hist. Soc.

Hertz, Emanuel. "Ties That Tugged at Lincoln's Heart," *New York Times Magazine* (June 21, 1931).

Horner Scrapbooks (24 vols.) in Lincoln Room, Univ. of Ill. Lib. Clippings made by Mr. and Mrs. Harlan Hoyt Horner.

Hunt, Eugenia Jones. "My Personal Recollections of Abraham and Mary Todd Lincoln," *Abraham Lincoln Quar.* (March 1945), 235–252.

Ingraham, Charles A. *Elmer E. Ellsworth and the Zouaves of '61.* U. of Chicago Press, 1925.

Kaine, John Langdon. "Lincoln As a Boy Knew Him," *Century Magazine* (Feb. 1913), 555–559.

Kasson, Mrs. John A. "An Iowa Woman in Washington, D. C., 1861–1865" (signed "Miriam"), *Iowa Jour. of Hist.* (January 1954), 61–90.

Keckley, Elizabeth. *Behind the Scenes.* New York, 1868.

Kunhardt, Dorothy Meserve. "Lincoln's Lost Dog," *Life Magazine* (Feb. 15, 1954), 83 ff.

Lamon, Ward Hill. *The Life of Abraham Lincoln from His Birth to His Inauguration as President.* Boston, 1872. Ghostwritten by Chauncey F. Black.

―― *Recollections of Abraham Lincoln, 1847–1865,* ed. by Dorothy Lamon Teillard. Chicago, 1895.

Leech, Margaret. *Reveille in Washington.* New York, 1941.

Lewis, Lloyd. "When Tad Lincoln Had a Girl in Chicago," *Midweek, Chicago Daily News* (Feb. 5, 1930).

Lincoln, Abraham. *The Collected Works of Abraham Lincoln* (8 vols.). The Abraham Lincoln Association Edition, Springfield, Illinois. Roy P. Basler, ed., Marion Dolores Pratt and Lloyd A. Dunlap, assistant eds. New Brunswick, N. J., 1953.

Magazine of History, Vol. 34, No. 1; Lincoln Number No. 31; Extra Number No. 133.

McMurtry, R. Gerald. "The Harlan-Lincoln Tradition at Iowa Wesleyan College," *Lincoln Herald* (October 1946), 11–21.

Mearns, David C. *The Lincoln Papers: The Story of the Collection with Selections to July 4, 1861* (2 vols.). New York, 1948. The Introduction is very valuable to the study of Robert Todd Lincoln.

Meserve, Frederick Hill. "My Experience in Collecting Historical Photographs . . ." *Lincoln Herald* (Spring–Summer 1954), 2 ff.

Monaghan, Jay, ed. *Lincoln Bibliography, 1839–1939* (Ill. State Hist. Lib. *Collections,* XXXI, XXXII). Springfield, 1943–1945.

Moss, M. Helen Palmes. "Lincoln and Wilkes Booth As Seen on the Day of the Assassination," *The Century Illustrated Monthly Magazine* (April 1909), 950–953.

New England Historical and Genealogical Register, Vol. 81, No. 383 (July 1927), 243–247, article on R. T. Lincoln.

Nicolay, Helen. *Lincoln's Secretary: A Biography of John G. Nicolay.* New York, 1949.

—— *Personal Traits of Abraham Lincoln.* New York, 1912.

Page, Elwin L. *Abraham Lincoln in New Hampshire.* Boston and New York, 1929.

Pendel, Thomas F. *Thirty-Six Years in the White House.* Washington, 1902.

Perling, J. J. *Presidents' Sons.* New York, 1947.

Perry, Leslie J. "Lincoln's Home Life in Washington," *Harper's New Monthly Magazine* (Feb. 1897), 353–359.

Poore, Ben: Perley. *Perley's Reminiscences of Sixty Years in the National Metropolis . . .* (2 vols.). Philadelphia, 1886.

Pratt, Harry E., ed. *Concerning Mr. Lincoln: In which Abraham Lincoln is Pictured as he Appeared to Letter Writers of his Time.* Springfield, Ill., 1944.

—— *Lincoln, 1840–1846 . . . Day-by-Day Activities . . .* Springfield, 1939.

—— "Little Eddie Lincoln—'We Miss Him Very Much,'" *Jour. Ill. State Hist. Soc.* (Autumn 1954), 300–305.

—— *The Personal Finances of Abraham Lincoln.* Springfield, 1943.

Randall, J. G. *Lincoln the President: Springfield to Gettysburg* (2 vols.). New York, 1945.

—— *Lincoln the President:* Vol. III: *Midstream.* New York, 1952.

Randall, Ruth Painter. *Mary Lincoln: Biography of a Marriage.* Boston, 1953.

—— "Lincoln's Faith Was Born of Anguish," *New York Times Magazine* (Feb. 7, 1954).

—— "Lincoln's 'Little Devils'?" *American Weekly* (Feb. 6, 1955).

—— "Tad Knew How to Keep Christmas," *Chicago Tribune Books* (Dec. 7, 1952).

—— "The Lincolns Were Good Neighbors," *New York Times Magazine* (Feb. 8, 1953).

Rice, Allen Thorndike, ed. *Reminiscences of Abraham Lincoln by Distinguished Men of His Time.* New York, 1886.

Roberts, Octavia. *Lincoln in Illinois.* Boston and New York, 1918.

Sandburg, Carl. *Abraham Lincoln: The War Years* (4 vols.). New York, 1939.

—— *Abraham Lincoln: The Prairie Years and the War Years* (1 vol. ed.). New York, 1954.

—— and Paul M. Angle. *Mary Lincoln, Wife and Widow.* New York, 1932. "The Documents," about half the book, contain many letters by Mrs. Lincoln.

—— *Lincoln Collector: The Story of Oliver R. Barrett's Great Private Collection.* New York, 1949.

"Secretary Lincoln and the Color Line," *Frank Leslie's Illustrated Newspaper* (Oct. 11, 1884).

Stevens, Walter B. *A Reporter's Lincoln.* St. Louis, 1916.

Stoddard, William O. *Inside the White House in War Times.* New York, 1890.

Taft, Dr. Charles Sabin. "Abraham Lincoln's Last Hours," *Century Magazine* (Feb. 1893), 634.

Tarbell, Ida M. *All in the Day's Work, An Autobiography.* New York, 1939.

—— *The Life of Abraham Lincoln . . .* (2 vols.). New York, 1909.

Trial of John H. Surratt in the Criminal Court for the District of Columbia, Hon. George P. Fisher Presiding, Vol. I, Washington Government Printing Office, 1867.

Thomas, Benjamin P. *Lincoln, 1847–1853 . . . Day-by-Day Activities . . .* Springfield, 1936.

Townsend, William Henry. *Lincoln and His Wife's Home Town.* Indianapolis, 1929.

—— "Lincoln Bribes Tad," *The Rotarian* (Feb. 1934), 39–40.

Villard, Henry. *Lincoln on the Eve of '61,* ed. by Harold G. and Oswald Garrison Villard. New York, 1941.

Wallace, Mrs. Frances [Todd]. *Lincoln's Marriage: Newspaper interview . . . Springfield, Ill., Sept. 2, 1895.* Privately printed, 1917.

Ward, William Hayes, ed. *Abraham Lincoln: Tributes from His Associates.* New York, 1895.

Warren, Louis A. *The Lincoln Kinsman* (periodical), Fort Wayne, Ind. Especially Numbers 10 and 13 on Robert Todd Lincoln and Tad Lincoln.

—— ed. *Lincoln Lore* (1929 to date). Periodical published by Lincoln National Life Foundation, Fort Wayne, Ind. Numbers 296, 549, 954, 979, and 1288 especially helpful in this study.

Weik, Jesse W. *The Real Lincoln: A Portrait.* Boston and New York, 1922.

Welles, Gideon. *Diary of Gideon Welles . . .* ed. by John T. Morse, Jr. (3 vols.). Boston and New York, 1911.

White, Charles T. "The Great Man's Son," *Magazine of History.* Vol. 35, No. 4; Rare Lincolniana No. 33; Extra No. 140, 1928.

Wilson, Rufus Rockwell, ed. *Intimate Memories of Lincoln.* Elmira, N. Y., 1945.

—— ed. *Lincoln Among His Friends.* Caldwell, Idaho, 1942.

—— *Lincoln in Portraiture.* New York, 1935.